READING, WRITING AND RHYTHMETIC
the ABCs of Music Transcription

Roberta Radley
Assistant Chair, Ear Training Department
Berklee College of Music

This book is dedicated in loving memory to my late mother, Mary Catherine Bernadette Lawler Radley.
My earliest musical mentor, she encouraged me to always shoot for the high notes of life.
I listen for your voice every day.

Published by Sher Music Company
P.O. Box 455
Petaluma, CA 94953

© 2016 by Sher Music Co.
All rights reserved. No part of this book or the audio files may be reproduced in any manner without prior written authorization from the publisher.

ISBN 1-883217-95-4

Printed in the United States of America

Editors: Roberta Radley, Bill Brinkley, Paula Loudenslager, Chuck Sher

CD mastering by Mark White, Gorgon Studios, Cambridge, MA

Cover artwork: adaptation of the original 1907 sheet music cover for "School Days"
(Gus Edwards & Will D. Cobb.)

All audio examples, cover adaptation & cover design, book design and production, music typesetting:
Wm.R.Brinkley & Associates, Watertown, MA. www.wrbrinkleydesign.com

Contents

Acknowledgements iv

Introduction v

1 Determining the Time Signature
Introduction 1
The Beat 1
The Time Signature 1
About Conducting 2
Adding Other Note Values 3
About the Tempo 4
Working with Familiar Songs from Memory 5

2 Memorizing "Rhythm Words"
Introduction 9
Counting and Conducting 9
Memorizing "Rhythm Words" 11
Introducing $\frac{4}{4}$ time 13

3 Is the Song in a Major or Minor Key?
Introduction 21
Is the Song in a Major or Minor Key? 21
Finding the Root of the Scale 22
Major or Minor? 23
Reading Rhythms in $\frac{3}{4}$ 25
Tapping 27

4 Exploring Major Key Melodies with Solfege
Introduction 35
The Major Scale 35
Learning the Solfege Language 35
Using the "Sol-Fa" System 37
Counting and Tracking Sixteenth Notes 39
Memorizing One-Beat Sixteenth Note
  Rhythm Words 39

5 Pitches + Rhythms = Being Organized
Introduction 47
The Tonic I Chord 47
Tendency Tone Pairs 49
Combining Pitch and Rhythm 51
$\frac{6}{8}$ Time Signature 54

6 Melody + Bass Line = Harmony
Introduction 61
Melody Is Harmony 61
Relating Harmony to the Tendency Tone Pairs ... 62
Duet Work: Melody and Bass Line 66
Transcribing the Bass Line 68
Eighth Note Triplets 71

7 Transcribing Popular Chord Patterns in Major
Introduction 77
Hearing Major and Minor Triads 77
Diatonic Triads in the Major Key 78
Using the Vertical Approach 79
Swing Eighth Notes 82

8 Exploring Minor Key Melodies with Solfege
Introduction 87
The Natural Minor Scale 87
Comparing Relative Scales 88
Comparing Parallel Scales 88
More About Rhythmic Syncopation 92

9 Transcribing Popular Chord Patterns in Minor
Introduction 99
Diatonic Triads in Natural Minor 99
Introducing the Harmonic Minor Scale 100
Memorizing Popular Minor Key
  Chord Progressions 103
Syncopated Sixteenth Note Rhythm Patterns .. 104

10 Mapping the Song Form
Introduction 109
Song Form 109
Letter "A" 109
Here Comes "B" 110
12-Bar Blues Form 111
Binary Song Form: Verse and Chorus 113
Introducing Quarter Note Triplets 114

11 Creating a Lead Sheet
Introduction 121
32-Bar Song Form 121
A A B A 121
A B A B 122
A B A C 122
Creating a Lead Sheet from a Transcription 123
Odd Time Signatures 128

12 Transcribing Jazz Solos
Introduction 131
Charting the Arrangement 131
Featuring the C Section 134
Transcribing the Jazz Solo: Do as I Say,
  Not What I Did 134
My 12-Step Program 135
Mixed Meters 138
Beat Is Constant 138
Metric Modulation 139

Answer Key 141

Discography 201

About the Author 211

ACKNOWLEDGEMENTS

The first "thank you" is to Mr. Chuck Sher who published my debut book *The "Real Easy" Ear Training Book*, which was an incredible opportunity and experience, fulfilling a lifetime's dream. Now I am honored to have my second book, *Reading, Writing and Rhythmetic, the ABCs of Music Transcription* added to Sher Music Co.'s catalogue. Throughout both projects, you've offered 110% encouragement and support. Keep swingin'!

Thanks to all my students, both in the "live" as well as "virtual" classroom. You have taught me a tremendous amount and have been an inspirational audience. Your contributions appear in every line of this book. I appreciate all the wonderful music you've shared with me, keeping my listening ear forever young.

Thank you to my dear friend, Paula Loudenslager, who devoted many hours to text editing. Your flair for writing, your eagle eye for detail, and your encouragement have meant a great deal. Thank you, girl friend!

Thanks to my colleague, Mark White, who put the polishing touch on the book's CD recordings. As an ear training book, it's imperative to me that my students be treated to the highest quality listening experience. Thank you, Mark, for your expertise and keen ear.

Having left the best for last, a huge "thank you" to my husband, Bill Brinkley, for contributing on so many levels to the making and realization of both books. From book design to the final touches of text editing and conceptual clarity, Bill has been there every step of the way with me and for me. An accomplished musician, he has offered me counsel on many musical aspects of the book. Bill's work ethic and drive to make things the best they can be is of the highest level and is one of the things I most admire about him. Behind every woman who writes a book on "transcription" is a great man. Thank you, sweetheart, you are the A in my ABC book.

INTRODUCTION

INTRODUCTION

Welcome to *Reading, Writing and Rhythmetic,* where we will explore the ABCs of music transcription, steering towards the successful destination of notating the music we hear. It is a challenging journey, but with a good map to follow, and fueled with a tank full of enthusiasm, motivation and patience, we'll make it!

WHY I WROTE THIS BOOK

Musicians come in all glorious shapes and sizes!

Some begin their journey by learning and making music "by ear." Is this you? You hear a song on the radio that appeals to you, you hum along and learn the lyrics by rote. You pick up your guitar and try figuring out the chords. Or, you listen to the song over and over, and eventually pick out the melody notes on your trumpet. Over time, and with lots of trial and error, you gain confidence in your intuitive approach to understanding music, but you lack the theoretical vocabulary to discuss the process. Your intuitive knowledge is primarily based on "playing it by ear" experience.

Others begin the journey with music lessons. Maybe this is you. You study with a private voice teacher and learn about proper vocal technique. You take an online music theory course and learn how to construct chords. Or, you play trumpet in the school orchestra and develop your reading skills. Though you might have the vocabulary to talk about music, you lack confidence in performing without a written piece of music in front of you. You might be academically educated and can "talk the talk," but inexperienced with "walking the walk."

Regardless of your musical situation, ear player or the schooled musician, or somewhere in between, this book will help you develop your ability to transcribe music. I have seen you in my ear training classroom at Berklee over the past four decades! My philosophy is to encourage each individual student to put his or her best foot forward in the learning process. Use what you know to get at what you don't know *yet.* And trust that you know more than you think you do!

The goal of this book is to help every student make the connection between what he or she hears and what that sound looks like on the page. In other words: *to see what they hear* (the "ear player") and to *hear what they see* (the "schooled musician"). This book provides a step-by-step process, the "ABCs," on how to achieve this two-way goal.

The book is designed for a wide and varied audience. You can work through it on your own, with a friend, a teacher, band members, or classmates. If you are a teacher, I hope you find that it enhances your work with your students, and adds to your own methods of teaching ear training.

Why Transcribe?

I often tell my students that I have learned more about music by transcribing than any book could ever have revealed to me. When I was a young, inexperienced newcomer to jazz, I wanted desperately to learn more about improvisation. My teachers advised me to transcribe solos, and so I did, and they were right!

My first transcription was Miles Davis' solo on the tune "When Lights Are Low." It took me almost a month to complete, but what he was playing was an inspiration!

Transcribing his solo, slowly, note by note, (and yes, with a keyboard by my side at all times!), I digested what he had to say in a deep and lasting way. To this day, I can still sing back the solo. It was one of the biggest ear training challenges I ever faced, but the rewards and results were worth it.

What are the Steps to Take?

Above all else, *listening* is the first and most important step to take. This is the inspirational moment when the music "grabs you." Enjoy this moment! I encourage you to put that pencil down and take the time to listen carefully and with an "open" ear. Can you sing back or play back the musical phrase? That's an excellent way to confirm that you've successfully heard and retained the musical idea, because if you cannot remember the phrase, there's nothing to translate.

Step two involves the translation process, the "brain training" part of ear training. *What* are the pitches and *how* are the rhythms notated? How do we *visualize* the music we *hear?* These are the analytical challenges we face when transcribing. How do we strengthen the skills needed for this second step in the transcribing process?

Being organized and taking small steps in the beginning will lead to giant steps down the road. There are many paths we can take toward learning the "ABCs" of the language of music, and we will take those paths throughout this book. Listening, singing, playing, reading, composing, are all activities to prepare for a successful journey to transcription proficiency. Using the tools of solfege to translate pitches into meaningful "*do, re, mi*'s," and learning to count and conduct as means of turning the groove into rhythmic symbols will prepare us for the ultimate goal of writing down the musical idea, the final outcome of the transcription process.

What is the secret to success formula? It's easy:

Listening (ear training) + Analysis (brain training) = Successful Transcription

Next is a brief description of each section featured in the book, our road map to follow.

Road Map of this Book

CD Icons

Two CDs accompany this book. The numbered CD icons indicate that there is an audio track. Some of these tracks demonstrate a lesson concept, and many represent an Activity performance, dictation or reading assignment. If the CD track contains several examples, you will hear my voice direct you from one example to the next. CD1 has tracks for Chapters 1–6 (tracks 1–77); CD2 has tracks for Chapters 7–12 (tracks 1–63).

Remember, this is an ear training book, so take every opportunity to listen. If a picture is worth a thousand words, certainly listening is everything when it comes to understanding an ear training concept.

INTRODUCTION

Visiting the Web

The focus of this book is to practice transcribing real music, not just textbook examples. The exercises on the accompanying CDs are a helpful means to this end, but not the ultimate goal. You will be asked to listen to hundreds of real music examples to develop and apply your transcription skills. There is no substitute for the "real deal" as inspiration, and no greater challenge than transcribing music, not simply exercises. The featured activity of each chapter will be "Takin' It to the Streets." Get out there on the Internet highway and enjoy the trip!

Activities and Answer Keys

The Activities are at the heart of this book. They are where you will use a variety of practice routines which will prepare you for the ABCs of transcription. At times you will be asked to sing, to play, to compose, to analyze, but the main intent of practice is to recognize rhythmic, melodic and harmonic ideas by ear and to be able to write them down. There is a wealth of dictation and transcription work here to keep you busy!

All answers are available in the Answer Key, giving you immediate feedback on your work, which will be particularly helpful if you're using the book solo and/or at your own pace. If at times the work is overwhelming, simply listening to the musical examples while viewing the answer key will be very helpful.

Going the Extra Mile

In this section, I often encourage you to take the practice to the next level, incorporating the practice into your daily listening and music-making activities. This is another way to "make it real," and another opportunity for you to own the idea in a deeper way.

Tips

Here I offer you additional strategies for transcription practice. I hope you will find these tricks of the trade helpful. Many of these tips have been contributed by students over the years.

Two for the Road

These are opportunities to have some fun quizzing your friends and classmates. Playing the teacher is a great opportunity to test your own knowledge of the material. And, if two heads are better than one, imagine what four ears can do!

Collecting Souvenirs

We will work with hundreds of song excerpts throughout the book as we develop our transcription skills. Add your own souvenirs to this song list and watch our collection grow! We can never get too much practice: there's always one more song down the road to visit.

VII

READING, WRITING AND RHYTHMETIC

Round Trip

Each chapter will conclude with a Round Trip activity to practice a concept covered in previous lessons. This "two steps forward, one step back" approach is essential as we build upon and develop our ability to transcribe the music we hear. Remember, mastery develops over time and with repeated practice.

Approaching the Fork in the Road

This is an opportunity to reflect upon and share questions, insights and strategies with classmates, bandmates and teachers about why we do what we do. It's not only what you do, but also how you do it, that can often make the difference in getting the most out of your practice time and studies. There isn't just one correct road to success, but you do want to be in the driver's seat, rather than the passenger's seat, in getting there.

Discography

Throughout the book, I will reference an extensive repertoire of song recordings for our "Takin' It to the Streets" transcription work. Over 300 songs featured or referenced in this book are listed in the Discography. Exercises are one thing, but hearing and being able to identify and transcribe musical concepts in the "real thing" is the ultimate challenge and rewarding experience. I encourage you to listen to as many of these recordings as possible as you practice the ABCs of transcription. Adding these songs to your audio collection is a worthwhile investment.

Now that you've studied the road map of how the book works, and are fueled up for the long journey, let's get started. As a musician, learning to trust your ear is a very satisfying, confidence-building experience. It's incredibly hard work, but undeniably worth it! Don't miss out on taking this trip of a lifetime…start your engines!

1 DETERMINING THE TIME SIGNATURE

INTRODUCTION

We're about to embark on the long and very interesting journey of analyzing and dissecting the music we listen to. The road will be a winding one, with many stops along the way before we reach our final destination—learning to notate our musical ideas and transcribe the music we hear.

Our first stop along the way will be determining the time signature. To do this, we'll use counting and conducting techniques to determine the time signature in a knowledgeable and confident way. Other tools (the metronome or click track) can also help us ensure accuracy in keeping time. Next, we will do some reading and performance activities in order to prime the engine for our transcription work.

We won't venture far from the neighborhood in this first chapter: we'll work with familiar songs to begin learning how to determine time signatures.

Are you ready, bags packed? Let's get this show on the road!

THE BEAT

What's the beat and how do we locate the beat when listening to a piece of music? Without thinking, you probably feel the beat by tapping your foot, bobbing your head, or snapping your fingers: that's what your body senses as the basic musical pulse. Get up and move to the music! When you're dancing, you're feeling the beat, and you might trip if you're not! Feeling a beat (or pulse) is an intuitive process, and not something you really think about. But if you're not a dancer, let's add a dose of intellect to the process.

What's the "look" of the beat when reading or notating the rhythms in a piece of music? In many cases, we represent the fundamental beat with a quarter note (♩). In this first chapter we'll use the quarter note as the beat representative.

Collecting Souvenirs

Watch Peter Gabriel's live performance (Secret World Tour, 1993) of his composition, "In Your Eyes." The musicians are expressing the beat throughout the performance…moving and dancing to the beat (the quarter note), and jumping up on the downbeat (the first beat of the measure). We'll talk more about the downbeat in the next section on time signatures.

THE TIME SIGNATURE

The time signature, (also referred to as the "meter") organizes the beats into small units called measures, or bars. Some of the beats get accented more than others in the measure. The strongest beat, the most accented beat, is the first beat of the measure, called the "downbeat."

There are two basic kinds of time signatures: simple and compound. A simple time signature has only one accented beat per measure, the first beat, or downbeat. Compound meters have more than one accented beat within the measure. In this chapter, we'll concentrate our work with the two simple meters of 2/4 and 3/4. Let's take a look at these two simple time signatures.

The top number in the time signature tells us how many beats are within each measure, and the bottom number tells us what kind of note value receives one beat (the 4 on the bottom represents the quarter note). So in 2/4 time, there are two beats per measure and the quarter note receives one beat. How would you interpret the 3/4 time signature?

Let's listen to a 4-bar phrase of steady quarter notes (beats) in each of the two time signatures, 2/4 and then 3/4. Notice how each downbeat is accented, announcing the beginning of each measure.

1 First, let's listen to the 2/4 example on Audio track 1.

2 Now, let's listen to the 3/4 example on Audio track 2.

Listening for the downbeat (the accented beat) will tell us what the time signature is!

ACTIVITY ONE: *Counting the Beats*

Let's return to Audio tracks 1 and 2 and count along with the quarter notes, the beats. This time we'll add more detail and locate exactly which beat we're singing within the measure by counting, "*one*, two; *one*, two," etc., for the 2/4 example, and "*one*, two, three; *one*, two, three," etc., for the 3/4 example. Accent the downbeat when counting the beats aloud.

ABOUT CONDUCTING

In addition to counting, conducting is another method for showing the exact placement of the beats within the measure. Conducting is an active tool with which we use arm and hand movements to represent a physical picture of the time signature. Take a look at the conducting patterns for 2/4 and 3/4, shown below.

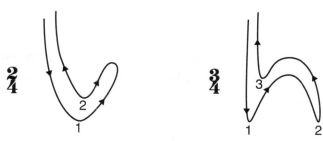

ACTIVITY TWO: *Conducting in $\frac{2}{4}$ and $\frac{3}{4}$*

Try conducting each pattern, while counting the beats at the same time. It is traditional to conduct with the right hand, but for our purposes of timekeeping, conducting with the left hand is fine too. Keep the conducting patterns small; we're not attempting to direct a full orchestra!

For $\frac{2}{4}$, think, "down, up," with a slight bounce at the end of each beat to breathe some life into the moves. There will be a slight angle to the right (away from your body) with this conducting pattern (imagine the shape of a fish hook).

For $\frac{3}{4}$, think, "down, out (away from your body), up," again with a small bounce at the end of each beat to keep an even flow to the beats. There are no red lights to stop for; keep it moving. If you're conducting with your right hand, "out" will also mean to the right (picture the shape of a triangle). If you choose to conduct with your left hand, it will be the mirror image, but again think, "down, out (this time to the left), up," for the conducting pattern.

Often students will ask if it's OK to conduct with their left hand because they're "lefties." I'm a lefty too! I suggest that conducting with the right hand is better because it frees up the left hand for writing. You will find conducting to be a very useful tool when it comes to transcribing the rhythmic details of a piece of music.

Tip: There are so many aspects of the music to pay attention to when transcribing, it can feel like you're in a traffic jam! Isolate the practice routine of conducting. Spend time daily simply conducting, until the arm and hand movements begin to feel like second nature.

ACTIVITY THREE: *Combining Conducting and Counting*

Let's return to the examples on Audio tracks 1 and 2, this time combining the techniques of conducting and counting the beats aloud as you listen. Remember to accent each downbeat as you perform. Give it a try, maestro!

ADDING OTHER NOTE VALUES

Now that we've established feeling and recognizing the beat (the quarter note), let's add some other note values to our rhythmic vocabulary list.

The half note (♩) gets two beats, and will fill one measure of $\frac{2}{4}$ time. When singing half notes or performing them on your instrument, hold the half note out for its full two-beat value.

The dotted half note (♩.) will receive three beats, and will fill one measure of $\frac{3}{4}$ time. The dot increases a note's duration by adding half its value to it. Thus, the half note (2 beats) + the dot (1 beat) = 3 beats total. Remember to sustain this dotted half note for the full count (1, 2, 3).

The eighth note (♪) will receive one half of a beat. Four eighth notes fill one measure of $\frac{2}{4}$. How many eighth notes are needed to fill one bar of $\frac{3}{4}$ time? Simply counting the beat is not sufficient for tracking eighth notes. Try counting, "1 + 2 +," when in $\frac{2}{4}$, or count "1 + 2 + 3 +" for $\frac{3}{4}$ time, in order to keep steady track of the half a beats.

A single eighth note has its own flag (♪). When you have a series of eighth notes, it is common to connect the flags, and "beam" them together:

Reading, Writing and Rhythmetic

Activity Four: *Conducting, Counting and Reading*

We'll add the third element, reading, in this activity. Each example acts as a "rhythm grid," marking the relationships of the longer and shorter note values directly back to the beat, the quarter note pulse. Follow the suggested practice plan (travel directions) listed below.

1. Listen to Audio tracks 3 and 4 as you read through the following two examples in 2/4 and 3/4 time. The examples will incorporate quarter notes, half notes, dotted half notes and eighth notes into the mix. Each audio track is sixteen measures long in total. The first eight bars present the rhythmic phrase along with the click track. The remaining eight bars include only the click track for your solo performance when practicing step 4.

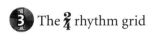

The 2/4 rhythm grid

The 3/4 rhythm grid

2. Add conducting as you listen and read through the examples.
3. Let's now include performing (singing or playing on your instrument) as you listen and read along with each example. Remember to sustain the notes longer than a quarter note, and count 1 + 2 + to track the eighth notes. With these three steps, you're in the passenger's seat, following along with the audio tracks.
4. Finally, try performing the 8-bar phrase on your own, with only the click track for accompaniment. You have now traded seats, moving into the driver's seat. Let your inner hearing take over the wheel…this is a great opportunity to develop self-confidence with tracking, reading and performing rhythms!

Tip: The metronome or a click track are great tools to use when practicing counting and conducting. They serve as "outside monitors" to ensure that the tempo remains steady. Practicing with these outside timekeepers ensures accuracy. And practicing on your own helps develop confidence in your own inner clock.

About the Tempo

Music is performed at a variety of speeds or "tempos." These tempos are sometimes indicated with metronome markings representing the beats per minute (bpm). For example, ♩ = 60 means one quarter note per one second, or 60 quarter notes per minute. This is similar to the speed markings on the highway, such as "60 mph" for a traveling speed of 60 miles per hour. Different styles of music render themselves to certain predictable ranges of speed or tempos. For example, a ballad or a reggae song is likely to be performed at a slow tempo, (ranging from ♩ = 48–60). A heavy metal rock or samba song will be performed at a fast tempo, (ranging from ♩ = 88–120). The tempo marking might be as general as the description "medium swing." If you want to be exact, providing the specific metronome marking is best.

Going the Extra Mile

Set the metronome or click track at a variety of speeds and practice performing the two 8-bar examples presented in Activity Four. Getting comfortable with various tempos will provide you with more skill, flexibility and readiness when dealing with rhythms in a variety of musical styles.

WORKING WITH FAMILIAR SONGS FROM MEMORY

Up to this point, we have been honing and preparing the tools of counting and conducting through listening, reading and performance activities. With these tools sharpened, we're now ready to put them to use for the purpose of determining the time signature of a piece of music. Let the transcribing process begin!

As mentioned in the Introduction on page vi, transcribing is a two-step process: first, listening carefully and ingesting the musical idea; second, translating that same musical idea. Both steps require time and effort. If one can't remember how the music sounds, there's nothing to translate. But if we start with familiar songs we hold in our memory, then we can proceed immediately to step two, the translation process. Let's take a trip down memory lane with some old favorites from our childhood, and determine if these golden oldies are in either $\frac{2}{4}$ or $\frac{3}{4}$ time.

Recall a simple children's song or folk song you already have committed to memory. Sing or hum your way through it. If the song has lyrics, they will play a very helpful role in determining where the downbeat (first beat) of the measure is. The lyrical syllables that are most accented will likely fall on the downbeat! Let's work with two classic songs, one in $\frac{2}{4}$ and one in $\frac{3}{4}$.

5 Sing through "Twinkle, Twinkle, Little Star." Notice that you're accenting TWINK-le twink-le LIT-tle star, HOW I won-der WHAT you are. This song is in $\frac{2}{4}$, with the accented syllables falling on the first beat of each $\frac{2}{4}$ measure. I'll demonstrate on Audio track 5.

6 And how about "Happy Birthday"? hap-py BIRTH-day to YOU, hap-py BIRTH-day to YOU…this song is in $\frac{3}{4}$ time. It's a little bit trickier because this song involves "pickup" notes, notes that happen before the first complete measure of the song. Again, I'll demonstrate on Audio track 6.

ACTIVITY FIVE: *Is the Song in $\frac{2}{4}$ or $\frac{3}{4}$ Time?*

Now it's your turn. Put your counting and conducting to the test with some or all of the following songs, and determine the time signature. Is the song in $\frac{2}{4}$ or $\frac{3}{4}$ time?

Start with the songs you know from memory, and search the Internet for the ones you're not familiar with (or need a refresher with the lyrics). Remember, when stating the lyrics, "feel" where the accented syllables fall; they should be falling on the downbeats, providing major clues. What did you discover?

Check the Answer Key (p.141) to see how you did.

Reading, Writing and Rhythmetic

1. "Amazing Grace"	9. "Old MacDonald"
2. "Brahm's Lullalby"	10. "Pennsylvania Polka"
3. "Frère Jacques"	11. "Silver Bells"
4. "Greensleeves"	12. "Take Me Out to the Ballgame"
5. "Jingle Bells"	13. "U.S. National Anthem"
6. "Joy to the World"	14. "When Irish Eyes Are Smiling"
7. "London Bridge Is Falling Down"	15. "Yankee Doodle Dandy"
8. "Mary Had a Little Lamb"	

Now sing or speak the lyric of each song along with the $\frac{2}{4}$ or $\frac{3}{4}$ backing tracks (Audio tracks 7 and 8) provided below. Each track is 16 bars long, so you will have plenty of measures to work with. Some songs will cover eight bars, some twelve, and some will take up the entire 16-bar track.

7 16 bars of $\frac{2}{4}$ with click track (has 2-bar pickup)

8 16 bars of $\frac{3}{4}$ with click track (has 2-bar pickup)

Notice that in each of these songs, regardless of the total length of the song, 4-bar phrasing is a universal standard. We will be exploring phrasing and song form in greater detail later in the book, but for now, pay attention to this 4-bar phrase standard.

ACTIVITY SIX: *Takin' It to the Streets*

Let's branch away from our memory bank of familiar songs and take the road less traveled. Let's listen to actual recordings of songs in $\frac{2}{4}$ or $\frac{3}{4}$ time. There are several resources (some of them free) available for streamed listening: YouTube, iTunes, Spotify, SoundCloud, Rdio, and Bandcamp just to mention a few. Perhaps some of these recordings live in your own listening library or CD collection.

Access one or more of these sites and listen to the following songs. Determine if the song is in either $\frac{2}{4}$ or $\frac{3}{4}$ time.

1. "Armando's Rhumba," Chick Corea, *My Spanish Heart*
2. "Be Good," Gregory Porter, *Be Good*
3. "Magalenha," Sergio Mendes, *Brasilerio*
4. "Mas Que Nada," Sergio Mendes & Brasil '66, *Greatest Hits*
5. "Minuet in G Major," from the Notebooks for Anna Magdalena, J. S. Bach
6. "Moon River," Andy Williams, *The Very Best of Andy Williams*
7. "Natural Woman," Aretha Franklin, *The Best of Aretha Franklin*
8. "Pomp and Circumstance, March No.1," Sir Edward Elgar
9. "Scarborough Fair," Simon and Garfunkel, *Parsley, Sage, Rosemary and Thyme*
10. "Someday My Prince Will Come," Miles Davis, *Someday My Prince Will Come*
11. "Só Danço Samba," Stan Getz, Joao Gilberto, *Getz/Gilberto*
12. "Stars and Stripes Forever," John Philip Sousa
13. "Sunrise, Sunset," *Fiddler on the Roof* soundtrack
14. "First Movement Theme," from Symphony No.5 in C Minor," Ludwig van Beethoven

1 DETERMINING THE TIME SIGNATURE

15. "The Times They Are a Changin'," Bob Dylan, *Bob Dylan's Greatest Hits*

16. "Waltz of the Flowers," from the Nutcracker Suite, Pyotr Tchaikovsky

Now check the Answer Key (p.141) to see how you did…or…try this activity with a partner!

Two for the Road

If two heads are better than one, imagine what four ears can do! Consider doing Activity Six with a partner rather than traveling solo. Discuss your strategies for arriving at the answers. Did you and your partner always agree?

Collecting Souvenirs

Add to the list with other songs you discover are in $\frac{2}{4}$ or $\frac{3}{4}$ time. Share your souvenirs with classmates or band members. We can build quite a sizeable collection if we pool our resources! Explore your band's song list; are some of the songs in $\frac{2}{4}$ or $\frac{3}{4}$? As you begin to do the research, you might find that some songs are in $\frac{4}{4}$ rather than $\frac{2}{4}$ time, and that some songs you thought were in $\frac{3}{4}$ might really be in $\frac{6}{8}$ time.

We will talk about these other time signatures in later chapters so don't discard these gems just yet.

ACTIVITY SEVEN: *Round Trip*

We've come full circle in this first chapter: it all starts with establishing the beat. Listen to the following recordings and identify which instruments are stating the beat, the basic rhythmic pulse. What instrument has you bobbing your head?

1. "Bits and Pieces," Dave Clark Five, *Glad All Over* (best to watch video if possible.)
2. "Blues March," Art Blakey & The Jazz Messengers, *Moanin'*
3. "Carmina Burana," Carl Orff
4. "Edelweiss," *Sound of Music* soundtrack (best to watch video if possible.)
5. "Eleanor Rigby," The Beatles, *Revolver*
6. "Four on Six," Wes Montgomery & Wynton Kelly Trio, *Smokin' at the Half Note*
7. "Funeral March," Frederic Chopin
8. "Lil' Darlin'," Count Basie & His Orchestra (best to watch video if possible; watch guitar player, Freddie Green, behind the trumpet solo.)
9. "Living for the City," Stevie Wonder, *Innervisions*
10. "Off the Wall," Michael Jackson, *Off the Wall*
11. "Penny Lane," The Beatles, *Magical Mystery Tour*
12. "Purple Haze," Jimi Hendrix, *Are You Experienced*
13. "Rolling in the Deep," Adele, *21*
14. "The Rose," Bette Midler, *The Rose*
15. "Someday My Prince Will Come," Miles Davis, *Someday My Prince Will Come*
16. "Stay with Me," Sam Smith, *In the Lonely Hour*
17. "There Will Never Be Another You," Chet Baker, *Chet Baker Sings*
18. "Time Has Come Today," The Chambers Brothers, *The Time Has Come Today*
19. "Uptown Girl," Billy Joel, *An Innocent Man*
20. "Where Did Our Love Go," The Supremes, *Anthology*

Check the Answer Key (p.141) to see which instrument established the beat.

7

There's a lot to juggle when listening to music in an analytical way! In this first chapter we concentrated on identifying the time signature, as we learned to conduct and count along the way. Continue to practice these routines with familiar songs you hold in your memory, or while listening to recordings. Seize the moment and grab every opportunity you can to practice. When you least expect it, a song will come into your mind, or a song will be playing on the radio: go for it, try to figure out the time signature and conduct and count along.

In the next chapter we will explore "rhythm words," attending to the rhythmic phrase itself in greater detail. But counting and conducting will remain essential tools for that task as well…keep practicing!

Approaching the Fork in the Road

One of my mottos is, "Ear training is 50% brain training." All of us grew up with songs we learned simply by rote. Over time and with repetition, we learned songs through pure recall and imitation, parroting what we heard. Without thinking, we became acquainted with music.

But as we developed into musicians, we wanted to understand the music on a deeper level, desired to "talk the talk" about music we had intuitively nurtured through "walking the walk." This is where the rubber meets the road and "brain training" comes into the equation. It isn't a question of merely hearing the music, it also means comprehending the music. What are the names of those notes we sing in the melody or in the chords we play? What do the rhythms we perform on the drums look like on the page? How do we write down the composition we've been working out in our head? All of these activities require a serious "brain-train" workout! In our musical journey, learning a song by rote is good for the short run, but not necessarily for the long trip ahead.

It's a balancing act between trusting one's intuitive gut reaction to the music and understanding the music intellectually. What do you think?

2 Memorizing "Rhythm Words"

Introduction

In Chapter 1 we addressed some of the big picture aspects of rhythm. We determined what the beat was, and then organized the beats within measures of 2/4 or 3/4. We tracked the beats by counting, and mapped out these simple time signatures with conducting patterns.

In this chapter we will dig deeper into the rhythmic details to determine what the actual rhythmic phrase we hear looks like when notated. Counting and conducting will continue to be valuable tools in determining these details, but I will propose another approach as well: memorizing small "rhythm words" for instant recognition. This will be the primary topic of this chapter.

We will also work with the most common time signature in popular music, 4/4 time, and apply the same tools of counting, conducting and "rhythm word" identification to this compound meter.

Let's hit the road and get started!

Counting and Conducting

One of the most challenging aspects of transcribing music is writing down the rhythmic value of a musical phrase. We can reference an instrument for the pitches, but what can we reference for rhythmic notation?

Counting and conducting are not only valuable tools for determining the time signature; they are also extremely useful in evaluating the rhythmic details of a musical phrase. In Chapter 1, we used a "rhythm grid," counting through the beats (quarter notes), counting through longer note values (half notes and dotted half notes) and attending to eighth notes by counting in half-beat increments (1 + 2 + etc.). Using a metronome or click track helped to ensure our counting accuracy.

We can reverse the process and use these same rhythm grids as excellent tools for notating the details of a rhythmic phrase when listening to music. Let's listen again to some of the songs from Chapter 1 that were in 2/4 and apply the rhythm grid approach to determine their rhythmic notation. Let's review the 2/4 rhythm grid introduced in Chapter 1.

Tip: When establishing the rhythm grid, set the grid to account for the smallest note value (fastest note) in the phrase. If the smallest note value is the quarter note, then simply tracking the beat is sufficient. But if the smallest note value is an eighth note, tracking and counting 1 + 2 + etc., as you listen to the phrase might be necessary. You might even want to assign each click of the metronome to represent the smallest note value, in this case, the eighth note, leaving no room for error.

Reading, Writing and Rhythmetic

Activity One: *Using the Rhythm Grid*

The following song excerpts use a variety of rhythmic values ranging from half notes to eighth notes. We'll revisit some of the songs we discovered were in 2/4 from Chapter 1, reserving songs in 3/4 for the next chapter. Consider setting your rhythm grid to accommodate the smallest note value, the eighth note, counting 1 + 2 +. Each melodic example will be accompanied with the click track representing the beat, the quarter note value. Our job is to determine only the rhythms for these melodies. We'll revisit some of these songs again in Chapter 4 for their pitch content, so stay tuned! I've figured out the first song to get your motor going.

9 "London Bridge Is Falling Down"

Note: What you hear as the "uneven" pair of eighth notes is notated as a dotted 8th, 16th note figure (♩. ♪). We'll be exploring sixteenth note patterns in greater detail in Chapter 4.

10 – **14** Now it's your turn. Try your hand at some or all of the following 8-bar song excerpts. The song titles are listed below with accompanying templates for you to write in your answers. Audio tracks 10–14 will provide a simple version of the melodies. Enjoy!

10 "Old MacDonald"

11 "Joy to the World"

12 "Mary Had a Little Lamb"

13 "Yankee Doodle Dandy"

14 "Pennsylvania Polka"

Check the Answer Key (p.142) to see the results.

2 MEMORIZING "RHYTHM WORDS"

Collecting Souvenirs

It is very common for sections of songs to be eight bars long. As you saw in Activity One, some entire songs are only eight measures! Notice that these eight bars often consist of two 4-bar phrases. Sometimes these two phrases repeat, with slightly different endings. Or the second phrase "answers" the first phrase. As we collect our song souvenirs throughout our transcription trip, pay attention to how musical ideas are organized within songs. We will be examining song form in greater detail in later chapters; start noticing the landmarks along the way.

Counting and conducting are very convenient and efficient tools to use with songs that incorporate very simple rhythmic patterns and a lot of repetition. These tools can be equally helpful when dealing with more challenging rhythmic patterns, where breaking the pattern down and analyzing through counting is essential. But let me suggest another possible approach in addition to counting.

MEMORIZING "RHYTHM WORDS"

We are going to make a vocabulary list of "rhythm words" and commit them to memory. Let me give you a good analogy with the English language.

When looking at the word "t-h-e," what do you see? Do you spell out the letters "t-h-e" or do you immediately react to these letters, recognizing them as the word "the"? When you were young and first learning to read and spell words, sounding out the individual letters was a good place to start, but you are now well past that point and can easily read words, sentences, and even novels. Rather than focus on the reading mechanics of sounding out and spelling individual words, you concentrate on the meaning of the statement.

Spelling out the letters of words is similar to counting, "1 + 2 +..." through a rhythmic phrase. I suggest that we develop a spelling list of short rhythm words, become comfortably familiar with them, and then commit these "words" to memory.

Let's start with a short list of two-beat rhythm words which are comprised of only half, quarter and eighth note combinations. Sound familiar? These were the same basic note values found in our rhythm grid from Chapter 1! For now, we won't include rests except for the whole rest (➡) in order to give us a chance to breathe in between the rhythm words. The good news is that the resulting list is short, with only eight possible combinations!

Note: Modern music notation uses a whole rest (➡) to indicate a bar of rest, regardless of what the time signature is.

ACTIVITY TWO: *Memorizing Two-Beat Rhythm Words*

Listen to Audio track 15 as you read the following 16-bar example in $\frac{2}{4}$ time. Each rhythm word will be introduced in one measure, and then followed by a measure of rest in which you are to repeat the word. Stating or singing the rhythm word is a great proactive way to "feed your inner hearing" and more powerful than just being a passive listener, so sing, sing, sing! Your inner hearing will thank you for it.

Each word is numbered for reference. Spend as much time as you need with this preliminary "filling up the gas tank" activity and commit the eight rhythm words firmly in your memory. In the next activity you will need to recognize and identify these same words when they are presented in random order.

Reading, Writing and Rhythmetic

15 Two-beat rhythm words

Activity Three: *Recognizing the Two-Beat Rhythm Word*

16 Let's do a test drive to see how well you've memorized the rhythm words from Activity Two. Listen to the following 12 examples and transcribe them in the 24-bar template provided below.

You will hear a sequence of one measure containing the rhythm word, followed by one measure of rest, allowing you a little bit of time for quick reflection and response. The words will be presented in random order, with some repeats, so listen carefully.

It might be helpful to reference the list of rhythm words from the previous activity as you listen, so you don't have to recreate and picture the "words" with your mind's eye. Referencing the "words" by their associated number will be handy for quick response. Feel free to pause between examples if you need extra time to determine your answers. Ready, set, listen!

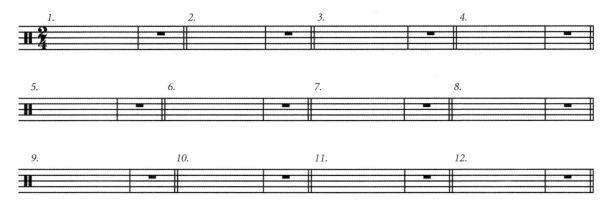

Tip: Make sure to listen first and not jump too quickly to the translation stage. Sing back what you hear before deciding what the word is. Taking that extra second or two to listen attentively will pay off.

Check the Answer Key (p.142) to see how you did.

Going the Extra Mile

Get extra mileage out of the Answer Key for reading practice. Remember, reading and writing is a two-way street. If you didn't do so well identifying the rhythm words, just spend some time reading through the Answer Key as you listen to the recording. Repeated exposure to the material will be good reinforcement. If you did great on this assignment, then simply read through the Answer Key template as you recite the rhythm words—use a metronome or click track, or be brave and go solo! Either way, don't forget to conduct!

2 Memorizing "Rhythm Words"

Two for the Road

Create your own short rhythm word examples and perform them for your partner. Make sure you are accurate in your performance (which is good practice in itself). Have your partner write down your example. How did they do? Now switch roles. I've created a sample below, but feel free to make things more challenging by lengthening the examples, requiring reflex reaction from your partner…and enjoy!

My sample example in 2/4

Let's now double the fun and combine two measures of 2/4 together. The result will be one measure of 4/4 time.

Introducing 4/4 Time

The most popular time signature found in contemporary music is 4/4 time, also called Common time (**C**). It is the first compound meter we will work with in this book: it is commonly felt as 2 + 2. You might ask: how do we know if it's two bars of 2/4 or one bar of 4/4? Here's how: the downbeat (beat one) of a 4/4 measure continues to be the strongest beat of the measure. But, beat 3 is also accented, just not as strongly as the downbeat. Beats 2 and 4 are weak beats. So, if the measure is 4/4, the pulses will be felt as "Strong, weak, less strong, weak." If it's really two measures of 2/4, the pulses will be "Strong, weak, Strong weak." Another factor useful in determining the difference is often the style of music. We'll explore that feature later in the chapter when we reference a variety of songs in 4/4.

Let's take a look at and practice with the conducting pattern for 4/4 in the next activity.

Activity Four: *Conducting in 4/4*

As with the 2/4 and 3/4 conducting patterns, the first beat will always be a vertical line downward, announcing the downbeat, and the final beat will come from the outside of the body (providing a clear preparation signal for the upcoming downbeat). Take a look at the 4/4 conducting pattern shown below and trace the picture: down, in (towards the body), out (away from the body), up. If you're conducting with the right hand (which is the standard): down, left, right, up. This pattern resembles a pendulum in motion. As you conduct, count the beats aloud, "1, 2, 3, 4," giving the strongest accent to the downbeat with a slightly less accent on beat 3. Keep the pattern flowing steadily, avoiding "dead spots" along the way.

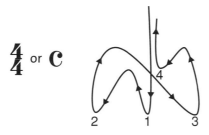

Reading, Writing and Rhythmetic

Activity Five: *Adding the 4/4 Grid for Counting and Conducting*

Follow along with the 8-bar rhythm grid below, counting and conducting in 4/4 as you listen to Audio track 17. This is similar to the practice routine in Chapter 1 with the 2/4 and 3/4 grids. We'll get our engine warmed up, moving through the different gears of whole notes (four-beat value) through eighth notes. The audio track is a total of sixteen measures long. The first eight bars present the rhythm grid along with the click track. The remaining eight bars include only the click track for your solo performance.

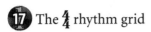 The 4/4 rhythm grid

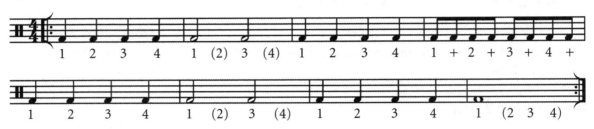

Note: In music notation, repeat signs (𝄆 𝄇) indicate that the measures enclosed by the repeat signs should be played again.

Activity Six: *Listening to and Conducting with Songs in 4/4*

Listen to the following 12 songs that are in 4/4 time. You can find these popular songs on the web or they might even live in your own private recording library of CD's and mp3's. First find the beat, and then conduct along.

1. "All I Have to Do is Dream," The Everly Brothers, *The Very Best of the Everly Brothers*
2. "Beat It," Michael Jackson, *Thriller*
3. "Birthday," The Beatles, *White Album*
4. "Burning Down the House," Talking Heads, *Speaking in Tongues*
5. "C Jam Blues," Duke Ellington, *Duke Ellington's Greatest Hits*
6. "Fire," Jimi Hendrix, *Are You Experienced*
7. "Jeepers Creepers," Louis Armstrong, *C'est Si Bon*
8. "A Little Night Music, First Movement," A. Mozart
9. "My Girl," The Temptations, *The Temptations Sing Smokey*
10. "River," Joni Mitchell, *Blue*
11. "Uptown Girl," Billy Joel, *An Innocent Man*
12. "Walkin'," Miles Davis, *Walkin'*

Collecting Souvenirs

Share your own examples of songs that are in 4/4 time with classmates or band members. Let them know how they can access the recordings for a listen. You shouldn't have any trouble finding examples…there are thousands of them out there!

ACTIVITY SEVEN: *Creating Compound Rhythm Words*

Let's add some compound rhythm words to our vocabulary list. We can simply create different combinations of the eight two-beat words listed in Activity Two, linking two words within one measure of 4/4. How many possible combinations are there? There are many more than eight!

I'll start the list with a few combinations; can you add to the list?

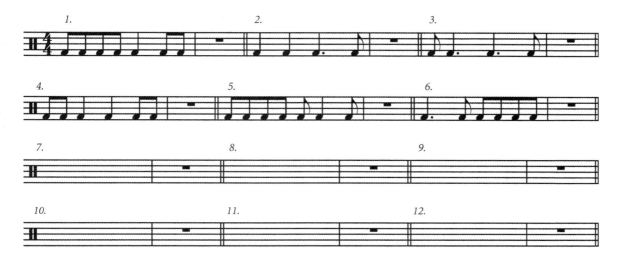

Tip: This is a perfect opportunity to talk about the "imaginary bar line" notation rule. Simply put, it divides the compound measure of 4/4 into two equal halves, 2 beats + 2 beats (see above). The eye can easily see the "two-beat words" as independent and separate. This convention makes music much easier to read as you become more adept at recognizing small rhythmic units rather than larger ones. And as listeners and transcribers, our job is made a little bit easier too, as we put our work with the rhythm words to practical use.

There are some common exceptions to the "imaginary bar line" notation. These exceptions are used because they are simpler to read than they would be if they followed the rule. There may be other exceptions, usually used for specific rhythmic phrasing.

Imaginary bar line common exceptions

Reading, Writing and Rhythmetic

Activity Eight: *Recognizing Compound Rhythm Words in 4/4*

🎧 Listen to Audio track 18 and identify the following 12 examples of compound rhythm words in 4/4. You will hear a pattern of one measure of the rhythm figure, followed by one measure of rest, allowing for some breathing room between each example. You might recognize some of these compound words from the list we created in Activity Seven. A template of 24 bars is provided below for you to write in your answers.

Follow the same recommended steps we took in Activity Three. Good luck!

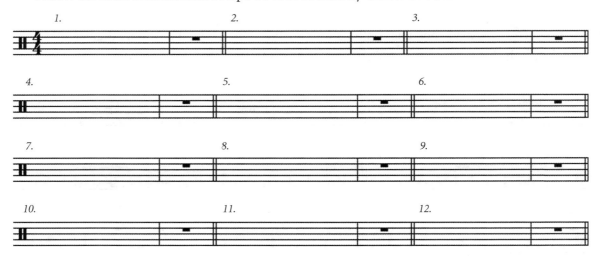

When you're ready, check the Answer Key (p.143) to see how well you did. These same compound rhythm words will reappear throughout many of the song excerpts used in Activity Nine's transcription workout. Previewing them now will get our engines primed and ears perked.

Two for the Road

Create an 8-bar example that incorporates some of our four-beat compound rhythm words. Make sure you can hear what you've written before you pass it to your partner. Have him or her read and perform it. Remind your partner that conducting is part of the performance! How did they do? Now reverse roles.

Activity Nine: *Takin' It to the Streets*

Let's revisit the 12 4/4 songs we listened to in Activity Six and extract some short passages for transcription. You should recognize some of our two-beat and compound rhythm words in action. As we look under the hood for close examination of the rhythm engine of music, consider using all the tools in the kit: conducting, counting, and recognition of rhythm words.

I've added more two-beat rhythm words to the list; these words incorporate some quarter and eighth note rests. We'll need these additions for our transcription work in this activity. Pull off the road and spend a little time practicing with these additions before you "take it to the streets" with the song excerpts.

Check the Answer Key (pp.143–145) when you're finished.

2 Memorizing "Rhythm Words"

Two-beat rhythm words with rests

Let's get back on the road and tackle the following songs. Each example indicates the particular clip to listen to. A template is provided for each example.

1. "All I Have to Do Is Dream" vocal melody, 1st verse

When I want you

2. "Beat It" vocal melody, 1st verse

They told him

3. "Birthday" bass and guitar riff

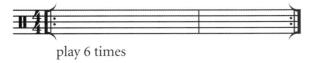

play 6 times

4. "Burning Down the House" vocal melody, 1st verse

Ah! Watch out

burn - in' down the house

5. "C Jam Blues" full band melody, 2nd chorus

play 3 times

Reading, Writing and Rhythmetic

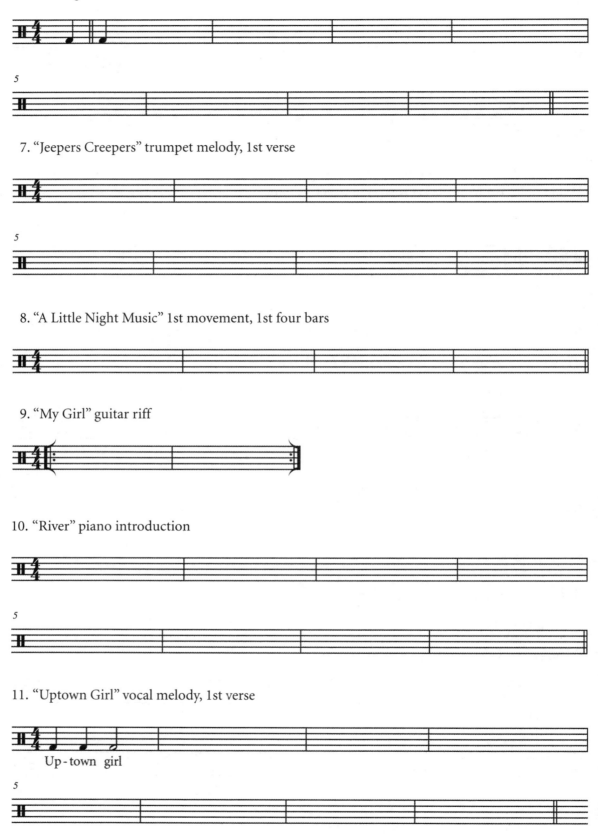

12. "Walkin'" introduction

Tip: Don't feel like you have to complete all the examples in one session. Taking breaks allows for a fresh set of ears and renewed concentration. Don't hesitate to pause or rewind the recording if you need to. We are not in a race. It's not about speed: it's about accuracy.

ACTIVITY TEN: *Round Trip*
Let's revisit the same songs we worked with in Activity One, but this time from the perspective of using our memorized vocabulary list of two-beat rhythm words. Do you recognize some favorites from the list? What were some patterns used frequently throughout these songs?

In the next chapter we'll add some three-beat rhythm words to our vocabulary list as we revisit some songs in 3/4 time. Conducting, counting, and reacting to rhythm words—what a powerful combination! With routine practice, we're becoming more and more rhythmically fluent.

We'll also explore one of the big picture aspects of the music from a tonal point of view and learn how to determine if the song is in a major or minor key. Are you ready?

Approaching the Fork in the Road
Let's take a moment to consider the benefits and drawbacks of hand-written notation vs. using notation software. Which road should we take?

I'm old fashioned and grew up in a time when notation software didn't exist. I got by with paper, pencil (never a pen!) and one big fat eraser, and transcribed by hand, technology-free. To this day this is my first inclination, to do my work by hand. I feel more connected to the process and can concentrate better. I like the feel of the pencil in my hand, deriving an artistic and physical pleasure from sketching and drawing the notes. Ah, the good old days! But there was one big drawback: how would I know that my answers were correct, or not, doing things this way?

The modern world has provided many wonderful technological tools for the musician, one of them being notation software. And one of the most helpful features of notation software is the playback feature. Having the opportunity to hear as you notate, or to hit playback and hear the immediate results of what you've written is a huge benefit for the transcriber. The playback feature tells no lies, and objectively plays back what you've notated. Compare this with the process of reading back and subjectively performing your own work. Are you really performing what's written on the page, or are you performing from memory? Of course, you could ask a third party to perform what you've written, but that's exactly the role of the playback feature.

What are your opinions and thoughts about the high road or the low road?

3 IS THE SONG IN A MAJOR OR MINOR KEY?

INTRODUCTION

The first two chapters of this book were devoted exclusively to working with rhythms. In this chapter, we'll begin working with the other essential musical ingredient: pitches (also called "tones" or "notes"). We'll begin our discussion with how notes relate to each other within a key, and then discuss how to determine if music is in a major or minor key.

The most important note to establish first is the root, which is the first note (or "tonic") of the scale. Finding the root will be our "Route One" destination. We can rely on intuition for starters, but I'll suggest some musical tips to get us there safe and sound, and with confidence. Once we've arrived at the root, we'll listen up from it to the third note of the scale to determine if we hear a major or minor third interval. It's this relationship from the root to the third of the scale that helps determine if the song is in a major or minor key.

We'll continue our rhythmic work in $\frac{3}{4}$. Reading will take the front seat in this chapter, setting the example for recognizing similar rhythmic phrases when listening and transcribing. Remember, reading and writing is a two-way street. In addition to conducting and counting, I'll suggest tapping as another tool for reading accuracy, focusing on feeling the difference between "on" the beat (downward movement) and "off" the beat (upward movement).

And, as is our tradition of "Takin' it to the Streets," we'll apply all our work to the real deal, listening to songs from our memory or recordings for practical practice.

Back on the road again…

IS THE SONG IN A MAJOR OR MINOR KEY?

Let's begin our work with the other essential musical ingredient: the pitches, (or tones, or notes). Most contemporary and popular music is tonal, meaning centered in a key. You might hear someone say, "The song is in the key of G." What that means is that the majority of notes in the song belong to the G scale, or that the melody seems to come to rest on the note "G." There are two types of tonal keys: major and minor. Some songs use notes from major scales, others from minor scales, and most songs are either in a major or minor key. How can we tell the difference between major and minor? Let's explore.

Trust your instincts. All of us have experience listening to and playing music. We've all heard and performed music in both major and minor keys. When listening, you might instinctively have the answer to the question, "Is this major or minor?" What are some of the contributing factors that support this intuitive approach?

If the song has lyrics, they may tell a story with an intended emotional impact on the listener. Our emotions are guided down one path or another, with the music playing a supporting role in this drama. Many times, but not always, we equate the major sound with happy, virtuous, positive lyrics; we associate the minor sound with sad, sinister, negative tales. The same thing can happen

READING, WRITING AND RHYTHMETIC

to us when watching a movie—the film score is playing with our emotions. Of course we can't always depend on these emotional responses to be so predictable.

Sometimes intuition alone isn't enough, so we'll take a more analytical route and examine the music independent of the lyrical message and our emotional response to determine if the song is in a major or minor key. What do the notes tell us? First, we need to locate the most important note of the key: the root, "1" or "tonic." From there, we can take the next step of determining if this is the root of a major or minor scale. Let's find that root!

FINDING THE ROOT OF THE SCALE

How do we find the root of the scale? Listen to the song from *beginning to end*, don't jump in too quickly and guess. In most cases, you'll find the root at the very end of the song. Why there? Because this is where the song comes to a point of complete rest; "dah-dah...the end," the musical idea has come home to stay. Listen to the last note of the melody, listen to the final note the bassist plays, and listen to the last chord of the song. It is 95% likely that in all three places, you'll hear the root of the scale.

Tip: A big mistake many beginning transcribers make is assuming that the first note of the melody is the root of the scale. Honor the yellow caution light and beware—many times the first note will *not* be the "1" of the key. It's better to take the full journey to the end of the phrase, or better yet, to the very end of the song to find the root.

ACTIVITY ONE: *Finding the Root of the Scale*

🔵**19** – 🔵**33** Listen to the following 15 melodic phrases on Audio tracks 19–33 and find the root of the scale. Remember to listen through to the end of the phrase. Sing out loud the pitch that sounds like the root. You probably won't know the name of the actual pitch you're singing. You're just getting the sense of what note feels like the home, i.e., which note sounds the most restful. This is the pure "ear training" step in the process.

1. "Bourrée," J.S. Bach
2. "Farandole," Georges Bizet
3. "Frère Jacques," traditional
4. "Glory, Glory Hallelujah," traditional
5. "Greensleeves," traditional
6. "Joy to the World," traditional
7. "Mary Had a Little Lamb," traditional
8. "Mexican Hat Dance," traditional
9. "Minuet," J.S. Bach
10. "Ode to Joy," Ludwig van Beethoven
11. "Scarborough Fair," traditional
12. "Sometimes I Feel Like a Motherless Child," traditional gospel
13. "We Three Kings," traditional
14. "When Johnny Comes Marching Home," traditional
15. "You Are My Sunshine," J. Davis and C. Mitchell

Finding out the actual name of the pitch you sang for the root is the "brain training" step, and you'll need some help from your instrument to do this.

Unless you have perfect pitch, you will need to refer to a tuning fork, your instrument, or a keyboard for the answer. (We will describe the differences between perfect or "absolute" pitch and relative pitch in an upcoming "Approaching the Fork in the Road" discussion…stay tuned!).

Sing the root as you try to find this pitch on your instrument. This process might feel like trial and error until you land on the right note, but that's OK. The real work was identifying the root by ear, by singing it. Locating the root of the scale is our first step in exploring relative pitch (how pitches relate to one another within a key).

Refer to the Answer Key (p.146) for the pitch name of the root for each of the 15 melodic phrases. How successful were you in matching the roots you sang to the actual pitches on your instrument?

For additional practice, sustain the root either by singing or playing it, as you listen to the melodies. This will confirm that you're hearing the anchor of the phrase, the root or "1" of the scale.

Going the Extra Mile
Try locating the root of the scale with other songs you're familiar with, following the recommended steps in Activity One.

Taking this first step, finding the root of the scale, is essential before venturing any further down the relative pitch path. "There's no place like home," as Dorothy said. "There's no two, three without a one to start from," is what I say. Once you've mastered the ability of determining the root, the second step, determining if this is the root of a major or minor scale, can then be made with sure footing. Let's take that second step.

MAJOR OR MINOR?

34 Is the song in a major or minor key? Listen to the two melodies on Audio track 34: one is in major, the other in minor. Both melodies have the same starting and ending pitch, C (the root of the scale). Both melodies share the same contour (shape). Which melody is in the key of C major; which one is in C minor?

How did you make your decision? As mentioned earlier in this chapter, you might have known intuitively which melody was major, which minor. But if we want to eliminate intuitive guesswork, let's consider something else.

We will be exploring major and minor scales in their entirety in upcoming chapters. But for now, we will focus on the relationship of the root to the third of the scale in order to decide if the song is in a major or minor key. If you hear a major third interval from the root to the third, the song is in a major key. If you hear a minor third interval from the root to the third, then the song is in a minor key. It's as easy as that!

What might not be so easy is quickly and confidently distinguishing between the sound of major and minor third intervals, so we'll take a small detour to give our inner hearing a chance to recognize major and minor third intervals. Listen to Audio track 35 which compares the two.

Reading, Writing and Rhythmetic

Activity Two: *Playing and Singing Major and Minor Third Intervals*

How do you learn to distinguish the sounds of major and minor third intervals? One way is to sing them. I firmly believe that if you can sing it, you can hear it. Another way of saying this is, that if you can't hear it, you can't sing it. (Ask any vocalist.) Practice the following routine.

1. Play the major or minor third interval on your instrument or keyboard and listen closely. Play the interval both ways: melodically and harmonically, as was demonstrated on Audio track 35.
2. To eliminate guesswork, play the intervals as you sing them. Playing ensures that your natural instrument, your voice, sings the correct notes.
3. Finally, sing the interval without the instrument or keyboard. This is the step where confidence in your inner hearing takes over the wheel.

Activity Three: *Recognizing Major and Minor Third Intervals*

Listen to Audio track 36 and identify the following 12 examples as either major or minor third intervals. As a beginner, you might need to use your instrument with this activity—that's OK! When your self-confidence is ready, you can go it alone and rely solely on your inner hearing ability.

Check the Answer Key (p.146) to see how you did.

Two for the Road

Quiz your partner: can they sing a major or minor third interval? Play major and minor thirds: can they identify which is which? Then of course, switch seats!

Equipped with the trio of intuition, the ability to find the root of the scale, and the ability to recognize major and minor third intervals, we're ready to give the melody the third degree and determine if it's in a major or minor key.

Activity Four: *Is the Melody in a Major or Minor Key?*

19 – 33 Let's return to the same melodies we worked with in Activity One (Audio tracks 19–33) and now determine if these melodies are in a major or minor key. We've already located the roots (and know the actual pitch names as well). Determine if you hear a major or minor third interval above the root: play or sing your chosen interval. If you choose the wrong answer, the "crash" of sound will help direct you to the correct answer. For example, if you think the song is in minor and play a major third interval, you'll certainly hear the collision of the two thirds!

Now check the Answer Key (p.146) to see how you did.

37 For fun, let's take a detour and listen to a couple of "twisted tunes." How would Beethoven's 5th symphony theme ("da-da-da-dum") sound in major? And, "Happy Birthday" in a minor key? Maybe not such a happy occasion!

3 IS THE SONG IN A MAJOR OR MINOR KEY?

ACTIVITY FIVE: *Takin' It to the Streets*

Is the song in a major or minor key? I've compiled a very short list of some of my favorites, from a variety of musical styles. Give these songs a listen. I've indicated the root of the scale for each example, so you can immediately "cut to the chase" and determine the major or minor quality.

1. "Alice in Wonderland," Bill Evans, *Sunday at the Village Vanguard* (C)
2. "All Along the Watchtower," Bob Dylan, *John Wesley Harding* (C♯) or
   Jimi Hendrix, *Electric Ladyland* (C)
3. "Another Day in Paradise," Phil Collins, *…But Seriously* (F♯)
4. "Beat It," Michael Jackson, *Thriller* (E♭)
5. "Carey," Joni Mitchell, *Blue* (D♭)
6. "Chim Chim Cher-ee," *Mary Poppins* soundtrack (C)
7. "Eleanor Rigby," The Beatles, *Revolver* (E)
8. "Every Breath You Take," The Police, *Synchronicity* (A♭)
9. "Goodbye Yellow Brick Road," Elton John, *Goodbye Yellow Brick Road* (F)
10. "Here Comes the Sun," The Beatles, *Abbey Road* (A)
11. "Human Nature," Michael Jackson, *Thriller* (D)
12. "Isn't She Lovely," Stevie Wonder, *Songs in the Key of Life* (E)
13. "Jeepers Creepers," Louis Armstrong, *C'est Si Bon* (G)
14. "Mas Que Nada," Sergio Mendez & Brazil '66, *Greatest Hits* (F)
15. "My Girl," The Temptations, *The Temptations Sing Smokey* (C)
16. "Ob-La-Di, Ob-La-Da," The Beatles, *White Album* (B♭)
17. "Que Pasa," Horace Silver, *Song for My Father* (C♯)
18. "Rolling in the Deep," Adele, *21* (C)
19. "Russians," Sting, *The Dream of the Blue Turtles* (C)
20. "We Will Rock You," Queen, *News of the World* (E)
    Check the Answer Key (p.146) to see if you agree.

Collecting Souvenirs

What are some of your own personal favorites? Consider if they're in a major or minor key and share your collection with classmates or band members.

We're off to a great start! We will explore the complete major scale in the next chapter. Time now to turn the wheel towards groove city and see what makes $\frac{3}{4}$ tick!

READING RHYTHMS IN $\frac{3}{4}$

In Chapter 2 we became familiar with simple two-beat rhythm words in $\frac{2}{4}$, and then coupled these simple words together, creating compound rhythm words in $\frac{4}{4}$. If we were to make a list of three-beat rhythm words, using only dotted half notes through eighth notes (not including rests), the list would amount to more than 20 possibilities. That's quite a list to take on and memorize! So, we'll use a different approach to address typical $\frac{3}{4}$ rhythmic patterns in this chapter. Let's put the task of reading in the front seat, as we continue to use our conducting and counting tools. Transcribing will remain in the back seat for the moment, but will certainly benefit from being an observant passenger.

25

Reading, Writing and Rhythmetic

Activity Six: *Reading in 3/4*

Read through the following 32-bar example, using the rhythm grid listed below the notes as a guide. The grid will use eighth notes (1 + 2 + 3 +) to accommodate the smallest (fastest) note value. Counting the smallest subdivision of the beat, the eighth note, will ensure accuracy throughout the reading process.

No specific tempo has been indicated, so to start, choose a comfortable tempo, and set the metronome or click track to that tempo. Use the click to represent either the quarter note ("1, 2, 3") or eighth note ("1 + 2 + 3 +"). Try both ways and see what works best for you. Remember to keep the durations accurate.

Are you ready? Give yourself two bars of 3/4 before you begin reading in order to have a firm hold on the tempo.

In the first two chapters of this book, we talked about the 4-bar phrase and the 8-bar section as the standard format for many songs. The reading example above takes things a step further and indicates how each 8-bar section relates to or differs from one another. "Rehearsal letters" are assigned to each section, designating their similarities or differences. Notice that we have two nearly identical sections (labeled as A), and then a new idea presented in the sections labeled B and C. The B and C sections share similarities in their first 4-bar phrases but have different endings. Should we call them both B's because they are 50% similar, or B and C because they are

3 Is the Song in a Major or Minor Key?

50% different? We could argue for either case. In later chapters we'll discuss song form in greater detail. Until then, here is a preview to get us thinking in that direction.

Two for the Road

You might want to try Activity Six with a partner. It's OK to lean on your partner (and vice versa) as you perform together. As the song says, "We all need somebody to lean on."

Tip: It's a good practice habit to record your performance. Often when you're in the moment of live performance you can miss important details. However, by listening to your recording you can assess things more objectively, detect mistakes, as well as acknowledge strengths in your performance. The recording tells no lies and you can learn a lot from it. You don't have to be in a recording studio to do this: simply push "record" on your smart phone!

TAPPING

Here's another counting approach I learned from a student. It's extremely helpful for reading syncopated rhythms: rhythms that accent the "+'s of the beat (also called offbeats). As you count, "1 + 2 + 3 +," tap down on the table for those attacks that hit "on" the beat (1, 2, 3), and lift up your hand for the attacks that fall "off" the beat (+, +, +). This adds a nice visual "down, up" to the counting system. As you perform this "down, up" pattern, count "1 + 2 + 3 +," or, count "on, off, on, off, on, off." Counting syncopated rhythmic figures will involve a lot of "+'s" or "off's." Your hand will be in the "up" position when these offbeat attacks occur.

ACTIVITY SEVEN: *Tapping as You Read*

Try reading through the 32-bar example of Activity Six once again, this time applying the tapping/counting approach just described. Compare this approach to conducting and counting. Which do you prefer?

Make reading music a regular part of your practice routine. It will have a powerful impact on your ability to recognize rhythmic patterns when listening and transcribing.

For the next leg of our trip it's time to switch places, and put reading in the back seat, transcribing in the front.

ACTIVITY EIGHT: *Recognizing the Two Measure Figures*

38 While looking at "Activity Six: Reading in $\frac{3}{4}$," listen to the six 2-bar excerpts on Audio track 38. Each excerpt occurs somewhere in Activity Six. The 2-bar figure might have occurred in more than one location, so scan through the entire 32 bars. When you've located the figure, write it down. A template is provided on the next page for you to write in your answers.

Reading, Writing and Rhythmetic

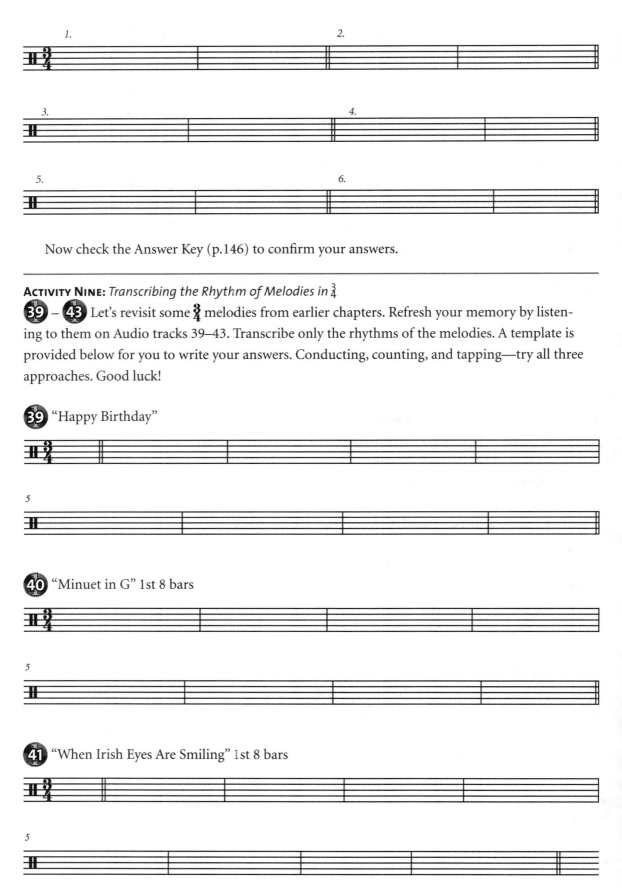

Now check the Answer Key (p.146) to confirm your answers.

Activity Nine: *Transcribing the Rhythm of Melodies in 3/4*

39 – **43** Let's revisit some 3/4 melodies from earlier chapters. Refresh your memory by listening to them on Audio tracks 39–43. Transcribe only the rhythms of the melodies. A template is provided below for you to write your answers. Conducting, counting, and tapping—try all three approaches. Good luck!

39 "Happy Birthday"

40 "Minuet in G" 1st 8 bars

41 "When Irish Eyes Are Smiling" 1st 8 bars

3 Is the Song in a Major or Minor Key?

42 "U.S. National Anthem" 1st 8 bars

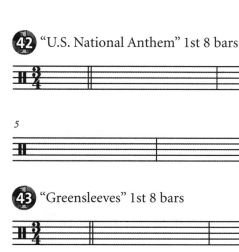

43 "Greensleeves" 1st 8 bars

Check the Answer Key (p.147) for results.

Going the Extra Mile

Let's take 3/4 to the streets and transcribe the rhythm of the following song excerpts. You'll need to research these songs on the web if you don't have them in your own collection of recordings. This challenge is meant only for the brave…are you game? I knew you would be!

Templates are provided for the following song excerpts.

1. "Scarborough Fair," Simon & Garfunkel, *Parsley, Sage, Rosemary and Thyme*
2. "Moon River," Andy Williams, *The Very Best of Andy Williams*
3. "Sunrise, Sunset," *Fiddler on the Roof* soundtrack
4. "Lucy in the Sky with Diamonds," The Beatles, *Sgt. Pepper's Lonely Hearts Club Band*
5. "Chim Chim Cher-ee," *Mary Poppins* soundtrack
6. "Piano Man," Billy Joel, *Piano Man*
7. "Open Arms," Journey, *Escape*
8. "Alice in Wonderland," Bill Evans, *Sunday at the Village Vanguard*
9. "Someday My Prince Will Come," Miles Davis, *Someday My Prince Will Come*

When you're finished, check the Answer Key (pp.148–150) to see how well you've done!

READING, WRITING AND RHYTHMETIC

1. "Scarborough Fair" vocals, 1st 24 bars

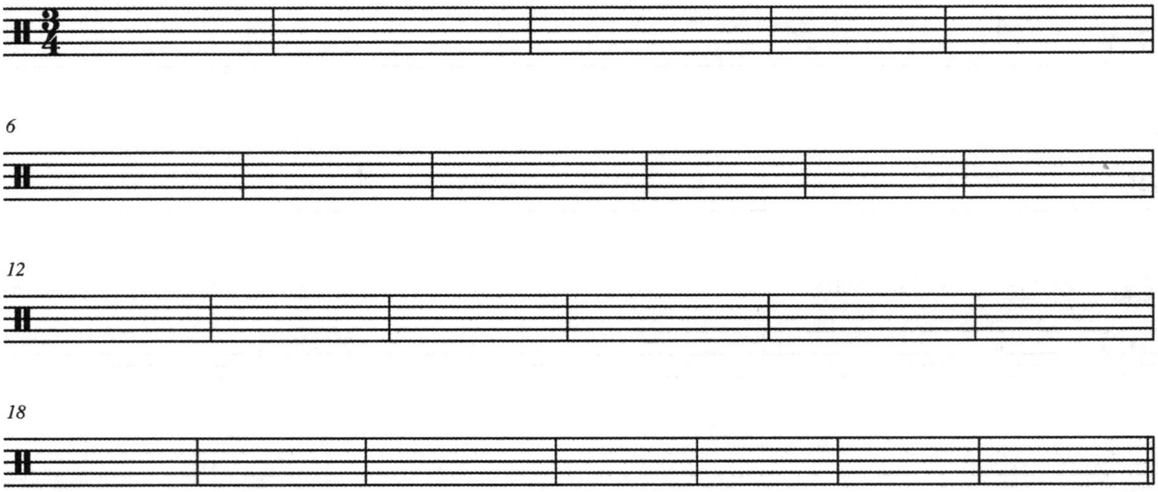

6

12

18

2. "Moon River" vocal, 1st 16 bars

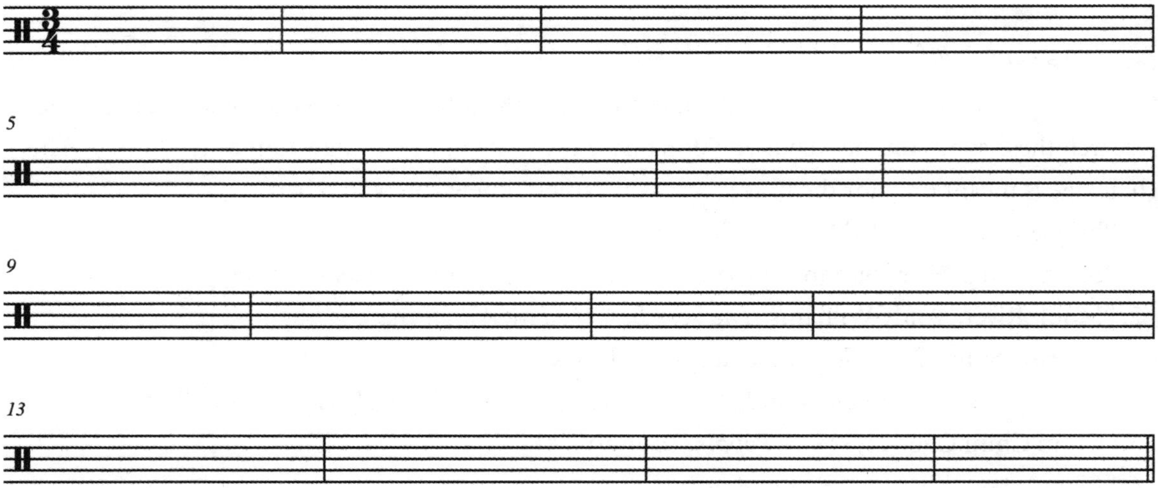

5

9

13

3. "Sunrise, Sunset" vocals, chorus (B section), 16 bars

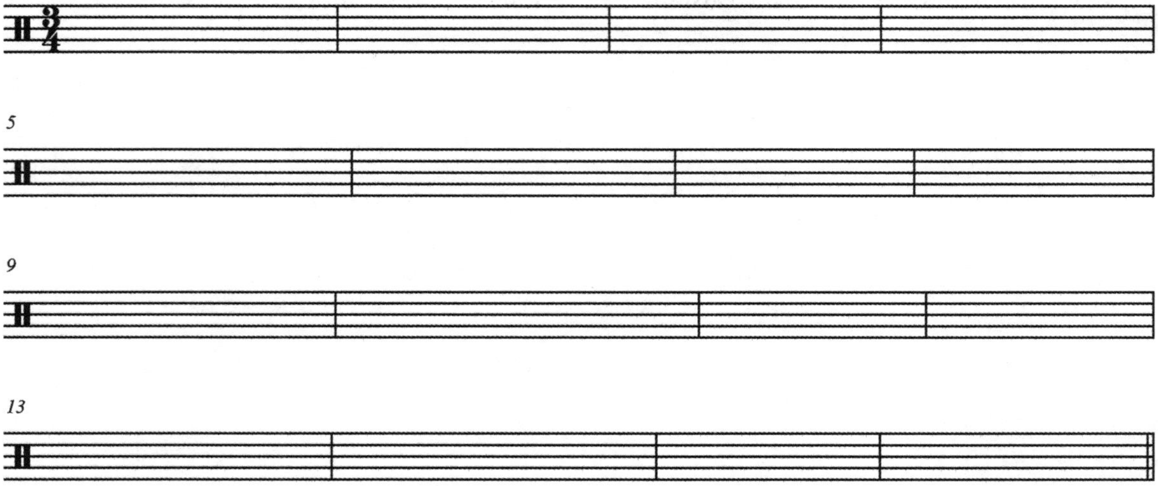

5

9

13

3   Is the Song in a Major or Minor Key?

4. "Lucy in the Sky with Diamonds" vocal, 1st 19 bars

5. "Chim Chim Cher-ee" vocals, 1st 25 bars

6. "Piano Man" harmonica introduction, 16 bars

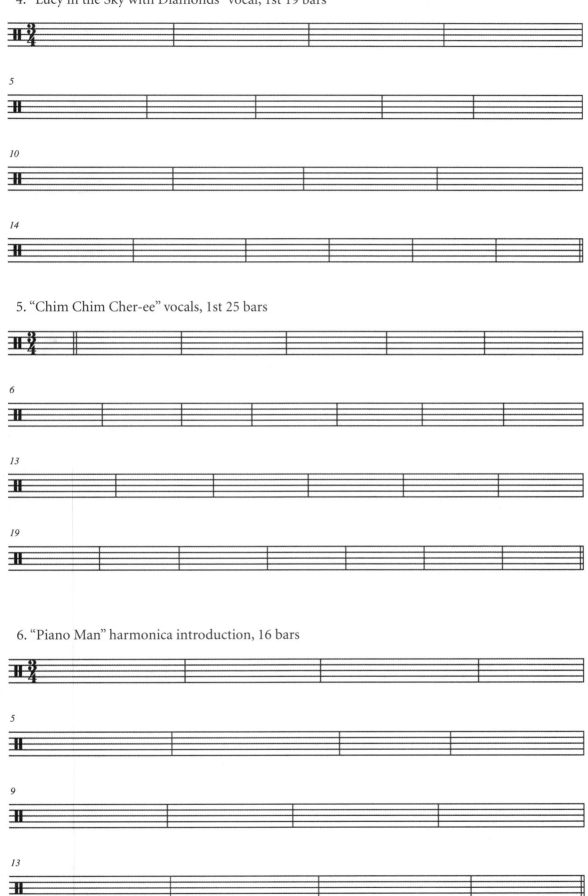

31

READING, WRITING AND RHYTHMETIC

7. "Open Arms" vocal, 1st 16 bars

8. "Alice in Wonderland" piano melody, B section, band entrance, 16 bars

9. "Some Day My Prince Will Come" piano chord introduction, 16 bars

ACTIVITY TEN: *Round Trip*

How many three-beat rhythm words can you come up with? Without using any rests, there are more than 20 possibilities. By adding rests to the mix, that number will increase dramatically. Go for it! Remember, ear training is 50% brain training—this is an excellent workout with numbers and notation.

We've made excellent headway in this chapter with our first dealings with tonality: we found the root, the "1" of the scale, and then determined if the song was in a major or minor key. In Chapter 4, we'll spotlight the major scale in its entirety and learn about the musical language of solfege. We'll also take our rhythm grid to new territories, exploring sixteenth notes: "a-one, a-two, a-one e + a, two e + a"…let's get this party started!

Approaching the Fork in the Road

"Is it OK to use your instrument when transcribing?" This is one of the most common questions my students ask. My short answer is, "Yes, but…"

Do whatever you have to do, use any support system you have (such as using your instrument) to become engaged in the game (work!) of ear training. As beginner transcribers, it's hard to trust inner hearing skills on their own. So, use your best musical friend, your instrument, for reference to ensure and confirm what your inner hearing heard. After all, most of us don't have perfect pitch so we will sometimes need to reference an instrument when transcribing.

Transcription is a balancing act. In the beginning, you might rely heavily on your instrument, but with experience and practice you'll depend less on it, as you gain more trust in your inner hearing skills. Further down the road, inner hearing will take the lead and your instrument will just double-check and confirm what your ear hears.

Using your instrument might initially seem like a short cut, but it's one which leads to trusting your inner hearing. Driving with inner hearing, you'll hit some pot holes along the way and make some mistakes. Transcribing might take longer, but in the long run, you'll be glad you used inner hearing to arrive at your destination as you develop self-confidence along the way.

4 EXPLORING MAJOR KEY MELODIES WITH SOLFEGE

INTRODUCTION

In Chapter 3 we focused on hearing and identifying the root of the scale, the "1" of the key, and learned to distinguish between the sound of major and minor keys. In this chapter we will explore the major scale in its entirety, and learn to identify how all seven pitches of the scale interact with each other. First we'll concentrate exclusively on how the scale tones connect by stepwise motion.

The "moveable Do" solfege system, the musical language that equates each scale tone to its numerical placement within the key: *do-re-mi*, easy as 1-2-3, will be introduced in this chapter.

We'll be singing, improvising and transcribing melodies, all using only stepwise motion within the scale. That's pretty amazing, but we can get big results from simple things. We will wrap things up with more rhythm words added to our list, adding sixteenth notes.

We have a few stops to make on this trip, so fasten your seat belts and let's get an early start!

THE MAJOR SCALE

44 Listen to the following scale on Audio track 44 as it ascends and descends by stepwise motion. Sound familiar? For many of us, we grew up with this scale, the major scale. Let's dig a bit deeper into understanding how this major scale works. As you listen to the C major scale (notated below), notice that each scale degree is identified by numbers. These numbers identify each note's placement, or function, within the scale and their distance from the root of the scale. In the last chapter we concentrated on the relationship between the root and the third of the scale (the major third interval), which determined that the scale was a major scale. Let's add in the other five notes and see what makes this major scale tick!

We'll spend some time listening to and singing through the major scale, "filling our tank" with major scale vocabulary "fuel" before we continue down the roads of recognition and transcription. But first, let's make a pit stop and learn another way of identifying scale degrees using the "solfege" system.

LEARNING THE SOLFEGE LANGUAGE

Many people refer to the seven pitches of the major scale simply by numbers, which makes perfect and logical sense. We will too, but we'll also use solfege syllables. Solfege is the musical language used to identify the names of the notes. The biggest advantage of solfege syllables over numbers is that they are only one syllable long, making them very easy to speak or sing. The solfege syllables within the major scale are: *do, re, mi, fa, sol, la, ti, do*. So for example, instead of saying, "seven," the one syllable "*ti*" does the trick.

There are two variations of the solfege language. In many countries, the "fixed Do" solfege language is used. In a fixed Do system, the note C is always called *do*, the note D is always called *re*, etc., regardless of the key the music is in. The names of the notes are always referred to by solfege, never by letter names. This fixed Do system is particularly useful for developing an absolute recognition of the pitch, but does not describe the function, the "why" of the notes.

Throughout this book, we will use the "movable Do" solfege language. The movable Do solfege language is very useful for developing relative pitch, understanding the "why" (the *function*) of the notes within the key. The movable Do solfege syllables equate exactly with numbers: *do* is the first note of the scale, scale degree 1; *re* is the second note of the scale, scale degree 2; *mi* is the third note of the scale, scale degree 3, and so on to *ti*.

The solfege names and numbers are interchangeable when using the movable Do solfege language. These solfege syllables are called "diatonic" because they refer to only those notes that are in the major scale. We will only be working within the major scale for the next few chapters.

ACTIVITY ONE: *Singing the Major Scale with Numbers and Solfege Syllables*

(44) Listen to Audio track 44 again while reading the example shown above. Then try singing along, using both numbers and solfege syllables.

Tip: The pronunciation of the solfege vowels are: a (ah); e (ay); i (ee); and o (oh).

Here's a phrase that might whet your appetite for a solfege meal: *do* (as in donut); *re* (as in raisin); *mi* (as in meat); *fa* (as in fava bean); *sol* (as in filet of sole); *la* (as in latte); and *ti* (as in tea). I often think of the "Do-Re-Mi" song from the *Sound of Music* as another fun way to remember the sound of solfege. I highly recommend you listen to it; for many of us, it's a trip down memory lane as Maria teaches the children the "ABCs" of "do-re-mi."

If you're new to the movable Do solfege language, equating the solfege syllables with numbers will be very helpful. If you have been trained with the fixed Do system, it might be very difficult and confusing to make the adjustment to the movable Do system. Suddenly "*do*" no longer just describes the pitch C! So, emphasizing the equation of movable Do solfege syllables with numbers is especially crucial.

In the next section I recommend a routine for more practice with the movable Do solfege language which doesn't associate the syllables with specific notes, or specific major scales.

4 Exploring Major Key Melodies with Solfege

Using the "Sol-Fa" System

The "Sol-Fa" system is a generic way of hearing how each solfege syllable relates back to *do*. In this chapter, we are using the C major scale for demonstration, but we could use any major scale when working with Sol-Fa. It's the best way to get away from thinking actual pitches, and instead, to focus on the function of each scale note as it relates back to the root of the scale, *do*.

Using a "tone ladder" with Sol-Fa will further illustrate how each scale degree relates "vertically" back to *do*. The tone ladder is provided below for you to use when practicing with Activity Two. Let's step on out…

Activity Two: *Stepping Your Way Through the Major Scale*

do'	1
ti	7
la	6
sol	5
fa	4
mi	3
re	2
do	1
ti,	7
la,	6
sol,	5

🎧 45 Let's begin our practice with the major scale using only stepwise motion to connect from one scale degree to the next. Stepping through the scale is the easiest and most user-friendly way of making your way through the scale. Listen to the series of stepwise scale phrases on Audio track 45. Each scale phrase is a graduated stepwise line that starts on *do*, ascends by step to a target scale tone, and then returns back by stepwise motion to *do*. The phrases start small (*do-re-do*; *do-re-mi-re-do*; *do-re-mi-fa-mi-re-do*; etc.) and extend further up and down the tone ladder as you go. First, simply listen to the stepwise scale phrase. Immediately following the phrase, you'll be given some time to repeat the phrase, singing with either numbers or solfege. Try both for the complete workout!

Tip: I suggest you use the tone ladder as a helpful visual guide. Point at the solfege/numbers as you listen and sing. At this early stage, it's unrealistic to expect to have all the solfege syllables memorized.

By the time you've made it through the entire recording, you'll have had quite an earful and mouthful of solfege syllables! Repeat this routine on a daily basis and before you know it, you will become a fluent native speaker of the solfege language.

Going the Extra Mile

Transpose the scale patterns on Audio track 45 into different keys and play them on your instrument. If you allow "*do-re-mi*" to take the lead, you'll be amazed how flawlessly your fingers will play, hitting all the right notes with accuracy and with confidence. Why? Because the process won't simply be mechanical or hit or miss: instead, you'll be bringing your ears along for the ride. Start with the key of C major, and expand out from there: key of G (one sharp), key of F (one flat) etc. This is a great way to engage your instrument, playing it by ear.

Activity Three: *Improvising a Stepwise Melody*

🎧 46 Let's add a dose of creativity to our practice routine by composing some stepwise melodies. Keeping the rhythms simple, take your time as you improvise stepwise through the scale. We're not attempting to create the greatest solo ever heard, we're practicing associating the scale tones with numbers and/or solfege syllables so we can recognize these kinds of stepwise patterns by ear. Let me demonstrate a few runs on Audio track 46 to get the engine warmed up. Then you give it a go…this can be a lot of fun!

READING, WRITING AND RHYTHMETIC

Tip: Refer back to the vertical tone ladder in Activity Two as you improvise. Mapping the up/down nature of your lines with hand movements is a physical way to describe the shape and direction of the melodies you've created. It's another way to stay focused and connected.

Two for the Road

Trade solos with your partner. Make sure the lines you create remain stepwise for now. And make sure you're singing with numbers or solfege: singing "la, la, la" isn't going to fuel our inner hearing for the long road ahead.

ACTIVITY FOUR: *Takin' It to the Streets*

There are many songs that are composed entirely of stepwise motion, or close to it. Let's listen to a few and translate them using solfege syllables and/or numbers. We will not attempt to notate these melodies in any specific key, or transcribe their rhythmic values. These well-known melodies are excellent examples of just how good a stepwise melody can sound!

I've provided the starting solfege syllable for each melodic excerpt; figuring out the rest is up to you. Remember, it's all about stepwise motion. Some melodies head straight up or down in one direction; some take a winding road, with twists and turns along the way, and there are no road signs, so pay close attention!

You might already know some of these songs and won't need to refer to a recording. Sing or hum a few bars to refresh your memory and then begin the process of translating. Working with songs from memory can be done anywhere, anytime, even when stuck in the car in a traffic jam!

If you're not familiar with some of these songs, please listen to a recording. I've recommended some of my favorite versions, but do some exploring and listen to other artists' renditions as well. Enjoy!

1. "Angels We Have Heard on High (Gloria)," traditional: starts on *sol*
2. "Blue Moon," Billie Holiday, *Solitude:* starts on *sol*
3. "Bye Bye Blackbird," Miles Davis, *Round About Midnight:* starts on *mi*
4. "Can't Help Falling in Love" (only this lyric), Elvis Presley, *Blue Hawaii:* starts on *sol*
5. "Fix You" (B section), Coldplay, *X&Y:* starts on *fa*
6. "Fly Me to the Moon," Frank Sinatra, *It Might as Well Be Spring:* starts on *do*
7. "Human Nature" ("tell 'em that it's human nature"), Michael Jackson, *Thriller:* starts on *mi*
8. "I Want to Hold Your Hand" (only this lyric), The Beatles, *Meet the Beatles!:* starts on *do*
9. "Joy to the World," traditional: starts on *do*
10. "Lean on Me," Bill Withers, *The Best of Bill Withers:* starts on *do*
11. "Minuet in G," J.S. Bach: starts on *sol*
12. "My Romance," Ella Fitzgerald, *Ella Fitzgerald Sings the Rodgers and Hart Songbook:* starts on *mi*
13. "Never on Sunday," Melina Mercouri, *Never on Sunday:* starts on *sol*
14. "Ode to Joy," Ludwig van Beethoven, *Ninth Symphony:* starts on *mi*
15. "One Note Samba" (B section, key change), Astrud Gilberto, *Getz Au Go Go:* starts on *la*
16. "Overkill," Men at Work, *Cargo:* starts on *sol*
17. "Canon in D," Johann Pachelbel: starts on *mi*

4 Exploring Major Key Melodies with Solfege

18. "Silver Bells," Johnny Mathis, *Merry Christmas:* starts on *mi*
19. "Smile," Nat King Cole, *The Nat King Cole Story:* starts on *do*
20. "St. Thomas," (B section), Sonny Rollins, *Saxophone Colossus:* starts on *mi*
21. "There Will Never Be Another You," Chet Baker, *Chet Baker Sings:* starts on *sol*
22. "Twinkle, Twinkle Little Star," traditional: starts on *do*
23. "The Way You Look Tonight," Frank Sinatra, *Nothing But the Best:* starts on *sol*
24. "Will You Be There," Michael Jackson, *The Essential Michael Jackson:* starts on *do*
25. "With a Little Help from My Friends," Joe Cocker, *With a Little Help from My Friends:* starts on *mi*

Check the Answer Key (p.151) to review the "road maps" of each melody. Do a little bit more exploring. Where did *do*, the root of the scale, appear in these melodies? In many cases it was the final note of the melody, but not necessarily the opening note.

Collecting Souvenirs

Search for additional examples of melodies that are made up of mostly stepwise motion. Can you determine the Sol-Fa? Share your mementos with classmates and band members.

That's been quite a workout with "*do-re-mi!*" Let's take a break and return to our rhythm work. The word for the day is "sixteenth note."

COUNTING AND TRACKING SIXTEENTH NOTES

Before we expand our "rhythm word" list to include sixteenth note figures, let's make sure we have a system for counting and tracking sixteenth notes. If we are in 2/4, 3/4 or 4/4 time, the sixteenth note receives only one quarter (one fourth) of a beat. We tracked eighth notes by counting "1 + 2 +" etc. We can track the sixteenth notes by counting "1 e + a, 2 e + a" etc., dividing the eighth note pulse into two smaller halves.

47 Listen to the following example in 2/4 on Audio track 47 as you read and count along. You will first hear the six measure rhythm grid to warm up the engine, then take to the road on your own during the next six bars, counting as you track the quarter notes, eighth notes and sixteenth notes.

The rhythm grid for sixteenth notes

With our engine warmed up, let's tackle some one-beat sixteenth note rhythm words.

MEMORIZING ONE-BEAT SIXTEENTH NOTE RHYTHM WORDS

Let's expand our rhythm word list to include one-beat sixteenth note figures. This time we will add some rests into the mix, but the list of possible rhythm words (12) remains relatively easy to memorize.

Reading, Writing and Rhythmetic

Activity Five: *Memorizing One-Beat Sixteenth Note Words*

48 Listen to the following 26-bar example in 2/4 on Audio track 48 as you read along. Each sixteenth note word will be introduced on the first beat, followed by a quarter rest on beat two, allowing you the opportunity to hear the rhythm word in isolation. Word "zero" (♪ ♪) counting "1 +") will start the engine, and then we'll cruise through the sixteenth note patterns from there. A "blank" measure will follow for you to quote the one-beat word.

When you sing back the rhythm word, try it two ways. Sing back, " la, la, la," for the rote experience, simply parroting what you heard. Then try singing it back with the "1 e + a" counting system to indicate the exact details of where the attacks are. Use the "1 e + a" grid written below each word for this approach. I think you'll find this analytical approach will give you better mileage down the road when reading and transcribing (remember, ear training is 50% brain training!). Each word will be numbered for quick referencing when doing the recognition workout in the following "Two for the Road" activity.

One-beat sixteenth note rhythm words

Tip: Notice with patterns 5 and 6, I offer alternate notations, depending on the duration of the pattern. If we consider the duration details, there are alternate ways to notate some of the other patterns as well. In order to keep the list short and manageable, I didn't include all the possibilities. But when transcribing, it's important that you consider the duration factor.

Two for the Road

Play the role of the teacher and quiz your partner on recognizing the one-beat sixteenth note rhythm words. Remember, your ability to accurately perform the rhythms is essential and good practice in itself. Have your partner reference the words in Activity Five by numbers to be speedy. Now reverse roles.

Activity Six: *Recognizing Two-Beat Sixteenth Note Words*

I've created several examples of two-beat sixteenth note rhythm figures by combining two words back to back. Can you recognize these "compound words?"

4 Exploring Major Key Melodies with Solfege

49 Listen to the following 16 examples of compound words on Audio track 49 and identify them. A template of 32 measures is provided below for you to write your answers in the odd-numbered measures. The even-numbered bars are moments of rest in order to separate each compound word from the next.

You will need to respond quickly, so identify each compound word by its associated numbers from the list given in Activity Five. I've done the first example for you (1+6). Don't hesitate to put the brakes on and pause between each example. You can then take the time in the silence to notate the compound rhythmic figures. Are you ready?

Two-beat compound words

Check your results with the Answer Key (p.152). How did you do? If you did a great job, then you've spent enough time with Activity Five's memorization process. If you feel you could have done better, you can tighten the bond between what you hear and what it looks like on the page by spending time reading through the Answer Key results as you listen to the audio recording. Listening and looking—a good combination.

Tip: Remember the imaginary bar line rule we talked about in Chapter 2 that divided a measure of $\frac{4}{4}$ into two equal halves? That rule made it easy on the reader's eye. When notating sixteenth note rhythms, there is an imaginary bar line that separates *each beat* within the measure. This rule is also for the purpose of making rhythms containing sixteenth notes easier to read. Can you imagine the possible chaos without it? Within one measure of 4/4 there are sixteen possible attacks and combinations thereof! Better to have a stop sign at each beat intersection for safe travel throughout the measure!

ACTIVITY SEVEN: *Takin' It to the Streets*

Transcribe the rhythms of the following 12 song excerpts listed below (templates provided). You already have a head start on this trip in that all the compound words from Activity Six will reappear throughout many of the songs. If you get stuck, refer back to Activity Six for refueling. Engines primed: get out on the Internet highway to give a listen!

1. "Don't Worry, Be Happy," Bobby McFerrin, *Simple Pleasures:* whistle introduction

2. "Esconjuros," Serge Mendes, *Brasilerio:* female vocals, 1st 8 bars (excluding pickup)

3. "Fix You," Coldplay, *X & Y:* vocal, B section (chorus)

4. "Humoresque No. 7 in G♭ Major, Opus 101," Dvořák, *Classic Perlman: Rhapsody:* 1st 16 bars

5. "I Want You Back," Jackson 5, *The Essential Michael Jackson:* bass line introduction

4 Exploring Major Key Melodies with Solfege

6. "Let's Dance," David Bowie, *Let's Dance:* bass line

7. "Livin' in America," James Brown, *Gravity:* background horns at chorus

8. "Sgt. Pepper's Lonely Hearts Club Band," The Beatles, *Sgt. Pepper's Lonely Hearts Club Band:* vocal, 1st 8 bars (excluding pickup)

9. "Sir Duke," Stevie Wonder, *Songs in the Key of Life:* horn introduction

10. "Stars and Stripes Forever," J. F. Sousa, *The U.S. Army Field Band:* introduction & 1st 16 bars

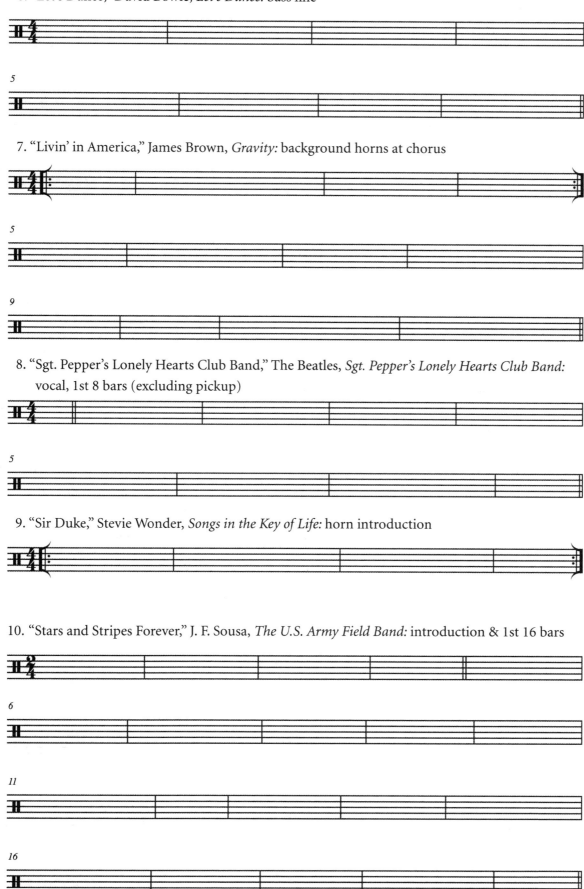

43

Reading, Writing and Rhythmetic

11. "Stayin' Alive," Bee Gees, *Saturday Night Fever* soundtrack: vocals, B section (chorus)

12. "We Will Rock You," Queen, *News of the World*: vocal, 1st 8 bars

Check the Answer Key (pp.152–155) to see how you did. We certainly got a lot of mileage out of our compound sixteenth note word list on this trip!

Going the Extra Mile
Determine both the pitches and the rhythms to "Joy to the World." We know from our past work with this carol that it's in 2/4 time, that it's in a major key, and that most of the melody notes connect by stepwise motion. It will also incorporate some of our new sixteenth note rhythm words. This will be the first time we've combined forces to produce a completed transcription of both the pitches and rhythms under one hood—a preview of our work to come in the next chapter. Get a jump-start!

🎧 50 Use the template provided below (key of C major) as you listen to "Joy to the World" on Audio track 50. Check with the Answer Key (p.155) to compare your results. En-"joy"!

"Joy to the World"

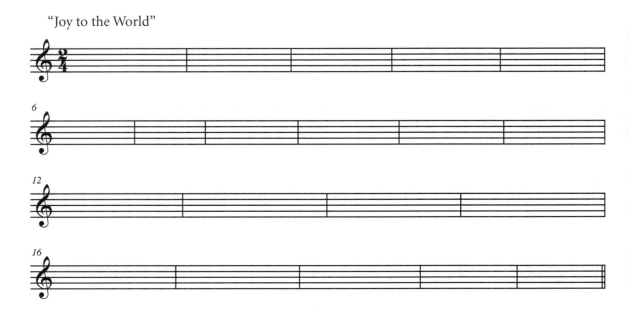

4 Exploring Major Key Melodies with Solfege

Activity Eight: *Round Trip*

Read through the following example in 4/4; this is a good review of the two-beat rhythm words presented in Chapter 2. I've included some rests in the example to make things a bit more challenging, and to provide places for you to catch your breath!

Set the metronome to a comfortable tempo, give yourself two measures "outside" before you begin: ready, set, conduct!

Now try this: convert the preceding 4/4 example into 2/4 at a tempo twice as slow. For example, one measure of 4/4 (♩ = 120) will now be one measure of 2/4 (♩ = 60). What was a quarter note in the original 4/4 example will now equal one eighth note in the slower 2/4 example. The template in 2/4 is provided below. I've converted the first two measures to help you get started. When you've finished, check the Answer Key (p.155) to see how you did.

This conversion process demonstrates how rhythms that sound identical can be notated two different ways, depending on the chosen tempo and time signature. Prove this by reading through the 4/4 example (♩ = 120) and then the 2/4 example (♩ = 60). With eyes closed, the listener would not know which example you were reading.

If you struggled with reading the $\frac{2}{4}$ example that incorporated sixteenth notes, you might benefit from relating it back to the more "user friendly" look of eighth notes in the $\frac{4}{4}$ version.

We're well under way on our trip, with a trunk filled with rhythms and scales. In the next chapter we'll strategize ways to combine these two musical items into one complete transcription. The key words are "be organized!"

Approaching the Fork in the Road

I'm often asked which is better: developing perfect pitch or relative pitch? This is one of the more controversial questions that comes up in my classroom. I see possible benefits to both sides of this ear training coin. But if I were a gambler, I'd toss the coin in favor of developing relative pitch skills.

Putting my efforts toward developing relative pitch is more practical for the kind of music I engage in, tonal music, music that is centered in a key. If you are a performer or composer of atonal music, music that is not intended to be key related, then attaining perfect pitch would be the better path to take. But then I ask: can someone actually develop perfect pitch or is it something that you're either born with or not? Anything's possible, but the amount of time and effort spent in the attempt to acquire perfect pitch might not be worth the time and the effort...and I'm not convinced that it can be done in the first place. One method might be to memorize a reference pitch (such as A440) and then relate the remaining eleven pitches to that note. But isn't that a form of relative pitch?

I choose to invest my effort in developing relative pitch. Once you know what key the music is in, what note is *do*, using relative pitch skills will ensure a successful trip from there. Using movable Do solfege syllables (or numbers) is the best GPS navigation system you'll ever need! It's an efficient, dependable and knowledgeable way to travel the road of tonal music. Once you get "*do-re-mi*" under your belt, you'll find it's a much easier and faster route to take as well.

I think there is a fascination that surrounds the idea of possessing perfect pitch vs. the more grounded reality of working hard at developing relative pitch. Consider the earned values of each. You know me, I'm the queen of metaphors! Just because someone can tell you the names of the colors used in a painting does not make him/her an artist. Simply identifying the pitches in a melody doesn't make someone a musician.

You can definitely develop relative pitch—guaranteed! I'm not so sure about the odds of developing perfect pitch.

5 PITCHES + RHYTHMS = BEING ORGANIZED

INTRODUCTION

In previous chapters we addressed the rhythm and pitches of a melody as two separate entities. Now, we'll incorporate them into one process, and strategize a variety of ways to accomplish these new challenges. Being organized is the key to success for this process.

We will continue working with the major scale, spotlighting the I major triad (*do-mi-sol*), and the significant role it plays in melodic development. "Tendency tone pairs" will also be introduced. These two-note combinations demonstrate tension/resolution within the scale, and can imply harmonic movement within the melody.

The compound meter of $\frac{6}{8}$ will be introduced. This is the first time we'll see a note value other than a quarter note representing one beat. We'll find out how $\frac{6}{8}$ is similar yet different from $\frac{3}{4}$ time. Are you ready? Start your engines!

THE TONIC I CHORD

In Chapter 3 we worked on locating the root of the scale, the *do* of the key. In this chapter we will develop the concept of *do* and discuss the tonic I chord. The term "tonic" means stable, or at rest within the key. As we are likely to find *do* at the conclusion of a melody, we're just as likely to find the I major triad (a three-note chord consisting of *do-mi-sol* of the key) there as well. Supporting *do* in the melody with the accompanying I chord provides a harmonic anchor, enhancing the sense of stability within the key. Nine times out of ten, you'll find the vocalist concludes the melody on *do*, with the accompanists (guitarist, pianist) playing the I chord, as the bassist plays *do*, the root of the I chord. All work together in concluding the song on solid, stable ground.

In fact, many melodies will outline (arpeggiate) the I major triad, featuring different combinations of *do*, *mi* and *sol*. As we continue our work, we will see how closely melody and harmony relate to one another in a song. Let's first explore outlining, or arpeggiating the I major triad: *do-mi-sol*. Then, we'll investigate some familiar melodies that feature arpeggiation of the I major triad.

ACTIVITY ONE: *Arpeggiating the I Major Triad*

51 Listen to Audio track 51 while reading the example shown on the top of the next page. The I major triad is featured in all its glory, including both root position and inverted arpeggios. Try singing along, using both numbers and solfege syllables. This will be a great start for recognizing these same patterns as they occur in the melody, in the harmonic accompaniment parts, or in the bass line.

47

Arpeggios of the I chord

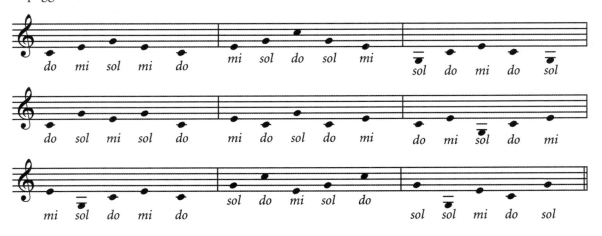

ACTIVITY TWO: *Recognizing the I Chord in Songs*

Now listen to the following song excerpts which feature I chord arpeggios and determine their solfege. Some songs will feature the I chord exclusively; others will demonstrate an enhanced version of it, including some additional scale tones which ornament the I chord. These ornamented versions will invite a discussion of our next topic: tendency tone pairs.

You might already be familiar with some of the songs and can recall them from memory. If not, I've suggested a version to listen to on the web. I've also indicated the specific snippet of the song to focus on by the lyric. Remember, you're listening for *do*, *mi* and *sol*'s.

1. "All of Me," Billie Holiday, *The Essential Billie Holiday:* "All of me…"
2. "Bicycle Built for Two," Nat King Cole, *Those Lazy Hazy Crazy Days of Summer:* "Daisy, daisy…"
3. "Black or White," Michael Jackson, *Dangerous:* "I took my baby on a Saturday bang…"
4. "First Suite in D," by Mouret (Masterpiece Theater theme song), *New York Trumpet Ensemble, 100 Hits: Greatest Classical Composers:* opening theme
5. "Jingle Bells," Harry Connick, Jr., *What a Night! A Christmas Album:* "Jingle bells, jingle bells, jingle all the way…"
6. "Just My Imagination," The Temptations, *Sky's the Limit :* "Each day through my window I watch her as she passes by…"
7. "NBC," TV theme
8. "Oh My Darling, Clementine," Malcolm Forest, *Legends:* "Oh my darling, oh my darling, oh my darling…"
9. "On Top of Old Smokey," Gene Autry, *The Essential Gene Autry:* "On top of old Smok(ey)…"
10. "Please Don't Talk About Me When I'm Gone," Willie Nelson, *Moonlight Becomes You:* "Please don't talk a(bout)…"

11. "Row, Row, Row Your Boat," Elizabeth Mitchell, *Kids' Club-Family Songbook:* "Merrily, merrily, merrily, merrily…"
12. "Someone Like You," Adele, *21:* "I've heard that you've settled down that you…"
13. "Taps," United States Navy Band, *Music for Honors and Ceremonies:* entire song
14. "U.S. National Anthem," U.S. Army Band, *A Patriotic Salute to the Military Family:* "Oh say can you see, by the dawn's early light…"
15. "When the Saints Go Marching In," Mel McDaniel, *30 Country Gospel Greats:* "Oh when the saints, go marching in, oh when the saints go marching (in)…"

Check the Answer Key (p.156) to see if you correctly identified the I chord arpeggios.

TENDENCY TONE PAIRS

Have you heard the saying, "All roads lead to Rome?" It's a similar musical journey in that most melodic roads eventually lead back to *do* or to the other two chord tones of the I chord, *mi* and *sol*. Let's listen to the following series of pitches, referred to as "tendency tone pairs." Within each pair, notice how the tension of the non-chord tones, *re, ti, fa* and *la*, immediately resolves back to notes of the I chord, target tones *do, mi* and *sol* via stepwise motion. *Sol* can be a chameleon at times, depending on the musical context. In the pair, *la* to *sol*, *sol* functions as the target tone, but in the pair, *sol* to *do*, *sol* is the unstable pitch on its way home to resolving to *do*. We will have a better understanding of the dual function nature of *sol* in the next chapter when we discuss harmonic function in greater detail.

52 ACTIVITY THREE: *Memorizing and Recognizing the Tendency Tone Pairs*

Practice singing the tendency tone pairs shown below along with Audio track 52. These are useful and practical patterns to memorize, as we will see how often these pairs play a significant role in melody after melody.

Tendency tone pairs

Two for the Road

Quiz your partner on identifying the different tendency tone pairs. To make things more challenging, change keys frequently. Make sure you first establish the new key for your partner by playing the new I chord. Then, switch seats.

Reading, Writing and Rhythmetic

Activity Four: *Sight-Singing Tendency Tone Pair Melodies*

Let's feed the transcription meter with some sight-singing. Sing through the four melodies shown below using solfege syllables. You'll notice that each melody contains several tendency tone pairs in action. Label the pairs with solfege. In fact, the work you did with memorizing these scale pairs in Activity Three will help you in the sight-reading process.

Check the Answer Key (p.156–157) to spot the tendency tone pairs.

1. "Twinkle, Twinkle Little Star"

2. "Happy Birthday"

3. "My Country 'Tis of Thee"

4. "Here Comes the Bride"

Now let's take our tendency tone pairs to the streets with the next activity.

5 PITCHES + RHYTHMS = BEING ORGANIZED

ACTIVITY FIVE: *Recognizing Tendency Tone Pairs in Songs*

Listen to the following song excerpts which feature tendency tone pairs, and transcribe, writing down the solfege syllables. Similar to Activity Two, I've identified the song snippet by the lyric.

1. "C Jam Blues," Duke Ellington, *Duke Ellingon's Greatest Hits:* entire song
2. "Dancing Queen," ABBA, *Arrival:* "See that girl, watch that scene, digging the dancing queen…"
3. "Freddie Freeloader," Miles Davis, *Kind of Blue:* first 8 bars
4. "I Just Called to Say I Love You," Stevie Wonder, *The Woman in Red:* "I just called to say I love you…"
5. "Just My Imagination," The Temptations, *Sky's the Limit:* "Each day through my window I watch her as she passes by…"
6. "Moonlight in Vermont," Ella Fitzgerald, *Ella and Louis:* "Pennies in a stream, falling leaves a sycamore…"
7. "One Note Samba," Astrud Gilberto, *Getz Au Go Go:* entire A section
8. "She," Elvis Costello, *The Very Best of Elvis Costello:* "She may be the face I can't forget… she may be the song that summer sings…"
9. "Star Eyes," Charlie Parker, *Bird at St.Nick's:* first 3 bars
10. "Theme Song from TV Show Jeopardy": opening theme
11. "Time After Time," Cyndi Lauper, *She's So Unusual:* "Lyin' in my bed I hear the clock tick and think of you…"
12. "Walkin'," Miles Davis, *Walkin':* opening 4 bars of solo
13. "We Can Work It Out," The Beatles, *Rubber Soul:* "Try to see it my way, do I have to keep on talking 'til I can't go on…"

Check with the Answer Key (p.157) to see how you did. What tendency tone pairs did you find were most popular in these examples?

COMBINING PITCH AND RHYTHM

Up to this point we've treated pitches and rhythmic components of melodies as two separate entities. Now it's time to combine these two components as we transcribe the melody. What is the key ingredient as we begin to intersect the two? Being organized!

53 Listen to the melody on Audio track 53. We're going to take this melody through an organized, step-by-step process. You don't always have to follow the steps in the same order, and don't try to combine too many steps at once. Being patient now will save you time and effort down the road.

Step 1: First, simply *listen*, becoming familiar with the melody. Can you sing it back, "la, la, la?" In my opinion, that's the best way to prove you've learned the melody. Remember, if you can't recall the melody, there's nothing to translate. Listen to the melody on Audio track 53 as often as you need in order to memorize and sing it back, "la, la, la."

Tip: I can't stress enough how important this initial step is: take the time to really listen and digest the music. This is the inspirational and fun part. There was something about the piece of music that grabbed your attention and piqued your interest. Enjoy it! Writing down the music is actually the last step in the transcription process, and has no lasting value if you skip over this first crucial step of listening. I can still remember some of the first jazz solos I ever transcribed…and that's many years ago!

51

Step 2: Next, provide a template, which has the key signature, time signature and the number of measures needed to complete the melodic transcription. This step will enlist several of your ear training skills as you: find *do* and then match it to a specific pitch to determine the key signature; find the downbeats to determine the time signature; and then count how many measures long the music lasts. That's a lot! But taking the time now to plan out your trip and establishing a good road map (template) will save you time in the long run.

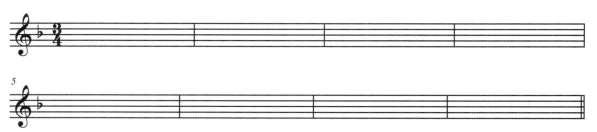

That's right, this melody is in the key of F major, is in 3/4 time and is eight measures long.

It's very helpful to have your eyes move through your template as you're listening. As your eyes travel the eight measures, you get a general idea of where the melody will locate along the way. Listen for repetition. Identify those pitches that fall on the downbeats and/or are of long duration (these are the skeletal notes of the melody). Do you recognize any familiar rhythmic motives as you listen? At this early stage in the transcription process, you're making a sketch, not writing down the final version in indelible ink. Oh, did I mention that a pencil with a big eraser is very handy at this stage?

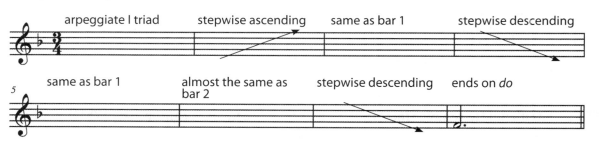

Step 3: If the example is lengthy and challenging to remember, you'll need to break it up into smaller phrases. Let's divide the melody on Audio track 53 into two 4-bar phrases. Think phrase to phrase, not note to note. You want to retain and appreciate the musical idea, not just a bunch of isolated notes and symbols on the page. You might want to start with the second phrase first. Sometimes, the last thing heard is the first thing you'll remember, so write it down.

Tip: When I was learning to speak Italian, the system used was a very clever "learn by ear" approach. You would first hear the entire sentence stated on the audio tape. Then, working backwards, you would hear the end snippet of the sentence, the final destination, and repeat it. Next, you'd hear the middle part connected to the end snippet and repeat that. Eventually you'd make it back to the very beginning of the sentence, hear it and repeat the whole thing. It worked! It was like taking a journey in which you knew all along where you were headed, rather than aimlessly traveling to an unknown destination. Somehow, this approach felt calm, without the anxiety of thinking I'm going to forget everything.

Step 4: As you begin the actual translation process, you might need to listen to the melody at a slower tempo than the recording. If you've been able to memorize the melody and can sing it back accurately, then you can be your own tape recorder, singing it back at a slower tempo as you listen for melodic details. "Rewind" in your head from memory as often as you need. In fact, I do most of the translation work with my inner hearing memory in silence, not when the actual music is playing. We'll be talking about software programs that can loop and slow down the music recording without changing the pitch in this chapter's "Approaching the Fork in the Road" section. Amazing stuff!

Step 5: Pick the element of the melody (pitches or rhythms) that comes easiest for you to identify, and start there. If it's the pitches, first find *do* (remember that you'll usually find *do* at the end of the melody). From there, you can determine the rest of the pitches as they relate to *do*. One way is to use solfege by ear and write down the syllables below in the template. Then go to an instrument to match *do* to a specific note to establish the key, and then play your solfeged melody to confirm if you're correct.

The other way is to first determine the key of the melody with an instrument, in order to write down actual pitches. Simply write in note heads of the pitches in the general vicinity within the measures. You'll be determining the rhythmic details as the next and final step. If you choose this route, I still recommend that you determine the notes by ear, using solfege, rather than randomly search for the notes on the instrument through hit or miss.

Step 6: If the rhythmic content of the melody seems more inviting, then start there. You've already determined the time signature, so using a combination of counting, conducting and recognition of familiar rhythm words, transcribe the rhythm of the melody. You can write out the rhythms above the template, leaving the measures blank until you've determined the pitches.

Reading, Writing and Rhythmetic

Tip: Here's a technique I learned from other teachers for "sketching" the rhythms. First, determine the rhythm grid by the smallest (fastest) note value. In this example, the smallest note value is an eighth note. Write out the rhythm grid (1+2+3+) above the staff. As you listen to the melody, put a slash mark through the numbers (1+2+3+) where you hear an attack. This is a very quick way to jot down the rhythms, not taking the time to write out the quarter or eighth note symbols. Then, in the silence, convert these slash marks into actual rhythmic notation.

Step 7: Put steps 5 and 6 together and you have your final results. Voilà!

Don't forget to double-check your final results either by using the playback feature of the notation software, or by playing the transcription on your instrument. Double-checking is always a smart idea!

In the next activity it's time for you to take to the road and experiment with these transcription steps on your own.

Activity Six: *Transcribing Melodies*

🎵 54 – 63 Transcribe the following ten melodies on Audio tracks 54–63, using the steps recommended above. You're on your own this time to establish the road map and templates for each example. Use your own manuscript paper or notation software. You will need to determine the key signature (the major key), the time signature (3/4 or 4/4), and how many measures, for each melody track. Remember, no matter which road you take in the transcription process, all roads start with listening. Be patient and with experience, you'll be able to tackle melodic and rhythmic aspects simultaneously, further down the road.

Check the Answer Key (pp.157–159) to see how you did. Wow! This was the first time you traveled 100% solo on the transcription trip. Congratulations, you've earned your driver's license!

Time to return to the rhythmic drawing board and take on a new time signature: 6/8.

6/8 Time Signature

Initially, we'll approach 6/8 time as two groups of three eighth notes (3+3), using the 2/4 conducting pattern. Remember from Chapter 1, the bottom number in the time signature represents what note value receives one beat. In 6/8, the 8 represents the eighth note (♪ = 1 beat).

You might ask: why 6/8 rather than 6/4? Good question! Logic doesn't always preside in our attempt to explain the "whys" in music. In most cases, music written in 6/8 is performed at a

54

moderate to fast tempo; seeing smaller note values on the page imparts this underlying psychological message of "play it fast."

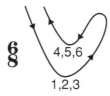

Similar to $\frac{3}{4}$, $\frac{6}{8}$ is also a compound meter, with the downbeat being the strongest beat, and beat 4 being slightly less accented. In one measure of $\frac{6}{8}$, the beats will be felt as "strong, weak, weak, less strong, weak, weak." Although there are six beats total within the $\frac{6}{8}$ measure, we'll use the "two" feel of 2 dotted quarter notes (♩. ♩.) as the basic pulse.

So, how do you know if the music is in $\frac{3}{4}$ or $\frac{6}{8}$? Are you hearing two measures of $\frac{3}{4}$ or one measure of $\frac{6}{8}$? This question comes up often in my classroom, and the answer isn't always easy to determine. The theoretical answer is: in $\frac{3}{4}$ you only feel one strong (accented) beat, the downbeat; in $\frac{6}{8}$, you feel two accented beats (beats 1 and 4). The style of music can also help determine which time signature is being used. For example, most waltzes are written in $\frac{3}{4}$. You might see some gospel feel or Afro-Cuban music notated in $\frac{6}{8}$. One other consideration is how many total measures result within the phrase: 16 bars of $\frac{3}{4}$ or 8 bars of $\frac{6}{8}$? It is more common to have 8-bar phrases, but this isn't always the case.

The bottom line is this: when listening, there is a very subtle difference between the two, and sometimes there isn't an absolute answer. These two meters have much more in common than not.

ACTIVITY SEVEN: *Conducting and Counting the $\frac{6}{8}$ Rhythm Grid*

64 Let's warm up our $\frac{6}{8}$ engine with the following rhythm grid. Simply read, listen and conduct along with Audio track 64 for the first eight measures. Then take the wheel for the next eight bars, performing the rhythm grid on your own along with the click track. You will get better mileage if you use the recommended counting system as you drive. This familiar warm-up routine is a great way to keep our inner hearing tuned up and ready for the road.

The $\frac{6}{8}$ rhythm grid

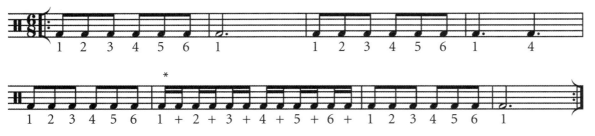

*You'll sometimes see this beaming:

Reading, Writing and Rhythmetic

ACTIVITY EIGHT: *Reading in 6/8*

Once again, let's put reading practice in the driver's seat, applying the conducting and counting tools presented in the previous activity.

Read through the following 32-bar example, using the rhythm grid listed below the notes as a guide. Where applicable, the counting system will accommodate the smallest (fastest) note value, in this case, the sixteenth note, by counting 1 + 2 + 3 + etc. In fact, you might try reciting the rhythms stating the numbers shown in the rhythm grid. Remember: in 6/8, all note values are receiving twice their normal duration value (♩=1 beat; ♪= ½ beat).

Choose a tempo that is comfortable for you. How? Before you begin, sing a measure or two of sixteenth notes to establish a tempo that won't break the speed limit. I suggest you use a metronome or click track to keep the tempo steady. You can set the metronome/click to represent the individual beat, the eighth note. Or, you can have the metronome/click represent the dotted quarter note, the basic "two" feel of the measure: this is more challenging and recommended only for the experienced driver. On your mark, get set, read!

Reading the Road Map: A B A C

1. Sing the first 8 bars (A).
2. Sing through the first ending (B).
3. Repeat the first 8 bars again (second A).
4. Skip over the first ending, and go directly to the second ending (C).

Tip: Don't forget to record your performance so you can review it later and work on those parts that were most challenging and need some extra attention.

5 PITCHES + RHYTHMS = BEING ORGANIZED

Two for the Road

Be a "live" tape recorder. Listen to and assess your partner's live performance of Activity Eight's reading example. How did they do? Can you point out places where they made mistakes and offer suggestions for improvement? Then, reverse roles.

ACTIVITY NINE: *Takin' It to the Streets*

We've racked up a lot of miles throughout this chapter. It's time to relax a bit and switch to cruise control. Let's listen to the following selections that are in $\frac{6}{8}$. Enjoy!

1. "All Blues," Miles Davis, *Kind of Blue*
2. "Be Ever Wonderful," Earth, Wind and Fire, *The Eternal Dance*
3. "Breaking the Girl," Red Hot Chili Peppers, *Greatest Hits*
4. "Call Me Back Again," Wings, *Venus and Mars*
5. "Don't Give Up," Peter Gabriel, *So*
6. "Don't Try to Explain," Keb' Mo', *Keb' Mo'*
7. "Gravity," John Mayer, *Continuum*
8. "Happy Xmas (War is Over)," John Lennon, *Power to the People: The Hits*
9. "I Me Mine," The Beatles, *Let It Be*
10. "Kiss from a Rose," Seal, *Hits*
11. "Love Letters," Patti Austin, *The Real Me*
12. "Mexican Hat Dance," Macarena Kids Party, *Macarena Kids Party*
13. "Morning, Peer Gynt Suite No. 1" (Edvard Grieg), London Philharmonic Orchestra, *50 Greatest Pieces of Classical Music*
14. "Norwegian Wood," The Beatles, *Rubber Soul*
15. "Piano Sonata No.9, Movement 1" (W.A. Mozart), Academy of St. Martin in the Fields, *The Complete Mozart Edition: The Symphonies, Vol. 1*
16. "Run Baby Run," Sheryl Crow, *Tuesday Night Music Club*
17. "Sailor's Hornpipe," 101 Strings Orchestra, *20 Best of Celtic Moods*
18. "Thick as a Brick," Jethro Tull, *The Very Best of Jethro Tull*
19. "When Johnny Comes Marching Home," Ross Moore, *Southern Son*
20. "With a Little Help from My Friends," Joe Cocker, *With a Little Help from My Friends*

It's possible that some of these songs might be interpreted as in $\frac{3}{4}$, $\frac{6}{4}$, $\frac{12}{8}$ or maybe even in $\frac{4}{4}$ (with eighth note triplets). What do you think, and why? We'll be working with triplets in the next chapter, comparing eighth note triplets in $\frac{4}{4}$ with $\frac{12}{8}$ time—stay tuned.

Going the Extra Mile

65 – **69** Are you ready to take the wheel once again and travel solo? Transcribe the following five songs on Audio tracks 65–69 (both the pitches and rhythms). I'll give you one clue: all songs are in $\frac{6}{8}$ (the click = ♩.). But you'll have to establish the other aspects of the template: the key signature and length of each song selection. You're likely to recognize some or all of these melodies, so you'll feel like you're traveling in familiar territory. Good luck! How was your trip? Check the Answer Key (pp.159–160) to find out.

READING, WRITING AND RHYTHMETIC

ACTIVITY TEN: *Round Trip*

Let's get back on the solfege trail for the last activity of this chapter. Practice with the following "alternate with *do*" pattern found on Audio track 70. It is quite similar to the stepwise pattern introduced in Chapter 4, Activity Two, found on page 37. In fact, you can use that earlier activity as a stepping stone for this current one.

do'	1
ti	7
la	6
sol	5
fa	4
mi	3
re	2
do	1
ti,	7
la,	6
sol,	5

70 Listen to Audio track 70. Each scale tone resolves directly back to *do* (*do-re-do; do-mi-do; do-fa-do,* etc.). Then, on your own, sing back the pattern using solfege syllables. You don't have to stay in tempo when singing. Take the time you need to first "inner hear" the target pitch before you sing out loud. If you're having difficulty hearing some of the larger intervals, link by step from *do* to the target pitch (e.g., sing *do-re-mi-fa*), then sing directly from *do* to *fa*. Linking by step ensures arrival at the target pitch correctly; guessing can be risky business. Use the tone ladder provided, or, close your eyes and visualize the notes in a particular key, on your instrument, or in the staff.

Going the Extra Mile

Practice the previous activity in a random fashion. It's a great way to stay in the moment, avoiding the back seat position of "auto pilot."

Being on auto pilot mode invites the temptation to be mindless, but remember, ear training is 50% brain training. Being consciously aware of what you're doing will help fill up your inner hearing tank. Here's an example: *do-mi-do; do-la-do; do-re-do; do-sol-do;* etc. How long can you keep the chain going? Coming back home to *do* each time, I imagine you could go for quite a while! And, if you record yourself, you'll have the chance to review and assess your workout. Go for it!

Approaching the Fork in the Road

Ah, sometimes technology can be our friend, making our musical lives a little bit easier.

We spoke earlier about the advantages of notation software programs for transcribing… mainly, the playback feature which gives us the immediate feedback of checking whether our written work is correct.

Other technological wonders are software programs that allow us to select a small portion of a recording, loop it, and/or slow down the speed without changing the pitch. There are several of these programs out on the market: Amazing Slow Downer, Transcribe!, Audacity, Anytune, etc., just to mention a few.

There is nothing more frustrating than not being able to comprehend what we hear. If the music is going too fast, it can sound like a blur of sound. Slowing it down gives us half a chance of understanding what's been played.

Looping allows us to zoom in on a short phrase and not be overwhelmed by a long phrase, and is a very efficient way to hear the phrase over and over, as many times as is necessary. I can remember the frustration of dropping the needle on my LP recording, hoping to land relatively close to the groove I was looking for…wasting so much time in the process, not to mention, butchering my records along the way!

5 PITCHES + RHYTHMS = BEING ORGANIZED

Or, I was able to slow down my LP's to half speed, but that also meant the music dropped an octave in pitch…not so handy when trying to transcribe a bass line!

This is not to say that we don't still have some organic work to do: it's our ears and brains that do the work of listening, comprehending, singing back and finally translating what we hear onto the page, but these technological tools provide a tremendous head start to getting to that point and allowing us to get to our role in the work process sooner than later!

We still are the ones in the transcribing driver's seat…but isn't it great to have a helpful tool sitting in the passenger seat!

6 MELODY + BASS LINE = HARMONY

INTRODUCTION

How do we determine the harmony of a song? In this chapter, we'll begin that journey by looking at the melody for harmonic clues. In most cases, the majority of melody notes are chord tones. We'll explore this concept methodically, leaving no melody note behind in our quest to determine the harmony.

We'll revisit the tendency tone pairs from Chapter 5 and learn how these pairs can suggest basic harmonies: the I, IV and V chords of the key. We've often seen how these tendency tone pairs exist within a melody. Let's take some simple, well-known melodies to the streets and determine the accompanying chords. Our motto is, "simple melody invites simple harmony."

In addition, we'll focus on hearing the bass line. For harmony, there is no better guide, as the bass line most often introduces the roots of the chords. Using the bass line plus the melody will provide most of the clues needed to solve the harmonic puzzle. We'll be transcribing bass lines and melody/bass line duets in this chapter, cracking the harmonic code with great success.

No chapter is complete without introducing a new rhythmic topic, so eighth note triplets will be featured, as we relate them back to the $\frac{6}{8}$ feel and then apply them as coming attractions, previewing the swing eighth note feel for Chapter 7. We'll double up on the concept about triplet feel and explore the question of whether the song is best notated in $\frac{12}{8}$, or in $\frac{4}{4}$ time with triplets.

We're fueled with a full tank of melodies, bass lines and chords. Back on the road again... full steam ahead!

MELODY IS HARMONY

Melody and harmony work together like Lennon and McCartney. In many songs, the majority of the melody notes will be chord tones of the accompanying harmony. In fact, composers often create the melody first, and then develop a chord progression to support this melody as the second step. The melody notes invite, or strongly suggest what chords to use in the harmony.

When transcribing a song it can be difficult to hear what the chords are by listening only to the rhythm section: there's so much sound to sift through, and making sense of it all can be both ear- and mind-boggling. Often the melody shouts out obvious harmonic clues, so let's listen to these clues.

Typically, the important melody notes are chord tones. What makes melody notes important? They may have long durations, may fall on strong beats (particularly the downbeat), and may be leapt away from, or not always be connected by stepwise motion. In other words, these are the melody notes that stand out to your ear when listening.

Reading, Writing and Rhythmetic

Relating Harmony to the Tendency Tone Pairs

Let's revisit the tendency tone pairs from the last chapter and see how they imply harmony.

The target tones (*do*, *mi* and *sol*) represent the tonic I major triad. The other scale tones (*re*, *fa*, *la* and *ti*) can also suggest harmony, representing chord tones of other diatonic chords. For now, let's restrict the harmonic possibilities of the other diatonic chords to include only the IV and V major triads.

Tip: There are three diatonic major triads built on *do* (1), *fa* (4) and *sol* (5) of the major scale. We identify individual scale notes with Arabic numbers: 1, 4 and 5; we identify these triads with Roman numerals: I, IV and V.

Again, *do*, *mi* and *sol* represent the I chord. *Sol*, *ti* and *re* can belong to the V chord. *Fa*, *la* and *do* are chord tones of the IV chord. Both the V and IV chords are unstable (non-tonic) in the key, needing to resolve back home to the tonic I chord. Remember, *sol* can be either a stable target note or an unstable note in the tendency tone series, depending on context. Even *do*, the tonic note of the scale, can sometimes imply instability, if it's associated with the non-tonic IV chord.

Using only the I, IV and V chords, the following harmonic associations can be applied:

tendency tones	re to do	ti to do	fa to mi	la to sol	sol to do
harmonic association	V to I	V to I	IV to I	IV to I	V to I

🎵 **71** As you listen to Audio track 71, pay attention to the harmonic cadences implied by the tendency tone pairs shown above. In each case, the first unstable tendency tone is accompanied by a complimentary unstable, non-tonic chord, creating a need to resolve back home to the stable, tonic I chord.

Activity One: *Harmonizing the Melody with I, IV and V Chords*

Let's take a look at some of the songs we transcribed in the previous chapter and now determine their implied harmonies.

As these children's songs are simple melodies, they will suggest simple harmonic accompaniments. It is safe to say that 95% of the time, using only the I, IV and V chords will work as simple harmonic accompaniment. This is what I call the "top-down" approach: relying primarily on the melody for harmonic clues.

6 Melody + Bass line = Harmony

Look for chord tone clues in the following melodies to determine where to use the I, IV or V chords in the harmonic accompaniment. Before checking with the Answer Key (pp.161–162), play your choices, letting your ear, not just your eyes, make the final decision. The Answer Key will provide some alternate harmonic solutions in parentheses. The melodies are notated in a variety of major keys. For the complete workout, supply both the actual chord symbols as well as the Roman numerals for your answers.

Tip: Keep in mind that some scale tones have more than one chord association, such as *do* (could be the I or IV chord) and *sol* (could be the I or V chord). How do you know which chord to choose? Again, you'll have to use an instrument to try both choices. Then decide which chord sounds "right."

1. "Frère Jacques"

2. "London Bridge Is Falling Down"

3. "Oh My Darling, Clementine"

4. "Old MacDonald"

5. "On Top of Old Smokey"

63

6. "Row, Row, Row Your Boat"

7. "Three Blind Mice"

8. "Twinkle, Twinkle Little Star"

Not every note in the melody implies a new harmony. Some of the ornamental or approach notes in the melody (those less important notes that resolve by step back to a target melody note) might only be melodic embellishments. Over-harmonizing simple songs is usually not musically appropriate. For example, "Row, Row, Row Your Boat" only uses the I chord throughout the entire song! This is probably why it works so easily as a round.

Two for the Road

Take a trip down memory lane and sing this famous round with your partner. Enjoy!

Collecting Souvenirs

Take a simple melody you're familiar with and determine its harmonic accompaniment. Remember, a simple melody usually suggests simple harmony. Share your example with classmates or band members (and vice versa), and watch the collection grow!

ACTIVITY TWO: *Takin' It to the Streets*

Your engine is warmed up from Activity One. Listen closely to the following melodies, looking for chord tone clues of the I, IV and V major triads. I've hand picked specific versions to listen to. Due to copyright laws, I cannot notate the melodies for your reference, so you'll have to make a sketch of the melodies yourself before making your final harmonic decisions. Remember, pay attention to only the "important" melody notes for harmonic clues. I've provided some melodic clues in the templates below.

Tip: Cut time (𝄵) is a fast 4/4 tempo, where the pulse is felt as two half notes rather than four quarter notes.

1. "Blowin' in the Wind," Bob Dylan, *The Freewheelin' Bob Dylan*

2. "I Still Haven't Found What I'm Looking For," U2, *The Joshua Tree*

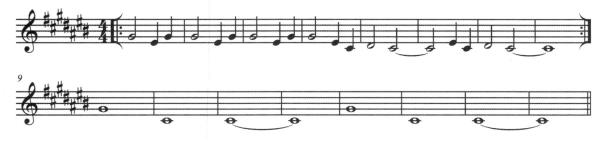

3. "Lean on Me," Bill Withers, *The Best of Bill Withers*

4. "Matilda," Harry Belafonte, *The Essential Harry Belafonte*

5. "Ob-La-Di, Ob-La-Da" (A section only), The Beatles, *White Album*

6. "When the Saints Go Marching In," Mel McDaniel, *30 Country Gospel Greats*

7. "You Are My Sunshine," Norman Blake, *O Brother Where Art Thou?*

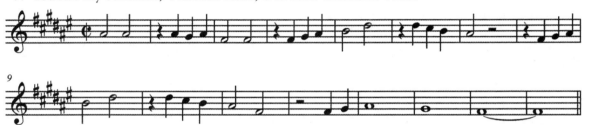

Check the Answer Key (pp.162–163) (which includes both the actual chord symbols and Roman numerals) to see how you did. When we work with the bass line, return to these recordings to see how the bass lines support your chord decisions. Melody and bass lines…a harmonious combo.

Duet Work: Melody and Bass Line

The melody, coupled with the bass line, often contains enough information to determine much of the harmony of a song. Let's try this approach with the next activity, where we hear only the melody and the bass line. When you were determining the harmony from only the melody line, at times there was more than one right answer. Now, however, with the two lines working together, the choices will be more limited, and there will likely be only one correct choice.

For example, if the melody line is *mi* and *sol*, accompanied by *do* in the bass line, the only choice is the I chord. If the melody is *sol* with the supporting bass note being *ti*, then the V chord is being stated.

Are you ready to take the wheel as we harmonize using both the melody and the bass line?

Activity Three: *Transcribing the Melody and Bass Line Duets*

72 – 75 Listen to the following four duets on Audio tracks 72–75. It's very likely you'll recognize the melodies! For each duet, first transcribe the melody, then the bass line. Being organized is key; don't attempt to transcribe both parts at the same time. The templates will provide opening clues for both the melody and bass parts.

6 Melody + Bass line = Harmony

After you've transcribed each example, write in what the resulting harmonies are, using either Roman numerals or actual chord symbols. For now, limit your harmonic choices to the I, IV or V chords. Then check the Answer Key (pp.164–165) to see how you did.

It's very possible that the resulting chords are not an exact match to those you chose when working with just the melodies in Activity One. The added influence of the bass line can play a significant role.

72 "Frère Jacques"

73 "Old MacDonald"

67

Reading, Writing and Rhythmetic

Two for the Road

Perform these duets with a partner. Sing the melody as your partner sings the bass line. Then reverse roles. Don't forget to sing using solfege syllables; they are helpful tools for achieving accurate intonation in your performance.

Transcribing the Bass Line

Why listen to the bass line? Because in most cases, that's where we'll hear the chord roots within the progression. Other chord tones may follow in the bass line, providing even more information about the harmony. Listen to the bass line as a diatonic phrase, rather than as a series of unrelated intervals. In other words, treat it as a "bass melody."

It can be challenging at times to actually hear this low frequency bass melody. Listen for clues in the lead melody which indicate what the accompanying chords might be. Assess important melody notes as potential chord tones. If the melody notes are *mi* and *sol*, listen for *do* in the bass line. This is a great way to use theory (remember, ear training is 50% brain training) to guide your ears towards identifying the correct bass notes.

Tip: It can be challenging to dig out the bass line from down under. Make sure to listen through excellent headphones or speakers to ensure best results. Listening through small computer speakers can make it nearly impossible to hear the bass notes. If you can't hear the bass notes, there's nothing to transcribe.

ACTIVITY FOUR: *Takin' It to the Streets*

Bass lines themselves can be interesting melodies. Let's listen to a few of them in popular recordings and transcribe them (templates are provided below). You can find these tunes on iTunes, YouTube, or perhaps in your own collection of CD's. Let's get to the bottom of the matter (pun intended!). Check the Answer Key (pp.166–168) to see how you did.

Note: In the following examples, ✗ means repeat the previous bar; ✗ means repeat the previous two bars.

1. "Ain't Too Proud to Beg," A section, The Temptations, *Motown's 1's*

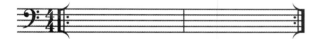

2. "All I Have to Do Is Dream," A and B sections, The Everly Brothers, *The Very Best of the Everly Brothers*

3. "Birdland," A section, Weather Report, *Heavy Weather*

4. "Carolina in My Mind," 1st A section, James Taylor, *James Taylor Greatest Hits, Vol. 1*

Reading, Writing and Rhythmetic

5. "Don't Stop Believin'," A section, Journey, *Escape*

6. "Every Breath You Take," 2 A sections, The Police, *Synchronicity*

7. " In the Midnight Hour," 1st A section, Wilson Pickett, *The Very Best of Wilson Pickett*

8. "Let It Be," A and B sections, The Beatles, *Let It Be*

9. "Ob-La-Di, Ob-La-Da," A section, The Beatles, *White Album*

10. "Piano Man," A section, Billy Joel, *Piano Man*

11. "Shoot the Moon," A and B sections, Norah Jones, *Come Away with Me*

12. "When Lights Are Low," 1st A section, Miles Davis, *Blue Haze*

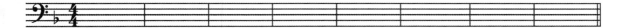

As you might have discovered, these bass lines are primarily influenced by the chord progression. We will return to several of these songs in the next chapter as we dig deeper into hearing the harmony.

It's time to get back on the rhythm road—destination: eighth note triplets.

Eighth Note Triplets

In the last chapter we explored $\frac{6}{8}$ time, a compound meter most commonly felt as two groups of three, and applied the same conducting pattern used for $\frac{2}{4}$. If we reverse gears and write this same $\frac{6}{8}$ figure in $\frac{2}{4}$, then we need to use what's called "eighth note triplets," shown below.

76 The time of three eighth note triplets is equal to the time of two normal eighth notes. Listen to Audio track 76. This example can be written out in either $\frac{6}{8}$ or $\frac{2}{4}$, with both notations sounding identical.

71

Reading, Writing and Rhythmetic

So, when is it best to write the music in 6/8 rather than 2/4 time? If the triplet feel persists throughout the music, then writing the song in 6/8 is the practical choice. But if the music goes back and forth between a duple feel (1 + 2 + etc.) and a triplet feel (1 trip-let, 2 trip-let, etc.), then using the 2/4 time signature is preferred, notating triplets where needed.

Let's practice switching back and forth between duple eighth notes and eighth note triplets in the next activity.

Activity Five: *Practicing Duple and Triplet Subdivisions of the Beat*

1. Set the metronome to a comfortable speed. Each click will represent the beat, the quarter note.
2. Practice breaking each quarter note (each click) into two equal parts—2 eighth notes. As you clap or tap out the eighth notes, count "1 +, 1 + etc." This should feel comfortable and familiar.
3. Next, divide the quarter note (each click) into three equal parts, counting "1-trip-let, 1 trip-let etc." Do a few of this series of triplets in order to get comfortable.
4. When ready, switch back and forth between these two subdivisions of the beat. For example: 1 +, 1 +, 1 trip-let, 1 trip-let. Mix the subdivisions up in a variety of ways: 1 +, 1 +, 1 +, 1 +, 1 trip-let, 1 trip-let, 1 +, 1 trip-let, etc. Spend enough time with this step until you feel very comfortable and confident in feeling and alternating between the two subdivisions.

Are you ready to tackle some transcribing in Activity Six? One, two, triplets!

Activity Six: *Transcribing Eighth Note Triplets*

(77) Listen to the 16-bar example on Audio track 77 and transcribe the rhythm. The example is in 2/4 and will incorporate some eighth note triplets along the way. Use the template provided below to write in your answers.

9

Before you check your results with the Answer Key (p.168), read and sing through what you've written. Did you catch any mistakes?

Two for the Road

As you count aloud the duple 1 + 2 + rhythm grid in 2/4, have your partner perform eighth note triplets above that grid. You'll get to hear the "three against two" of this interaction. Then switch roles.

Going the Extra Mile

For added challenge, see if you can perform both parts together on your own. Try tapping the 1 + 2 + as you say the triplets aloud. Or, tap the 1 + 2 + with your left hand as you tap the triplets with your right hand. It's quite a feat of coordination and can feel like a tug of war between your two hands. Nothing ventured, nothing gained. Go for it!

Is the Music in 12/8 or 4/4 with triplets?

It's the same question we posed regarding 6/8 time and 2/4 time involving triplets. If you consistently hear a triplet groove throughout the song, then notating it in 12/8 is best. In fact, you're likely to find many more examples of songs in 12/8 as opposed to 6/8 (similarly, most songs are in 4/4, rather than 2/4). Let's take 12/8 on the road in the next activity.

ACTIVITY SEVEN: *Takin' 12/8 to the Streets*

Listen to the following songs on the web that are best felt and notated in 12/8 time. You will consistently hear the triplet groove throughout. Several of these songs fall into the blues shuffle or 12/8 ballad genres. As you listen, conduct using the 4/4 pattern (similar to using the 2/4 pattern when conducting 6/8). I've included a baker's dozen. Enjoy!

1. "Always with You, Always with Me," Joe Satriani, *Surfing with the Alien*
2. "At Last," Etta James, *At Last!*
3. "Higher Ground," Stevie Wonder, *Innervisions*
4. "House of the Rising Sun," The Animals, *The Animals*
5. "I Only Have Eyes for You," The Flamingos, *Flamingo Serenade*
6. "Lateral Climb," Robben Ford, *Truth*
7. "Memory," *Cats* soundtrack
8. "Oh Darling," The Beatles, *Abbey Road*
9. "Summertime," Janis Joplin, *Pearl*
10. "Surfer Girl," The Beach Boys, *Surfer Girl*
11. "The Way You Make Me Feel," Michael Jackson, *Bad*
12. "You Really Got a Hold on Me," Smokey Robinson and the Miracles, *Ooo Baby Baby: the Anthology*
13. "Unchained Melody," The Righteous Brothers, *Just Once in My Life*

Going the Extra Mile

Let's put Joplin's version of "Summertime" under the "metroscope" and transcribe the rhythm of the lead guitar line in the 8-bar introduction. The template provided below starts with a 1-bar pickup.

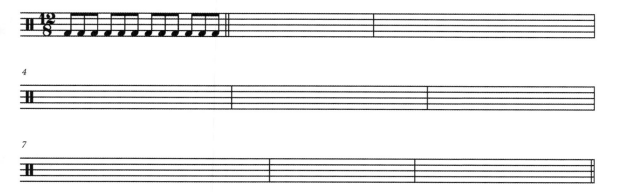

Check the Answer Key (p.168) to see how you did. We will revisit this song in a later chapter when we discuss minor key tonality.

Reading, Writing and Rhythmetic

Triplets have been around for a long time! Listen to: Bach's "Jesu, Joy of Man's Desiring," Beethoven's "Moonlight Sonata," or Ravel's "Bolero" just to mention a few of the classics.

We will fast forward in time in the next activity, listening to a jazz classic that incorporates eighth note triplets within the context of 4/4 time.

Activity Eight: *Takin' Eighth Note Triplets to the Streets*

It's time to sit back and enjoy the ride. Listen to a recording of Bobby Timmons' "Dat Dere" as you read along with the rhythmic score shown below (A sections only). My favorite version is from the Art Blakey and the Jazz Messengers' album, *The Big Beat*.

"Dat Dere," Bobby Timmons

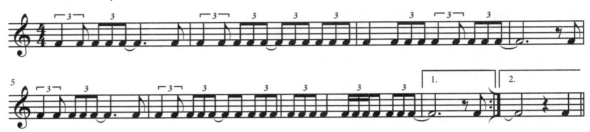

Tip: Sher Music Co. publications are a wonderful resource for checking your transcription work. Their collection of lead sheets are very accurately notated. This particular song, "Dat Dere," appears in *Volume 2 The Real Easy Book (Tunes for Intermediate Improvisers)*. This series in fact reflects specific performances of the songs. It's a worthwhile investment to have some of these "fake books" in your home library.

With the majority of the rhythms being triplets, why is this song notated in 4/4 rather than 12/8? Because this is a jazz tune, incorporating a "swing eighth note feel." If you listen to the rhythm section, and not simply the melody, you'll detect an overall 4/4 feel.

Have you heard the term, swing eighth note feel before? If not, you've come to the right place: that is our rhythmic destination for the next chapter. Feeling eighth note triplets provides a good introduction for feeling swing eighth notes. Get hip!

12/8 Feel

Is the music in 12/8 or 4/4 with triplets? Or, perhaps it is somewhere in between. Some songs share the best of both worlds and are referred to as having a "12/8 feel." Three examples of this crossover groove are: McCoy Tyner's "Blues on the Corner," *The Real McCoy*; Stan Getz's version of "Con Alma," *The Very Best of Stan Getz*; and John Coltrane's "Like Sonny," *A Giant Step in Jazz*.

Similar to Bobby Timmons' "Dat Dere," these are jazz tunes that exist primarily in the world of 4/4 swing, yet establish the impression of being in 12/8 time. For example, with "Blues on the Corner," when McCoy Tyner plays the "head," (the melody), he definitely establishes a 12/8 feel. But when it comes to soloing, he's back in the comfortable world of 4/4 swing. We'll revisit this song in an upcoming "Round Trip" activity, and see how we could notate the head in either 12/8 or 4/4. Until then, give the recording a preview test drive.

ACTIVITY NINE: *Round Trip*

Transposing is a great way to get mileage out of our movable *do* solfege syllables. Take some of the duets from Activity Three and notate them in a few different keys. This will be a good workout with both the treble and bass clefs. If you listen to the lines inside your head with solfege syllables, it's unlikely you'll make mistakes. You'll stay more musically engaged as you write. Bringing your ears along for the ride is like wearing your seat belt when driving. If your eyes and brain fall asleep at the wheel, your ears will keep you alive.

Tip: One of the wonderful features of notation software is the transposing tool. A simple click of the mouse can do the trick—how convenient! But if you do it the old fashioned way, by hand, by ear (using numbers or solfege), you might benefit more. What do you think these added benefits might be?

Approaching the Fork in the Road

In every chapter of this book, I have encouraged you to sing as a *pro*active way of listening. Why? Because "If you can sing it, you can hear it." We all have a voice, a built-in instrument that we can take anywhere, anytime. Singing a musical idea will show whether we have heard it correctly. You could pick up your instrument and search for the notes, but that does not prove that you have internalized the musical idea in your inner hearing. Singing back the music accurately ensures that you have "fed your inner hearing" correctly.

It's not always easy to sing back the music, but going the extra mile, making the effort to do so will pay off. It's not about the singing performance per se: it's about demonstrating that you've internalized the music you heard.

I've encouraged you to first take in the idea without thinking, singing it back, "la, la, la." This allows you to be open-minded and not judge the notes prematurely. The mind can do funny things at times, pre-guessing what it wants to hear rather than hearing what actually happened. If I've said that ear training is 50% brain training, then the other 50% might be devoted to this experiential activity of pure listening.

Once the musical idea has been firmly planted in our inner hearing, then the brainwork can begin. This is when we use conducting and counting to determine the rhythmic elements, and where we use the solfege language to translate the pitches and how they function within the tonality. How can singing be helpful for this translation stage?

If your inner hearing "owns" the idea, then you can sing it back at a slower tempo in order to have time to translate the "la, la, la's" into a meaningful description. You can take a small portion of the idea, loop it in your mind's memory tape recorder, playing it over and over in your head as you begin the analysis process. It's challenging to keep the sound in your head; sing it aloud, it makes the sound more "real" and accessible.

When you're introducing your inner hearing to new musical patterns, such as a new scale/solfege series, sing it back *slowly*! This is not about vocal facility; it's about having the time to consciously make the connection between the sound and the function of the pitches as you sing. If you feel you're on "auto pilot" in the singing process, then you're going too fast and I'm likely to give you a speeding ticket! Ear training really works best when we travel slowly through the process. Remember, we're not singing for the stage, we're singing to fuel our inner hearing tank.

"If you can sing it, you can hear it,"... and it is likely that you can transcribe it.

7. Transcribing Popular Chord Patterns in Major

Introduction

In the last chapter, we examined the melody for possible clues to hearing the harmonic accompaniment. We looked for chord tones within the melody and discovered that a majority of the melody notes were in fact chord tones. We used very simple songs and discovered that a simple melody invited simple harmony, primarily the diatonic I, IV and V major triads within the major key. I referred to this approach as a "top-down" way of searching for harmonic clues.

Next, we researched the bass line for additional harmonic clues. We found that many bass notes were also chord tones. In particular, the root of the chord was prominent, introducing each chord within the progression. In this chapter, we'll continue to work with the bass line and add the "bottom-up" or "vertical" approach to identifying the chords in a song.

What is the vertical approach? It involves listening upward, from the root to the third of each chord, to determine if we hear a major or minor third interval. It is this relationship of root/third that best identifies the quality of the chord as being major or minor.

This chapter's primary destination is recognizing diatonic chord progressions in a major key. We'll focus on listening to and memorizing common chord patterns. Learning to recognize these common chord patterns ("harmonic landmarks") in songs will save time when we're transcribing.

We continue our rhythmic work with the swing eighth note feel. Our work with triplets in the last chapter will serve as good preparation for this new rhythmic venture.

We have lots of ground and groove to cover in this chapter. Make sure you have a full tank of energy and enthusiasm...let's get started!

Hearing Major and Minor Triads

In Chapter 3, we practiced identifying major and minor third intervals in order to determine if the song was in a major or minor key. The relationship of the root to the third of the scale made the difference. We can now use that previous practice with major and minor third intervals to identify major and minor chord qualities. If we hear a major third interval between the root and third of the triad, the chord is a major triad. Can you make an educated guess as to what makes a minor triad minor? Let's find out.

① Remember: it's the interval between the root and third of the triad that is the distinguishing factor. Listen to Audio track 1 which compares the sound of C major and C minor triads. We can refer to these two triads as parallel, meaning they share the same root.

Comparison of C major and C minor triads

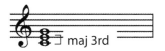 

Reading, Writing and Rhythmetic

When listening to any chord, the third is the most important chord tone to identify because it determines the quality of the chord. When chords are changing quickly in the progression, we often don't have enough time to hear all the chord tones (root, third and fifth), so recognizing the interval between the root and third becomes very important.

Two for the Road
Before attempting the quiz in Activity One, brainstorm with your partner about ways to practice hearing major and minor triads. Don't forget that playing and singing the triads is a great place to begin: if you can sing it, you can hear it!

Activity One: *Identifying Major and Minor Triads*

② Listen to Audio track 2 and identify the 12 triads as either major or minor. Pay close attention to the relationship between the root and the third of the triad and ask yourself, "Is it a major or minor third interval?" Check the Answer Key (p.169) to see how you did.

Activity One is an excellent workout for identifying individual chord qualities as major or minor triads, "out in space." Now, let's situate these triads within the context of the major key and discover their diatonic placement.

Diatonic Triads in the Major Key

③ Let's look and listen to the seven diatonic triads within the major key. In Chapter 6 we got a jump-start introduction with the three primary major triads: I, IV and V. Let's add to that list and examine *all* of the diatonic triads. Audio track 3 features the diatonic triads in the key of G major. All triads are played in both block form and arpeggiated for the complete listening experience. Diatonic triads are the same in all major keys: I, II–, III–, IV, V, VI– and VII° (diminished).

Tip: In the last chapter we identified the three diatonic major triads with Roman numerals: I, IV and V. We will identify the diatonic minor triads with Roman numerals as well. We continue using all upper case Roman numerals for labeling the diatonic chords: I, II–, III–, IV, V, VI– and VII°. A more traditional system uses lower case Roman numerals to designate the minor and diminished triads: I, ii, iii, IV, V, vi and vii. You are welcome to use either system, and it's good to be aware of both.

7 TRANSCRIBING POPULAR CHORD PATTERNS IN MAJOR

USING THE VERTICAL APPROACH

Our first step in hearing the chords vertically is to recognize the diatonic bass notes, which in most cases represent the root motion of the chord progression. The second step is very similar to what we did in Activity One: identifying whether we hear a major or minor third interval from the root up to the third of each chord. In the next activity, let's get a bit more practice hearing diatonic bass lines before stepping on up the triad.

ACTIVITY TWO: *Hearing Diatonic Bass Lines*

🔊 4 – 15 Listen to the 12 diatonic bass lines in the key of E♭ on Audio tracks 4–15. Each example is five measures long, and played where written (i.e., in "concert" pitch). You can identify the bass notes using numbers, solfege syllables, or actual pitch names in the key of E♭. Whichever route you choose to take to identify the bass notes, I highly recommend you first sing back the bass line from memory, "la, la, la," ensuring you've heard the diatonic phrase and not simply a series of unrelated pitches. Bass lines are melodies too! See the sample template and Answer Key for the first example, shown below.

Check the Answer Key (pp.169–170) to see how you did. For additional proactive listening practice, sing the bass lines using numbers and/or solfege syllables as you review the Answer Key.

Going the Extra Mile

Transpose the bass lines from Activity Two into three different keys. Using numbers or solfege syllables will make this a successful trip. Bring your ears along for the ride, singing the numbers or solfege syllables as you write.

ACTIVITY THREE: *Practicing the Vertical Approach*

🔊 16 Let's combine our workout of hearing the bass line with the second step of the vertical approach: listening from the root up to the third of the chord to confirm that we hear a major or minor third interval. What better way to do this than to sing, sing, sing!

1. Listen to the following chord progression in the key of F, on Audio track 16.
2. Sing the bass line twice, using numbers then solfege syllables.
3. Then, sing from the root up to the third of each chord, noticing its major or minor quality. For example, with the first chord, sing "1, 3, major third," or "*do, mi,* major third."

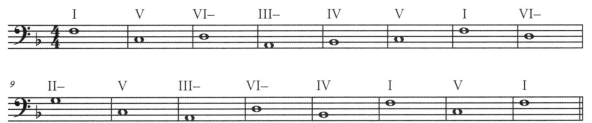

Did any chord patterns sound familiar in this progression? If so, which ones? In the next activity, we'll listen to some of the more common patterns found in popular music.

79

READING, WRITING AND RHYTHMETIC

ACTIVITY FOUR: *Memorizing Popular Chord Patterns*

17 Become familiar with the common chord patterns listed below (performed on Audio track 17) and try to memorize them. It is well worth your effort, as you discover these chord patterns in songs in different genres, but particularly within pop, rock, country and jazz music.

What's the best way to go about memorizing these chord patterns? Spend some time every day with only one or two patterns, following the same practice routine outlined in Activity Three. These are all diatonic chord patterns; simply memorizing the root motion will get you well past the halfway mark on your journey.

Common chord patterns:

Pattern 1:	I	IV	I	V	I
Pattern 2:	I	V	IV	I	
Pattern 3:	I	IV	V	I	
Pattern 4:	I	VI–	IV	V	I
Pattern 5:	I	VI–	II–	V	I
Pattern 6:	I	V	VI–	IV	I
Pattern 7:	I	IV	V	VI–	

Sometimes variations occur within these popular chord patterns. For example, Pattern 7 demonstrates how VI– is substituted for the I chord at the end of the phrase, creating a small surprise in the resolution, keeping our ears on their toes!

Two for the Road

Play these common chord patterns on your instrument and have your partner identify them. Then switch roles. Playing the chord patterns provides excellent hands-on experience. Play the chord patterns in a variety of keys. Before you know it, you'll own these chord patterns and start to recognize them in songs. Let's see how you do in the next "Takin' It to the Streets" activity.

ACTIVITY FIVE: *Takin' It to the Streets*

Listen to the following songs on YouTube, iTunes or from your own recording library. Each song will highlight one or more of the common chord patterns you memorized in the last activity. Go for it! There is no better way to practice hearing chord progressions than by listening to real music. Rote exercises can go in one ear, out the other: real music stays with you for a lifetime's journey!

Tip: With 25 songs to work with, pace yourself! Select only one to three songs per practice session, and then review these same songs on the following day. Following the "24-hour rule" will allow for a fresh set of ears and a recharged brain.

1. "All I Have to Do Is Dream," The Everly Brothers, *The Very Best of the Everly Brothers* (key of E, first A section)
2. "Always with You, Always with Me," Joe Satriani, *Surfing with the Alien* (key of B, A section)
3. "At Last," Etta James, *At Last!* (key of F, A section)
4. "Blowin' in the Wind," Stevie Wonder, *Up-Tight* (key of B♭, entire song)
5. "Blue Eyes Cryin' in the Rain," Willie Nelson, *Red Headed Stranger* (key of E, A and B sections)
6. "Come Away with Me," Norah Jones, *Come Away with Me* (key of C, B section)
7. "Don't Stop Believin'," Journey, *Escape* (key of E, A section)

8. "Every Breath You Take," The Police, *Synchronicity* (key of A, two A sections)

9. "Hey, Soul Sister," Train, *Save Me, San Francisco* (key of E, A section)

10. "Hiding My Heart Away," Adele, *21* (key of B, chorus)

11. "Hold My Hand," Hootie and the Blowfish, *Cracked Rear View* (key of B, entire song)

12. "I Still Haven't Found What I'm Looking For," U2, *The Joshua Tree* (key of C♯, A and B sections)

13. "Lean on Me," Bill Withers, *The Best of Bill Withers* (key of C, entire song)

14. "Let It Be," The Beatles, *Let It Be* (key of C, A section)

15. "Love Letters," Patti Austin, *The Real Me* (key of B♭, A section)

16. "Love Is a Verb," John Mayer, *Born and Raised* (key of E, A section)

17. "Mandeville," Bill Frisell, *Rarum V* (key of E, entire song)

18. "Ob-La-Di, Ob-La-Da," The Beatles, *White Album* (key of B♭, A section)

19. "So Lonely," The Police, *Message in a Box* (key of C, entire song)

20. "Someone Like You," Adele, *21* (key of A, chorus)

21. "Stand by Me," Ben E.King, *Be My Valentine: From Him to Her* (key of A, entire song)

22. "This Boy," The Beatles, *Meet the Beatles!* (key of D, A section)

23. "Viva La Vida," Coldplay, *Viva La Vida or Death and All His Friends* (key of A♭, A section)

24. "You Are My Sunshine," Norman Blake, *Oh Brother, Where Art Thou?* (key of F♯, entire song)

25. "You Send Me," Sam Cooke, *The Best of Sam Cooke* (key of G, A section)

Tip: Our goal is to recognize the basic chord patterns you've memorized from Activity Four. You might hear some small variations (some seventh chords, inversions, or an occasional Vsus4); and the chord patterns might not always begin with the I chord.

As you transcribe chord patterns found in popular songs, you'll likely start to memorize those patterns without making a conscious effort to do so. This will be a bonus benefit you've earned for your hard work and effort.

Check the Answer Key (pp.170–173) to see how well you did. If you find it challenging to recognize chord patterns in real music, try spending time listening to the songs as you read along with their chord charts. For most of us, hearing the harmony in real music is ten times harder than hearing the same harmony in a homemade exercise. You are *not* alone...hang in there! We are on this transcribing road for the long haul.

Collecting Souvenirs

Can you find some of your own examples of songs that spotlight these common chord patterns? Inspired by songs that catch your own personal interest is great motivation for the often bumpy road named "transcribing."

Tip: Chapters 6 and 7 introduced you to some strategies for transcribing "the changes," the chord progressions found in popular music. If you would like to continue this harmonic hearing work in greater detail and with additional in-depth practice routines, please refer to my other book, *The Real Easy Ear Training Book: A Beginning/Intermediate Guide to Hearing the Chord Changes,* published by Sher Music, as an additional resource.

I've got rhythm...do you? Let's turn our attention to the swing eighth note feel that breathes life into jazz and makes you want to snap your fingers on beats 2 and 4!

Swing Eighth Notes

The Feel

It's difficult to describe the swing eighth note feel if you've never listened to swing or jazz music. My first and best word of advice is that you have to spend a considerable amount of time *listening* to swing and jazz music for an honest and authentic education about the swing feel that uniquely characterizes jazz music. No two jazz musicians swing in exactly the same way, so you'll need to listen to a wide range of jazz artists. And there are many great artists to recommend! I'll use the alphabet to organize the names of just a few: Louie Armstrong, Art Blakey, John Coltrane, Miles Davis, Duke Ellington, Ella Fitzgerald, Dizzy Gillespie, Herbie Hancock, Chuck Israels, Keith Jarrett, Wynton Kelly, Abbey Lincoln, Wes Montgomery, Oliver Nelson, King Oliver, Charlie Parker, Sonny Rollins, Sonny Stitt, McCoy Tyner, Sarah Vaughan, Dinah Washington, Lester Young, and Joe Zawinul. The list goes on and on!

Make it a point to listen as often as you can in order to acquire the swing feel. You've got to live it.

The Look

Swing eighth notes look exactly like "straight" eighth notes, but don't sound the same. Straight eighth notes divide the beat (the quarter note) into two equal halves; swing eighth notes do not. They tend to sound closer to an eighth note triplet feel (♩♪).

(18) Listen to Audio track 18 as you read the following comparison of the swing eighth note notation and the eighth note triplet division of the beat. They sound identical, but which notation would you prefer to read?

What is the origin of swing eighth note feel? It was born out of jazz performance, not notated on the page. One feature of swing/jazz performance is syncopation, which can look fairly complicated when notated. Although swing eighth notes can sound like triplets (especially at slower tempos), standard eighth note notation is used for "swing" eighth note notation. Can you imagine how complex the notation could be with triplets and ties?

7 Transcribing Popular Chord Patterns in Major

Activity Six: *Comparing Straight Eighth and Swing Eighth Note Feel*

Read through the following 16-bar example, applying both the straight eighth note and swing eighth note feel for comparison. If you're performing a Latin, pop or rock piece of music, you're likely to interpret the rhythms with a straight, even feel. If the music is swing, jazz or hip-hop, you're more likely to swing the rhythms.

When swinging the eighth notes, did you happen to recognize this jazz gem? It's "Doxy," written by Sonny Rollins. You can view the lead sheet in Sher Music's publication *The Real Easy Book, Vol. 1*. A lead sheet is a sketch of a song, notating a simple version of the melody and chord changes. We'll be exploring setting up lead sheets in a later chapter. If you listen to the following artists' renditions of "Doxy,"—Sonny Rollins, Dexter Gordon, Miles Davis, Cal Tjader, John McLaughlin (there are many others)—you'll notice that no two musicians interpret the song exactly the same.

Activity Seven: *Transcribing Swing Eighth Notes*

🎵 19 – 30 Transcribe the following 12 examples of swing eighth note patterns played on Audio tracks 19–30. Each example is four bars long. A sample template with the Answer Key for example 1 is provided below. All examples will feature "call and response" phrasing, with the second 2-bar phrase "answering" the first.

You might recognize some of our two-beat rhythm words from earlier chapters, but they won't sound quite the same. Before transcribing these examples, take a trip down memory lane and practice the rhythm words with a swing feel. You'll also notice that these examples will employ more syncopation, more off-beat attacks and ties, which are characteristic of swing and jazz music. This makes things a bit more challenging.

ex. 1

Check the Answer Key (p.174) to see how swingin' you are! For additional practice, read and sing back each example, first with a straight feel, and then swing it!

83

Reading, Writing and Rhythmetic

Two for the Road

Create your own 4-bar rhythm examples and have your partner sight-read them. Have your partner perform your examples with both a straight and swing eighth note feel. Then switch roles. Back-to-back comparison of straight and swing eighth note feel can really drive home the differences.

Activity Eight: *Takin' It to the Streets*

It's time to sit back and enjoy the ride. Listen to the following excerpt from Miles Davis' performance of "When Lights Are Low," as you read along with the rhythmic transcription shown below. You're listening to his one chorus of improvisation (1:15–2:20) from the *Blue Haze* album. Though Miles is not overly syncopated in his delivery, he still swings hard, making simple phrases of quarter and eighth notes come alive! Notating his feel with swing eighth notes makes reading this example easy on the eyes. Enjoy!

"When Lights Are Low," solo chorus, Miles Davis, *Blue Haze*

7 TRANSCRIBING POPULAR CHORD PATTERNS IN MAJOR

ACTIVITY NINE: *Round Trip*

The top-down and vertical approaches can work hand in hand to determine the chord progressions found in popular music. In Activity Five, you recognized common chord patterns by using the vertical approach: first determining the bass notes (the chord roots), and then determining chord qualities as being either major or minor. Let's return to some of those same songs to examine the melodies with the top-down approach. You'll discover that the majority of melody notes are also chord tones. It comes full circle. You can start with the melody (top-down), or you can start with the bass line (bottom-up) to arrive at the same answer—one approach reinforces the other.

Approaching the Fork in the Road

Is it sometimes OK to let knowledge of music theory lead the way when transcribing? Of course. Use what you've got and go from there. For some of us who have had a lot of academic training in music but little hands-on transcription experience, using our knowledge of music theory can help set up harmonic and melodic expectations. This theoretical knowledge can be very handy, particularly when identifying chord progressions.

Knowing the common chord patterns we've studied in this chapter is great preparation for predicting chord patterns in songs we transcribe. For example, by knowing that many pop and rock tunes contain only diatonic harmony, we can start with that expectation when listening to them. Knowing that the bass line is likely to represent mainly chord roots is another good organizer. Theoretical knowledge helps to establish limits and a predictable template for transcribing. Instead of starting from scratch, you have a head start with knowing what's likely to happen.

Of course, it doesn't stop with theory: you still have to listen for the final answer. If ear training is 50% brain training, then what is the other 50%?

8 EXPLORING MINOR KEY MELODIES WITH SOLFEGE

INTRODUCTION

It's time to venture into new tonal territory in this chapter as we explore the natural minor scale. We'll adapt many of the same activities we used with the major scale to use for practice with the natural minor scale.

We'll visualize the minor scale in a variety of ways in order to become proficient in seeing and hearing the scale in different keys. Seeing the scale written out in the staff, seeing the scale on the keyboard, and visualizing the scale on your instrument will get us closer to the final stages of transcribing—writing down the musical idea.

And indeed, we'll be writing down the musical idea, as we "take it to the streets" with transcribing popular minor key melodies.

We'll explore rhythmic syncopation in greater detail in this chapter, paying particular attention to whether notes are on or off the beat. In the last chapter, we warmed up with swing eighth note reading activities. In this chapter, we'll put transcribing behind the wheel. We'll listen to how the jazz pros put their magic touch to making a melody come alive and really swing.

It's time to get out the map as we explore the sounds of minor and cap it off with a trip to Birdland, the land of swing. Ready for the count off? Let's hit the road, Jack!

THE NATURAL MINOR SCALE

31 In Chapter 3 we learned how to determine whether a song was in a major or minor key. We found that the relationship between the root and third of the scale made the difference. We've spent the last several chapters examining the major scale; now, it's time to visit the other side of the tonal fence and become familiar with minor scales. There are several different kinds of minor scales, but we'll start with the "big mama" of minor scales, the natural minor scale in this chapter. Listen to Audio track 31 as you read through the C natural minor scale shown below.

Notice the new solfege syllables and how they equate to the each note's numerical placement within the scale: *me* = b3, *le* = b6 and *te* = b7. You pronounce the vowel "e" like "ay" in the word, "say."

87

Comparing Relative Scales

32 The natural minor scale is also called the "relative" minor scale. "Relative" means that this minor scale shares the same pitches as the major scale starting a minor third above the root. For example, the C natural minor scale is related to the E♭ major scale, and therefore, will share the same key signature. Though these two scales share the same notes, they do *not* share the same *do*, and will not sound the same as a result. Listen to Audio track 32 and compare the two relative scales shown below. This is a great example of how simply looking at the notes is not enough; you also have to *listen* to determine if you're hearing a minor or its relative major scale.

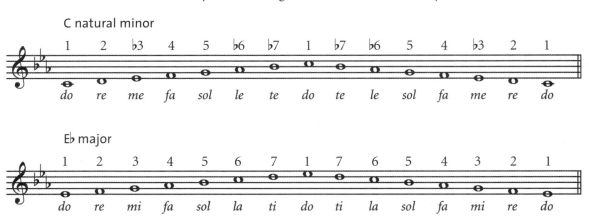

Tip: Do you remember how to locate the *do* of a melody? That's right, at the end, not necessarily at the beginning of the song. This applies to songs in minor as well. How do you know if the song is in the key of C natural minor or E♭ major? Listen and look to the end of the melody. The key signature alone will not tell you if the song is in the relative major or minor key.

Comparing Parallel Scales

33 Let's now compare the sounds of the C natural minor and C major scales. They are called "parallel" scales because they both start on the same root, but do *not* share the same pitches. Listen to Audio track 33, comparing these two parallel scales, paying particular attention to how the sounds of the 3rd, 6th and 7th scale degrees of the major and minor scales differ.

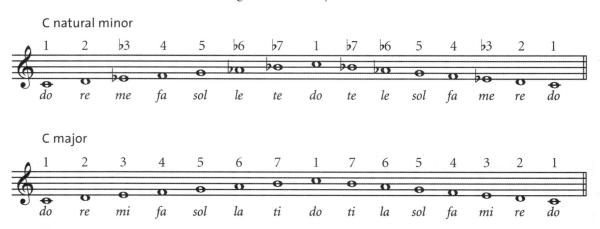

Enough talk of theory for the moment, let's get our ears engaged in the action!

8   Exploring Minor Key Melodies with Solfege

Activity One: *Singing Parallel Minor and Major Scales with Numbers and Solfege Syllables*

Comparing parallel minor and major scales and focusing on their differences is the best way to get them firmly planted in your inner hearing. Revisit Audio track 33 and sing along, using numbers and solfege syllables. Then try singing the scales on your own, letting your inner hearing do the driving. Don't forget to steer the wheel with numbers and solfege syllables as you navigate through both scales.

Tip: In minor, we now have numbers that can be tongue-twisters to say, such as "flat three," or "flat seven." Using our one-syllable solfege names, "me" (♭3), or "te" (♭7), will roll off the tongue much more easily.

do'	1
te	♭7
le	♭6
sol	5
fa	4
me	♭3
re	2
do	1
te,	♭7
le,	♭6
sol,	5

Activity Two: *Stepping Your Way Through the Natural Minor Scale*

34 In Chapter 4, we "stepped" our way through the major scale, singing graduated stepwise phrases that started with and then concluded on *do*. Let's apply this same routine to the natural minor scale. Listen to Audio track 34 and sing along using numbers and solfege syllables. Use the tone ladder provided alongside this activity as a helpful visual guide. The minor scale, with its three new solfege syllables, is new territory for our inner hearing. Traveling the tone ladder will provide a helpful visual map for remembering these new syllables.

Going the Extra Mile

Can you sing the scale pattern starting on a different *do*? If you've internalized the sound of the minor scale, you should be able to drive smoothly through another key or two, without any outside help from your instrument. Go for it!

We'll go the extra mile with the next activity, adding some tips for visualizing the minor scale in a variety of ways.

Activity Three: *Visualizing in Different Keys*

The tone ladder is a great visual tool for seeing how scale degrees relate generically to one another, using solfege syllables. The tone ladder does not actually display the scale tones in any specific key. But in fact, the movable Do solfege syllables can make the transposition into any key quite easy. Let's have solfege transport us through the different keys. Pick a key, any key, and visualize it following the steps outlined below. These steps are preliminary practice routines for "seeing" the scales in a variety of ways, getting us closer to the final destination of writing down the musical idea.

1. Actually write out the scale pattern in the new key: this will increase your ability to quickly identify the notes on the staff.
2. A paper keyboard has been provided on the next page. Use it to visualize the scale on the keyboard.
3. Can you imagine, and/or actually play the scale pattern on your instrument?

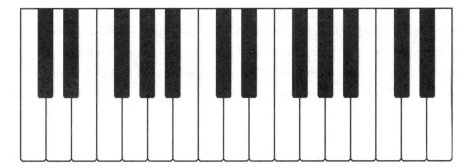

Repeat these steps on a daily basis, trying a new key each time. You want to be ready to cruise through any key, not stalling out due to a faulty engine.

Activity Four: *Improvising a Stepwise Melody*

In Chapter 4, we improvised a simple, stepwise melody. Now, we'll use that same exercise but with a slightly new twist in our work with the natural minor scale. In addition to singing your improvised line, visualize it. It's not necessary to write down the rhythmic details of your performance, simply visualize the notes.

Try applying the three steps of Activity Three for visualizing your improvised stepwise melody: seeing the notes written in the staff, seeing the notes on the keyboard, and seeing the notes on your instrument.

Two for the Road

Trade solos with your partner. Let's try this activity with the same twist we applied in Activity Four. Write down your solo and ask your partner to perform it. We can take two roads. You can simply give your partner the notes, giving him/her the freedom to perform with their own rhythms. Or, you can give them a fully written out solo, rhythms and all. Pick any minor key to write down your solo; your partner will perform it using solfege syllables, demonstrating the ability to read and hear what you've written, regardless of key. Keep it simple and don't over-complicate things rhythmically. Simple is good; complicated can cause a train wreck and not necessarily be musically tasteful. Then of course, switch roles. Have fun with this! I've provided a sample solo below to get the engine warmed up.

My sample solo

8 Exploring Minor Key Melodies with Solfege

do'	1
te	♭7
le	♭6
sol	5
fa	4
me	♭3
re	2
do	1
te,	♭7
le,	♭6
sol,	5

ACTIVITY FIVE: *Takin' It to the Streets*

What would our practice be if we didn't "take it to the streets?" Let's explore the following minor key melodies and transcribe them. Remember to first spend time listening thoroughly to each melody, until you're able to confidently "la, la, la" it back from memory. Then follow the transcription steps suggested below.

1. First, find *do*, the tonic of the key. Remember, *do* is most likely to be found at the end of the phrase.
2. With *do* established, next determine how the scale notes relate to each other, using numbers or solfege syllables. All melodies will remain 100% in the natural minor scale. I'll give you the first few starting notes for each melody in solfege. Use the tone ladder for guidance. This is the step where our inner hearing is really being put to the test.
3. Next, write out the melodies in their actual key. This is an opportunity to experience notating in a variety of keys, increasing our fluency in writing, reading and ultimately playing in different keys. I'll tell you the key for each melody, but you will need to provide the template from scratch, setting up the key signature.
4. We won't notate the rhythmic details of the melodies; let's simply focus on the pitches for now. Just write note heads on the lines and spaces in the staff. Remember, there are only seven pitches to choose from in natural minor.
5. Before referring to the Answer Key (pp.175–178), play through your transcriptions to double check your answers. Playing along with the actual recordings will help capture the rhythmic feel as well. There is no substitute for the hands-on practice of playing your instrument. To get things started I've done the first example, "Afro Blue," shown below. Enjoy!

ex. 1

Tip: A couple of these songs will incorporate the blue note, "se," ♭5 of the scale. There is a close relationship between the sound of the minor scale and the blues scale (*do, me, fa, se, sol, te*). We will delve into the blues in greater detail in Chapter 10 when we discuss popular song forms. The 12-bar blues form is at the top of the list.

1. "Afro Blue," Abbey Lincoln, *Abbey Is Blue* (key of C–, A section: *do, sol, me*)
2. "Ain't No Sunshine When She's Gone," Bill Withers, *The Best of Bill Withers* (key of A–, A section: *sol, te, do*)
3. "Another Day in Paradise," Phil Collins, *…But Seriously* (key of F♯–, verse: *sol, le, te*)
4. "Billie Jean," Michael Jackson, *Thriller* (key of F♯–, 1-bar bass line: *do, sol, te*)
5. "Blue Bossa," Joe Henderson, *Back Road* (key of C–, A section: *sol, sol, fa, me*)
6. "Evil Ways," Santana, *Santana* (key of G–, verse: *sol, fa, sol*)
7. "Equinox," John Coltrane, *Coltrane's Sound* (key of C♯–, 12-bar blues: *sol, me, do*)
8. "Farandole," Georges Bizet, *The Best of Bizet* (key of D–, 2 A sections: *do, sol, do*)
9. "Fever," Peggy Lee, *The Best of Peggy Lee* (key of A–, first 8 bars: *fa, me, fa*)
10. "Kiss from a Rose," Seal, *Seal: Hits* (key of G♯–, intro: *do, re, me*)

READING, WRITING AND RHYTHMETIC

11. "Mas Que Nada," Sergio Mendez and Brasil '66, *Greatest Hits* (key of F–, vocal intro: *do, me, sol*)

12. "Mr. P.C.," John Coltrane, *Giant Steps* (key of C–, 12-bar blues: *do, do, re, re*)

13. "New World Symphony, 4th Movement," Antonín Dvořák, *Bernstein: The 1953 American Decca Recordings* (key of E–, first 8 bars: *do, re, me*)

14. "Rolling in the Deep," Adele, *21* (key of C–, 8-bar chorus: *sol, te, sol*)

15. "Russians," Sting, *The Dream of the Blue Turtles* (key of C–, instrumental line, 8-bars repeated: *do, sol, fa*)

16. "Sixth Sense," Dave Brubeck, *In Their Own Sweet Way* (key of G–, A section: *me, re, do*)

17. "Softly as in a Morning Sunrise," McCoy Tyner, *Coltrane "Live" at the Village Vanguard* (key of C–, A section: *do, sol*)

18. "Sonnymoon for Two," Sonny Rollins, *Jazz 1—Timeless Legends* (B♭ blues, 12-bar blues: *do, te, sol*)

19. "Summertime," Miles Davis, *Porgy and Bess* (key of B♭–, two A sections: *sol, me, sol*)

20. "Superstition," Stevie Wonder, *Talking Book* (key of E♭–, horn line: *do, do, fa*)

21. "We Three Kings," Dolly Parton, *Home for Christmas* (key of B–, A section: *sol, fa, me*)

22. "We Will Rock You," Queen, *News of the World* (key of E–, chorus: *me*)

23. "When Johnny Comes Marching Home," Ross Moore, *Southern Son* (key of D–, entire song: *sol, sol, do*)

24. "While My Guitar Gently Weeps," The Beatles, *White Album* (key of A–, two A sections: *sol, do, re*)

25. "Wrapped Around Your Finger," The Police, *Synchronicity* (key of A–, instrumental line: *sol, le, sol*)

It continues to amaze me how a melody made up of primarily stepwise motion can sound so good! Sting's "Russians" demonstrates this simple feature. By the way, Sting borrowed this instrumental theme from Prokofiev's composition, "Lieutenant Kije Suite," as a direct quote. Sting obviously did his listening and transcription homework! Listen to the Prokofiev original when you can: it's a stunning and beautifully somber piece of music.

Collecting Souvenirs

Can you find examples of simple minor key melodies in your own recording library, or from memory? Sometimes, when you least expect it, a familiar song will pop into your head. Take a minute to explore it: does it sound major or minor? Can you find *do* and then figure out the rest of the melody using solfege? The process of transcribing starts with listening but doesn't have to end with writing it down. Seizing those on-the-spot moments for figuring out something about the music is well worth it.

I promised you a trip to Birdland: time to fly the coop!

MORE ABOUT RHYTHMIC SYNCOPATION

In the last chapter we worked with swing eighth notes, a notation system commonly used within a swing or jazz style of music. What goes hand in hand with these two styles of music is a heightened sense of syncopation, accenting the off beats, the "+'s" ("ands") of the beats. Reading these kinds of syncopated rhythms can be challenging, and transcribing these syncopated rhythms can be even more so because syncopation obscures the clarity of where the beats are falling. Is the rhythm falling on or off the beat? That is the question.

8   Exploring Minor Key Melodies with Solfege

(35) Back-to-back comparison might be helpful. For example, when transcribing the following example on Audio track 35, I might not be sure if the example should be notated as figure A or B. I recommend singing both notated versions and then determining which version is a closer match to the audio example. You try it: which do you think is the better match? That's right, it's figure B. The phrase first attacks off beat 1 (on the +) and then "sits" on beat 3.

Figure B was inspired by Roland Kirk's performance of the B section of "Serenade to a Cuckoo." When you get a chance, listen to the real thing on his *I Talk with the Spirits* recording.

I recommend that you commit to memory a list of syncopated figures typical in swing and jazz music. Even with such a list, it will often come down to the comparison test: which one is a closer match? Swing eighth notes are already "messing with" the time, making it challenging to determine if a figure is hitting on or off the beat.

Activity Six: *Memorizing Four-Beat Syncopated Rhythm Words*

(36) Let's commit to memory some common four-beat rhythm words that incorporate syncopation along with the swing eighth note feel. Listen to the following 12 examples on Audio track 36 as you read through the notation. Each 1-bar figure will be followed by one bar of rest, clearly separating each word. Sing along as you listen and read to further ingest the feel of the rhythmic phrase. Some of these words are almost identical, so pay close attention to the details. An eighth note's placement can make a big difference in the feel (falling on or off the beat).

Let's test-drive these patterns with the next activity.

Reading, Writing and Rhythmetic

Activity Seven: *Is It A or B?*

Visit the web and listen to the following 12 excerpts of opening 4-bar phrases from popular jazz songs. Each example will feature one of the syncopated patterns we memorized in the previous activity. You will be given two notations to choose from. Is it version A or B? Listen closely, because both notations are almost identical, differing only by an eighth note's placement. The visualization has been done for you already. Rather than having to create the notation from scratch, choosing between A and B gives you a 50–50 chance of being correct!

Check the Answer Key (p.178) to see how you did.

1. "Bessie's Blues," John Coltrane, *Crescent*

2. "Four," Miles Davis, *Workin' with the Miles Davis Quintet*

3. "I Mean You," Thelonious Monk, *Art Blakey's Jazz Messengers with Thelonious Monk*

4. "The Kicker," Horace Silver, *Song for My Father*

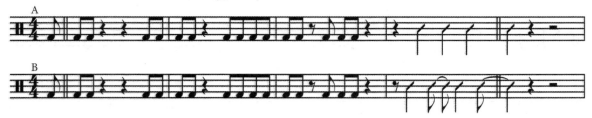

5. "Lullaby of Birdland," Sarah Vaughan and Clifford Brown, *The Definitive Sarah Vaughan*

8 Exploring Minor Key Melodies with Solfege

6. "Most Like Lee," Lee Morgan, *Cornbread*

7. "Pent-Up House," Sonny Rollins, *Sonny Rollins Plus 4*

8. "Satin Doll," Ella Fitzgerald, *Ella Fitzgerald with the Duke Ellington Orchestra*

9. "Stolen Moments," Oliver Nelson, *The Blues and the Abstract Truth*

10. "Tenor Madness," Sonny Rollins, *Tenor Madness*

11. "Unit 7," Wes Montgomery and Wynton Kelly Trio, *Smokin' at the Half Note*

12. "Yardbird Suite," Charlie Parker and Miles Davis, *Birdsong*

ACTIVITY EIGHT: *Reading Syncopated Rhythms with Swing Eighth Note Feel*

Let's take our new rhythm words out for another test-drive with the following 12-bar blues reading example. The example will incorporate quite a bit of syncopation, with plenty of ties and rests to "blur the beat." Don't forget our tools of conducting and the metronome to ensure a steady ride. Try performing the example at a variety of tempos. Ready?

Does this example sound familiar? That's right, it's Charlie Parker's "Au Privave." Listen to his version from the album, *The Genius of Charlie Parker*. Sing along as you listen to really get the swing feel into your soul.

Two for the Road

Create a 2-bar example in 4/4 that incorporates some syncopation and perform it for your partner. Have your partner transcribe your example. Then reverse roles. Remember, an accurate performance is good practice for you, and gives your partner a shot at success.

ACTIVITY NINE: *Takin' It to the Streets*

Let's revisit "Softly as in a Morning Sunrise," and spotlight the swingin' delivery of five jazz artists' interpretations: trumpeter Chet Baker, tenor saxophonist Michael Brecker, bassist Paul Chambers, vocalist Bobby Darin, and pianist McCoy Tyner.

Transcribe the rhythm only for the first 16 bars (two A sections) of this jazz standard from each artist's performance and "compare notes." No two people play it quite the same way. Enjoy the spice of life!

1. Chet Baker: *Chet Baker/Wolfgang Lackerschmid Artists Favor*
2. Michael Brecker: *Live at Jazz Baltica 2003*
3. Paul Chambers: *Paul Chambers Quintet*
4. Bobby Darin: *Bobby Darin: That's All*
5. McCoy Tyner: *Coltrane "Live" at the Village Vanguard*

Check the Answer Key (pp.178–180) for results. If you found some of these challenging to transcribe, take the time to listen as you review the answer, putting the notation and the swing feel together.

8 EXPLORING MINOR KEY MELODIES WITH SOLFEGE

ACTIVITY TEN: *Round Trip*

Take some familiar melodies that are in major and sing them in parallel minor. Do the same with some of the minor melodies we worked with in this lesson and sing them in parallel major. What a difference a *mi* or a *me* can make! Changing one or two notes in the melody can give the line an entirely new flavor and feel. From an ear-training point of view, it's a great practice routine. Comparing major and minor back-to-back really brings out each one's unique features. Don't forget to reinforce the differences by singing the melodies using solfege syllables.

Going the Extra Mile

Sing through the following mixed Sol-Fa passage. The phrases will twist in and out of major and minor. There's a wonderful lyric from Cole Porter's "Every Time We Say Goodbye" that says, "There's no love song finer, but how strange the change from major to minor…" He supports this lyric by changing the harmony from IV major to IV minor. We'll be exploring minor key harmony in the next chapter: stay tuned!

do re mi re | *do re me re* | *do re mi me* | *do re me mi re*

do mi sol mi | *do me sol me*

do mi sol la sol mi | *do me sol le sol me*

do ti la ti | *do te le te* | *do sol la ti* | *do sol le te*

do sol la sol | *do sol le sol* | *do te le sol* | *sol la ti do*

do re mi fa sol la ti do | *do te le sol fa me re do*

Approaching the Fork in the Road

Do we always have to write down a musical idea in order to call it "transcribing?" That depends on how loose or strict we want to be in defining the term "transcribing."

We spent time in this chapter with a variety of ways of visualizing the music. We have the generic Sol-Fa tone ladder to reference how scale tones relate to one another within the key, be it a major or minor key. We have the option of seeing and/or playing the musical idea using our instrument or the keyboard. Visualizing the pitches in the staff gets us almost to the finish line, absent the rhythms. So how far along in the process do we need to go in order to call it "officially" transcribing?

I always emphasize the importance of the process rather than just the final destination. As they say, "It's not whether you win or lose, it's how you play the game." Consider the purpose of your work. Does crossing the transcription finish line mean you've successfully written down the musical idea? Or have you gained enough knowledge along the way? To me, the most important reason for transcribing a musical idea is to learn something from or about it. What inspired you to listen in the first place? What did you learn about the music or the artist as a result? Have you really taken enough time to listen and internalize the music? To me, these are the questions to be answered.

True story: When I was a transcribing maniac, I couldn't wait to get the notes scribbled down on the page, but with hindsight I wish I had taken more time to really listen rather than to write. I now wonder why I was in such a rush to end the race.

9. Transcribing Popular Chord Patterns in Minor

Introduction

In this chapter, we'll become familiar with some of the popular chord progressions found in minor keys. We'll apply the same listening approaches for identifying chords as we did with major keys: listening to the bass line for chord roots, listening to the melody for additional chord tone clues, applying the vertical approach to identify the quality of the third of the chord above the root, and lastly, memorizing popular minor key chord patterns.

Two new minor scales will be introduced in this chapter: the harmonic minor and traditional melodic minor scales. We'll discover that minor songs are often a combination of different minor scales working together: a recipe for adventure!

We'll also spend time with syncopated sixteenth note rhythm patterns.

Time to get back on the road again.

Diatonic Triads in Natural Minor

Let's examine the diatonic triads in the key of C natural minor. Do they look and sound familiar? Yes, these are the same chords we found in the relative major key of E♭, only this time they revolve around C as *do*, the tonic in the key of C minor. Let's get our harmonic journey underway with Activity One.

Activity One: *Singing Diatonic Triads in Natural Minor Using Solfege Syllables*

🎧 37 Listen to Audio track 37 as you view the diatonic triads in C natural minor shown below. Each chord is labeled with both Roman numerals and solfege syllables. Make the listening experience more proactive by singing along using solfege syllables when the triads are arpeggiated. Change vocal register if needed.

Tip: As individual scale degrees show their exact numerical relationship back to the tonic: 1, 2, ♭3, 4, 5, ♭6, and ♭7 in the natural minor scale, the Roman Numerals will do the same in labeling the chords: I–, II°, ♭III, IV–, V–, ♭VI, and ♭VII.

READING, WRITING AND RHYTHMETIC

Two for the Road

38 How will we know if the chord progression is in the minor or relative major key? Listen to the following two progressions on Audio track 38. Which progression is in C minor? Which one do you hear in E♭ major? Discuss the reasons for your answers with your partner. It's not just getting there, it's *how* we get there that can make the difference.

It's time to fasten our seat belts as we begin the drive to recognizing minor key chord progressions on our own. What's the first step? That's right: listening to the bass line. Let's do so in the next activity.

ACTIVITY TWO: *Hearing Diatonic Bass Lines in Natural Minor*

39 – **48** Identify the ten minor key bass lines played on Audio tracks 39–48. Each example is four measures long. Remember, listening first is most important in the transcribing process. Can you sing back the 4-bar phrase with confidence, "la, la, la?" In fact, let's not write down the bass lines, let's commit them to memory, and then sing them back using solfege syllables. Not writing down the bass lines will force you to trust your memory. Later in the chapter, some of these same bass lines will reappear as the basis for recognizing common minor key chord patterns found in popular songs. Don't write down your answers just yet.

OK, now check your memory with the Answer Key (p.181).

Two for the Road

Compose some of your own bass lines in natural minor. Perform them for your partner and have him or her sing back the answers in solfege. Similar to Activity Two, don't have your partner notate the answers, have them sing your bass lines back from memory. How did they do? Now you know the "route-ine," have your partner take the wheel.

Once we have the bass line established, we're more than halfway home in identifying the chord progression. We can never get too much practice with hearing the bass line!

Collecting Souvenirs

It's time to do a bit of research on YouTube, iTunes, or in your own listening library. Listen to Stevie Wonder's bass line from "They Won't Go When I Go," on his album *Fulfillingness' First Finale* as he plays right up the natural minor scale, adding in *ti* at the very end: *do, re, me, fa, sol, le, te, ti, do.* Very simple, yet very cool! Where did this *ti* come from? Let's find out in the next section.

INTRODUCING THE HARMONIC MINOR SCALE

49 Another scale that is often used for the harmonic component of a minor song is, logically enough, called the "harmonic" minor scale. This scale is very similar to the natural minor scale, but contains the major 7th degree, *ti*, in place of *te*, the ♭7. Listen to Audio track 49 as you compare the two C minor scales shown on the next page.

100

9 Transcribing Popular Chord Patterns in Minor

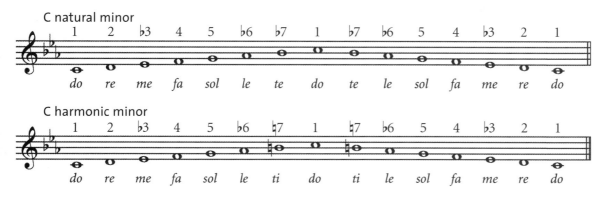

The harmonic minor scale has an exotic sound, created by the unique augmented second interval between the ♭6 (*le*) and ♮7 (*ti*). You can also spot the harmonic minor scale, because *ti* will always need an accidental before it to cancel out the ♭7 found in the key signature. This is the one instance where the eye has an advantage over the ear in detecting if the song is in a major or minor key, and in this case, harmonic minor specifically.

Tip: All minor scales use the relative minor key signature as their home base. If a *ti* or *la* appears in the melody, they will require adding accidentals, providing clear signals to the reader that the melody is not in natural minor, and very unlikely to be in the relative major key.

ACTIVITY THREE: *Takin' It to the Streets*

Let's revisit Janis Joplin's performance of "Summertime," from the album *Pearl*. We transcribed the 12/8 rhythms of the opening guitar solo line back in Chapter 6; now let's transcribe the pitches. The solo line is performed 100% using the G harmonic minor scale. The Answer Key (p.181) will provide the solfege. Try writing out the line in the actual key of G harmonic minor and compare notes. Due to copyright laws, I can't provide you the finished product, but you can put all the ingredients together on your own: 12/8 time signature and rhythms + solfege = finished product, written out in the key of G harmonic minor.

Here is the pickup measure to get you started.

Let's focus on why the harmonic minor scale is so influential on the chords that result from it. With the leading tone, *ti*, present, we now have the possible progression of a V to I– cadence, rather than V– to I–. Listen to the chord pattern in the next activity that uses all the diatonic triads from natural minor, with the exception of replacing V– with V. It's a good pattern to memorize.

ACTIVITY FOUR: *Hearing the Cycle 5 Chord Pattern in Minor*

🔊50 Listen to the following chord progression on Audio track 50. Rather than moving stepwise through the natural minor scale, the roots are organized in a series of diatonic intervals of a fifth, known as "cycle 5." The one twist harmonically is that the V– is replaced with a V major chord. Let's listen proactively with singing.

1. As you listen, sing the root motion, using both numbers and minor key solfege syllables.
2. Add the vertical approach, singing up from the root to the third of each chord, noting its major or minor third quality. For example, with the first chord, sing "1/♭3, minor third," or "*do/me*, minor third."

101

Reading, Writing and Rhythmetic

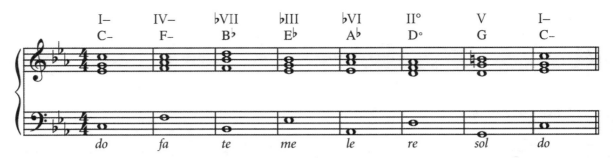

Tip: Notice in the example above the smooth connection from chord to chord. There are many instances of either common tones or stepwise motion linking the chords. This is called "voice leading." These voice-led lines are often easier to sing because you don't have to inner-hear and perform leaps. For more in-depth explanation and practice with the concept of voice-leading, refer to Chapters 5 and 6 in my *Real Easy Ear Training Book*.

Collecting Souvenirs

Listen to the following recordings as examples of the cycle 5 pattern in action. Don't be surprised if you hear a suggestion of the relative major key at times. In other words, are you hearing the chord phrase as IV–, bVII, bIII in minor, or as II–, V, I in the relative major key?

1. "Autumn Leaves," Eva Cassidy, *Songbird* (key of Bb–)
2. "Black Orpheus," Paul Desmond, *Take Ten* (key of G–)
3. "Europa," Carlos Santana, *Precious Lounge Moments* (key of B–)
4. " I Will Survive," Gloria Gaynor, *I Will Survive* (key of A–)

Going the Extra Mile

There's one more minor scale to be aware of: the "traditional melodic" minor scale.

True to its name, this scale was used in earlier times where the choice of the 6th and 7th scale degrees was determined by their direction within the melodic line. Listen to Audio track 51. No one says it better than Bach in an excerpt from his "Bourée in E minor" featured below. Don't forget to listen to a real recording of this Bourée when you get a chance.

51 "Bourée in E minor," J.S. Bach

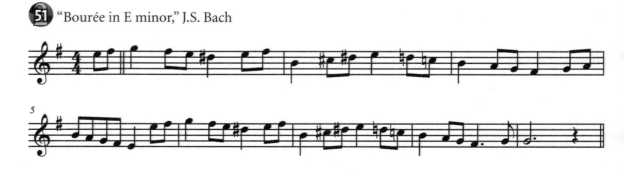

9 Transcribing Popular Chord Patterns in Minor

This traditional melodic minor scale is still used in today's music. In combination with the natural and harmonic minor scales, we often find that a typical song in minor might employ all three minor scale varieties, making for a rich harmonic texture. Though listening to the bass line might be our first step in hearing the chord progression, it cannot be our final or only step. Applying the vertical approach for chord qualities and examining the melody for chord tone clues is also essential. Before we "take it to the streets," let's make a pit stop and refuel by memorizing some popular minor key chord patterns.

Memorizing Popular Minor Key Chord Progressions

Committing to memory a few chord patterns typically found in minor key songs will save us quite a bit of time when transcribing.

Activity Five: *Memorizing Popular Chord Patterns in the Minor Key*

52 Let's revisit some of the same bass lines we worked with in Activity Two and add in the chords. Listen to Audio track 52. These are common chord patterns often found in minor tunes. It's a good idea to memorize them in order to be prepared for transcribing the chord changes. Knowing what to expect, we don't have to reinvent the wheel when listening to minor key harmony.

What are some of the most effective ways of memorizing these chord patterns? Pick one or two patterns each day and sing along as you listen. As you do, follow these steps:

1. Sing the root motion using numbers and/or minor key solfege syllables. In the majority of cases, remembering the root motion will awaken the chord pattern in your memory bank.
2. Apply the vertical approach to confirm the chord qualities. Sing from the root up to the third of each chord: is it a major or minor third interval you're singing?
3. There is no match for hands-on-the-wheel experience. Play the chord patterns on your instrument.

Pattern 1: (natural minor)	I–	IV–	V–	I–	
Pattern 2: (natural minor)	I–	♭VII	♭VI	♭VII	I–
Pattern 3: (harmonic minor)	I–	IV–	V	I–	
Pattern 4: (harmonic minor)	I–	IV–	I–	V	I–
Pattern 5: (harmonic minor)	I–	♭VI	V	I–	
Pattern 6: (harmonic minor)	I–	II°	V	I–	

Going the Extra Mile

Improvise over some of these popular minor key chord patterns. You might find that playing it "blues style" can adapt very well within minor.

Activity Six: *Takin' It to the Streets*

Listen to the following songs on YouTube, iTunes or from you own recording library. Each song will highlight one or more of the common chord patterns you memorized in the last activity. It has been my experience that most minor songs keep it simple and to the point harmonically. The listening options are fewer than you've experienced with major key harmony. Hearing these popular chord patterns in real music will convince you of the value of memorizing the patterns beforehand.

103

READING, WRITING AND RHYTHMETIC

1. "Afro Blue," Abbey Lincoln, *Abbey Is Blue* (key of C–, 16-bar A section)
2. "Ain't No Sunshine When She's Gone," Bill Withers, *The Best of Bill Withers* (key of A–, 8-bar A section)
3. "All Along the Watchtower," Jimi Hendrix, *Electric Ladyland* (key of C–, 2-bar repeated phrase, entire song)
4. "The Animal," Steve Vai, *Passion and Warfare* (key of D–, 14-bar minor blues)
5. "Another Day in Paradise," Phil Collins, *…But Seriously* (key of F♯–, 2-bar repeated phrase, A section)
6. "Beat It," Michael Jackson, *Thriller* (key of E♭–, 8-bar A section)
7. "Black Orpheus," Paul Desmond, *Take Ten* (key of G–, first 5 bars)
8. "Blue Bossa," Joe Henderson, *Back Road* (key of C–, 8-bar A section)
9. "Contemplation," McCoy Tyner, *The Real McCoy* (key of C–, 16-bar phrase, entire song)
10. "Django," Grant Green, *Idle Moments* (key of F–, 8-bar intro/same as last 8 bars of song)
11. "Equinox," John Coltrane, *Coltrane's Sound* (key of C♯–, 12-bar minor blues)
12. "Fever," Peggy Lee, *The Best of Peggy Lee* (key of A–, 8-bar phrase, entire song)
13. "Fragile," Sting, *Nothing Like the Sun* (key of E–, 8-bar A section, 8-bar B section)
14. "House of the Rising Sun," The Animals, *The Animals* (key of A–, 11-bar phrase, entire song)
15. "Livin' on a Prayer," Bon Jovi, *Cross Road* (key of E–, 8-bar A section)
16. "Mr. P.C.," John Coltrane, *Giant Steps* (key of C–, 12-bar minor blues)
17. "Red Rain," Peter Gabriel, *So* (key of E–, 10-bar B section, chorus, song starts with B section)
18. "Rolling in the Deep," Adele, *21* (key of C–, 8-bar C section, chorus)
19. "Sixth Sense," Dave Brubeck, *In Their Own Sweet Way* (key of G–, 8-bar A section)
20. "Softly as in a Morning Sunrise," Paul Chambers, *Paul Chambers Quintet* (key of C–, 8-bar A section)
21. "Song for My Father," Horace Silver, *Song for My Father* (key of F–, 8-bar A section)
22. "Tango Till They're Sore," Tom Waits, *Rain Dogs* (key of F–, 8-bar A section, 8-bar B section)
23. "Three Sheets to the Wind," Joe Satriani, *Unstoppable Momentum* (key of C–, 8-bar A section)
24. "The Thrill Is Gone," B. B. King & Eric Clapton, *80* (key of A–, 12-bar minor blues)
25. "You Know I'm No Good," Amy Winehouse, *Back to Black* (key of D–, 8-bar A section (verse), 8-bar B section (pre-chorus), 8-bar C section (chorus, modulates to key of A–)
    Check the Answer Key (pp.181–185) to see how you did with "hearing the changes."

Collecting Souvenirs

Can you find some songs that are in a minor key and transcribe the chords? Do you recognize any of the chord patterns we memorized?

Moving along, let's steer towards more work with sixteenth note patterns in the next section…but this time with a bit more funk to the feel.

SYNCOPATED SIXTEENTH NOTE RHYTHM PATTERNS

53 Let's return to our work with sixteenth notes, but increase the difficulty by using more syncopated patterns. We can apply much of the work we did with eighth note syncopation by visualizing the rhythms using smaller note values. Listen to Audio track 53 as you read through the

9 Transcribing Popular Chord Patterns in Minor

two examples shown below. Notice how both examples sound exactly the same, given the tempos indicated.

ACTIVITY SEVEN: *Rewriting Eighth Note Patterns with Sixteenth Note Patterns*

Take the following 4-bar rhythm examples that use eighth notes and convert to a 2-bar phrase using sixteenth notes. Read through both examples, paying attention to how they have the potential of sounding exactly the same. How so? That's right, the tempo of the eighth note example would have to be twice as fast as the example using sixteenth notes.

Check your notation with the Answer Key (p.186).

Reading, Writing and Rhythmetic

How will we know whether to notate using eighth or sixteenth notes? The answer goes all the way back to the beginning of our rhythm journey in Chapter 1. Where do we feel the beat? What is the tempo of the song? Though it might be more challenging to read and notate with sixteenth notes, we must be true to the beat with our notation. Another consideration is the style of music we're dealing with. In most cases, songs in a funk, reggae or pop ballad style are typically felt at a medium to slow tempo, and therefore, use lots of sixteenth notes. We'll verify this with the musical selections found in the upcoming "Takin' It to the Streets" activity. But first, let's do one more swing around the block with some reading.

Activity Eight: *Reading Syncopated Sixteenth Note Patterns*

It's time to test-drive syncopated sixteenth note patterns with the following reading example. I highly recommend you practice this at a slow tempo first, so that there is no guesswork involved. Start in first gear. Then gradually up the tempo, second gear, third gear, until you reach the speed limit of ♩=60 and cruise along from there. Does this remind you of a familiar song? That's right, it's Michael Jackson's "Man in the Mirror" from *The Essential Michael Jackson* recording. It's interesting to hear how something that grooves along so naturally can appear quite complex when written down.

Tip: Did you know that sixteenth notes can swing too? Listen to the following hip-hop example as you get up on the dance floor! I've transcribed the rhythm of the 8-bar horn line (starts at 0:59) on "I Got It Goin' On," from Us3's debut album, *Hand on the Torch*. Check it out!

Now it's your turn to take the wheel and transcribe the rhythms in the next "Takin' It to the Streets" activity.

Activity Nine: *Takin' It to the Streets*

Listen to the following ten song excerpts and transcribe the rhythms. The majority of the rhythmic figures will involve some sixteenth note syncopation. Phrases will be short, and often repetitive, allowing you to first sing back the phrase before writing things down.

Transcribing Popular Chord Patterns in Minor

1. "Back on the Block," Quincy Jones, *Back on the Block* (8-bar phrase, vocals starting at 0:04, "Back, back on the block…")
2. "Blame It on the Boogie," Michael Jackson, *The Essential Michael Jackson* (8-bar phrase, vocals starting at 0:40, "Don't blame it on the sunshine…")
3. "Chameleon," Herbie Hancock, *Head Hunters* (4-bar phrase played 4x, horn melody starting at 1:29)
4. "Get Up, Stand Up," Bob Marley, *Burnin'* (8-bar phrase, vocals starting at 0:08, "Get up, stand up…")
5. "Human Nature," Michael Jackson, *Thriller* (8-bar phrase, vocals starting at 0:50, "If they say why…")
6. "Hylife," Marcus Miller, *Afrodeezia* (8-bar phrase, horn melody starting at 1:12)
7. "Kalimba," Sergio Mendes, *Brasiliero* (14-bar vocal phrase, starting at 0:35)
8. "Rockit," Herbie Hancock, *Future Shock* (8-bar phrase, synth melody starting at 0:44)
9. "Say It Loud," James Brown, *Say It Loud—I'm Black and I'm Proud* (10-bar phrase, background horns starting at 0:03)
10. "Strasbourg/St. Denis," Roy Hargrove, *Earfood* (8-bar phrase, horn melody starting at 0:19)

Check the Answer Key (pp.186–188) for results. If the funk fooled you, spend time reviewing the answers as you listen to the examples.

ACTIVITY TEN: *Round Trip*

Keeping major and minor straight can be challenging at times! Is the song in a major or minor key? Does the song modulate between a major and minor key, and if so, are they relative or parallel keys? And then there's "modal interchange" harmony. What's that?

If a picture is worth a thousand words, then listening to an example of modal interchange might be the easiest way to answer the question.

Listen to the following modal interchange example on Audio track 54.

   I   VI–   II–   V   ♭VI   ♭VII   I
     C   A–   D–   G   A♭   B♭   C

There is no question that C is *do*. But are we in the key of C major or minor? Most of the chords describe the key of C major, but there is a taste of the key of C minor with the A♭ and B♭ chords. A♭ and B♭ have been borrowed from the parallel C minor key and used in the context of C major.

55 – **59** Listen to Audio tracks 55–59. Can you identify the modal interchange chords in the following five progressions? There are only three possible modal interchange chords to choose from: IV–, ♭VI and ♭VII.

1. First identify the bass line.
2. Then apply the vertical approach to determine if you're hearing a major or a minor triad.
3. Voilà! These are popular modal interchange chord patterns and should be memorized. Check the Answer Key (p.188) to see how you did.

READING, WRITING AND RHYTHMETIC

Collecting Souvenirs

Can you find examples of modal interchange songs? Here are a few to get the list started:

1. "But Not for Me," Chet Baker, *Chet Baker Sings*
2. "The Entertainer," Scott Joplin, *Ragtime*
3. "Have a Heart," Bonnie Raitt, *Nick of Time*
4. "In My Life," The Beatles, *Rubber Soul*
5. "Tell Her About It," Billy Joel, *An Innocent Man*

Approaching the Fork in the Road

Transcribing and memorizing musical ideas is most definitely a two-way street with lots of intersecting benefits. I can't think of one reason not to go down this road!

Throughout this book we've spent time memorizing small rhythm words and more recently memorized a small repertoire of common chord patterns. Having these patterns available makes it easier to identify them when they appear in songs we transcribe. It's like traveling down an old familiar road rather than embarking upon a maiden voyage each time.

In this chapter, I encouraged you at times *not* to write down the transcription, but rather to commit it to aural memory. There will be times when you've left the directions at home and will need to travel without a map, relying on past experience and a good set of ears to get you where you're headed, safe and sound. It puts a little more gas in the tank to ensure that you've engaged your ears in the memorization process. You'll be better prepared for the next song down the road, and the next song.

Turning the car around, how does transcribing songs help our musical memory? One of the biggest advantages of transcribing the song yourself, learning it by ear, rather than from reading, is that you've earned it and have it almost memorized as a result! Make it a goal to transcribe one song a week and watch your repertoire of memorized tunes grow as you get great ear training mileage as well.

Two for the Road

Talk with your partner about some of the other benefits to having a memorized repertoire of songs. To get the ball rolling, read what I have to say in the *Real Easy Ear Training Book*, "The Benefits of Memorizing," on page 27. Can you add to the list?

The road less traveled? Not this one. Let's make this two-way street of transcribing and memorizing a regular route!

10 MAPPING THE SONG FORM

INTRODUCTION

Up to now, we have traveled locally, visiting rhythmic, melodic and harmonic details of 4- and 8-bar phrases. It's time to hit the road on a more extensive journey, examining how these smaller musical phrases fit together within the song as a whole. We will begin to examine the ABCs of song form.

Our song form journey starts with letter A, the first musical idea. In some songs, our only destination is "A." But in much of today's popular music, there are often two, or maybe three different musical ideas expressed, extending our trip into new musical territory. In this chapter we will focus on song forms that involve only one (A) or two (B) ideas. We will begin to define the terms "verse" and "chorus" and how these terms relate to the A and B themes.

The 12-bar blues form will also be spotlighted in this chapter. You'll have a chance to compose your own original blues!

Quarter note triplets will fuel our rhythmic work. We can continue to get excellent mileage out of several of the same practice routines we applied to eighth note triplets to our new work with quarter note triplets.

So let's get back on the road, but this time with a greater understanding of the road map of song form.

SONG FORM

What is song form? It's how the different sections of a piece of music are put together and organized. Up to this point in the book, we've transcribed the rhythmic, melodic or harmonic details of short musical phrases (4–8 bars long). Now it's time to see how these small musical phrases connect and relate to each other in the big picture of the entire song—the song form. Understanding song form is an important concept. That, and noticing the amount of repetition that's involved in the song's organization, will make it easier to memorize a song, because you can reduce the piece of music to one, two, or maybe three ideas.

LETTER "A"

How do we begin to break down the big picture and identify song form? The first thing to do is to listen for repetition of a musical idea (or the *lack* of a repetition). Let's label the first musical idea we hear section "A." If we hear that musical phrase repeat literally, or with minimal variation, then we've heard "A A." Sing through "London Bridge Is Falling Down" in your head. The 8-bar musical phrase repeats several times, only the lyrics change. Keeping things simple by expressing only one musical idea makes it easy to remember the song. "Less is more" is easy on our memory. Listen to the following songs listed in Activity One (from your memory, your music library, or the web). They also express only one musical theme, the A theme.

109

ACTIVITY ONE: *Takin' the "A" Theme to the Streets*

Listen to the following selections which state only one musical "A" theme throughout the entire song. Most, but not all, of these songs use standard 8-bar phrases. Many of these arrangements also include a short instrumental breather between verses, giving the listener a chance to ponder what's been said before moving ahead in the story. Enjoy!

1. "All Along the Watchtower," Bob Dylan, *John Wesley Harding*
2. "Don't Worry, Be Happy," Bobby McFerrin, *Simple Pleasures*
3. "Hey Joe," Jimi Hendrix, *Are You Experienced*
4. "House of the Rising Sun," The Animals, *The Animals*
5. "I'm Walking to New Orleans," Fats Domino, *Hit's of the 60s*
6. "It Was a Very Good Year," Frank Sinatra, *Nothing But the Best*
7. "Matilda," Harry Belafonte, *The Essential Harry Belafonte*
8. "Nobody Knows You When You're Down and Out," Eric Clapton, *Unplugged*
9. "People Get Ready," Blind Boys of Alabama, *Higher Ground*
10. "Rocky Raccoon," The Beatles, *White Album*
11. "Scarborough Fair," Simon & Garfunkel, *Parsley, Sage, Rosemary and Thyme*
12. "Spoonful," Howlin' Wolf, *The Chess 50th Anniversary...*
13. "This Old Man," nursery rhyme
14. "We Will Rock You," Queen, *News of the World*
15. "Whole Lotta Love," Led Zeppelin, *Led Zeppelin II*

Every song you listened to in Activity One contained lyrics. In fact, it was only the changing lyric that distinguished one A section from those that followed. The music was the glue, the constant. It was the lyric that made one verse different from the other verses. Simply defined, a verse is a set of lyrics. We'll define the term "verse" in greater detail as we continue our discussion of song form terminology later in the chapter.

HERE COMES "B"

If a new musical idea is presented after the "A," we'll call that the "B" section. Sing "Twinkle, Twinkle Little Star" in your head. That's right, this 12-bar song form can be analyzed as "A B A." In this case, it's both the music and the lyrics which distinguish the A section from the B section.

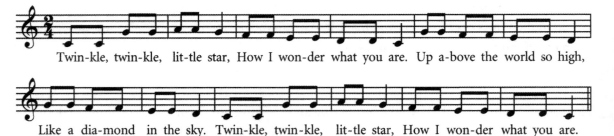

Note: It is not surprising that children's songs are short, involve one (A) or two (B) simple themes, and use a lot of repetition. Most children learn these songs by rote, so they need to be easy to remember.

Speaking of the 12-bar song form, there is none more popular than the standard 12-bar blues form. Let's explore the blues in the next section. It will be a great opportunity for us to test drive our ability to distinguish A and B sections. Let's "get our kicks" as we cruise on down the highway with Nat King Cole's classic "Route 66" playing on the car radio (from the album *The World of Nat King Cole*). We're just about to learn that this blues follows the "A A B" format.

12-Bar Blues Form

The blues is a song form that every musician needs to know and experience. It is universal, simple, and an opportunity to experiment with improvisation and have some fun!

What are some of the common characteristics of the blues?

- Standard blues harmony is simple, usually incorporating only the I, IV and V chords.
- The melody and improvisation is often drawn exclusively from the blues pentatonic scale (shown below).
- The 12-bar song form is one of the most telling features of the blues.

Let's explore this song form in greater detail.

Typically, the 12-bar blues form is broken down into three 4-bar melodic phrases: either A A A or A A B. Let's take a look at the following example that demonstrates the A A B format.

Tip: The blues pentatonic scale is *do, me, fa, sol* and *te*. Sometimes "*se*" (♭5) is included as well. The melody above features this scale.

A blues using lyrics makes it easy to determine if the format is A A A or A A B. The lyrics alone tell us. From my listening experience, most blues with lyrics follow the A A B format. The two A phrases "ask" the same question, and the B phrase "answers" the question. Listen to John Mayer's delivery of "Every Day I Have the Blues," from his *Where the Light Is: John Mayer Live…* album. It's a great example of this "question (A), question (A), answer (B)" format. Here are the lyrics:

A: Every day, every day I have the blues

A: Every day, every day I have the blues

B: Well you see me worried, baby, cause it's you I hate to lose

With instrumental blues, it can sometimes be more challenging to determine whether the format is A A A or A A B. Absent the lyrics, and with the addition of the musician's artistic freedom to interpret the melody, it can be difficult to hear whether the A theme is being restated or not.

For a comparison of A A A and A A B, let's listen to two blues composed by Sonny Rollins. "Sonnymoon for Two," from *Jazz 1 – Timeless Legends*, is a good example of the A A A form. His blues "Tenor Madness," from the recording *Tenor Madness*, features the A A B form. Can you hear the difference?

READING, WRITING AND RHYTHMETIC

Note: Both songs are available in Sher Music's *The Real Easy Book: Tunes for Beginning Improvisers* if you'd like to read through the lead sheets as you listen.

One standard variation of the A A B format that occurs often in instrumental blues is when the original A theme is transposed onto the IV chord in measures 5 and 6. Two good examples of this variation of A A B are John Coltrane's "Equinox" and "Mr. P. C." Listen to these two classic jazz blues when you get a chance. They are also included in *The Real Easy Book* just mentioned if you'd like to read along as you listen.

In the following activity, you'll test drive your knowledge of recognizing the blues form as being A A A or A A B.

ACTIVITY TWO: *Is It A A A or A A B?*

Listen to the following 20 examples of 12-bar blues and determine if the song form is A A A or A A B. Then check the Answer Key (p.189) to see if we agree.

1. "Bag's Groove," Milt Jackson, *The Birth of the MJQ*
2. "Bessie's Blues," John Coltrane, *Crescent*
3. "Born Under a Bad Sign," Albert King, *Born Under a Bad Sign*
4. "C Jam Blues," Duke Ellington, *Duke Ellington's Greatest Hits*
5. "Crossroads," Cream, *Wheels of Fire*
6. "Freddie Freeloader," Miles Davis, *Kind of Blue*
7. "Gate Walks to Board," Clarence "Gatemouth" Brown, *Texas Swing*
8. "Going to Chicago Blues," Ernestine Anderson, *When the Sun Goes Down*
9. "Hound Dog," Elvis Presley, *The Essential Elvis Presley...*
10. "If You're Goin' to the City," Mose Allison, *The Best of Mose Allison*
11. "Johnny B. Goode," Chuck Berry, *The Anthology*
12. "Lateral Climb" (14 bars), Robben Ford, *Truth*
13. "Love Me Like a Man," Bonnie Raitt, *The Bonnie Raitt Collection*
14. "Night Train," James Brown, *Gold: James Brown*
15. "Saturday Afternoon Blues," Ben Webster, *The Soul of Ben Webster*
16. "Stagger Lee" (13 bars), Taj Mahal, *Giant Step*
17. "She Walks Right In," Professor Longhair & the Meters, *Best of Professor Longhair*
18. "Stormy Monday," The Allman Brothers, *The Allman Brothers Band at Fillmore East*
19. "Sweet Home Chicago," Robert Johnson, *The Complete Recordings*
20. "The Thrill Is Gone," B. B. King & Eric Clapton, *80*

Tip: Check out Jean-Louis Locas' YouTube video *The Blues Workshop* when you get a chance. You're in for a treat! It is a terrific tutorial on the blues. Accomplished bassist, Jean-Louis Locas has been touring with Cirque du Soleil for more than ten years. I had the pleasure of meeting him in my online classroom.

10 MAPPING THE SONG FORM

Going the Extra Mile

Now that you've got a good idea about how the blues is organized, you're going to compose your own original 12-bar blues! Will your blues follow the A A A or A A B format? You don't have to write down your blues. Because it's only 12 bars long, and with some repetition involved, it should be easy to remember. Teach it to your band members by ear and perform it at your next gig!

BINARY SONG FORM: VERSE AND CHORUS

Let's continue to explore the binary relationship between A and B. The vast majority of popular music presents only two primary ideas. Why? Because the listener can retain only so many new ideas, and the composer wants the audience to remember his/her song, leaving the show whistling that happy tune!

Let's start with songs that have lyrics. In many cases with songs that have A and B sections, the A is called the *verse* and the B is called the *chorus* or the *refrain* (refrain means "to repeat" in Latin). The A section, the verse, sets the stage of the story. This is where the lyrics change as the story develops. The B section, the chorus, is the message of the song. This is where the lyrics are a constant and repeat. The title of the song often lives in the B section. It's the chorus that the composer hopes you'll leave the show whistling.

Let's identify the verse and chorus of songs in the next activity.

ACTIVITY THREE: *Hearing the Verse and Chorus*

Listen to the following 20 songs. In every case, the A section represents the verse, and the B section represents the chorus. The lyrics not only tell the story, but also define the song form. You'll notice that not all of the songs organize the A's and B's in the same order. Some might state two or more verses (A's) before getting to the chorus (B); some might alternate between the two (A B A B); and some songs might start right in with the chorus (B) first, and then backtrack to the verse (A).

As you listen, identify which sections are the verse (A) and chorus (B) and write them down as they occur. For example, with Dylan's "Blowin' in the Wind," the answer is: A A A B, A A A B, A A A B, then B. If an introduction, instrumental interlude, or ending occurs, you might want to mark them down as well. In Chapter 12 we will take this string of events and reduce them into one musical map—the chart.

1. "Blowin' in the Wind," Bob Dylan, *The Freewheelin' Bob Dylan*
2. "Carey," Joni Mitchell, *Blue*
3. "Compared to What," Less McCann & Eddie Harris, *Swiss Movement*
4. "Get Up, Stand Up," Bob Marley, *Legend*
5. "Give Peace a Chance," John Lennon, *Serve3: Artists Against Hunger & Poverty*
6. "Higher Ground," Stevie Wonder, *Innervisions*
7. "Hotel California," The Eagles, *Hotel California*
8. "Human Nature," Michael Jackson, *Thriller*
9. "I Just Called to Say I Love You," Stevie Wonder, *The Woman in Red*
10. "I Still Haven't Found What I'm Looking For," U2, *The Joshua Tree*
11. "Iko Iko," The Dixie Cups, *Chapel of Love*
12. "Jingle Bells," Roberta Radley, *Swing-a-Jing-a -Lingin'*
13. "Let It Be," The Beatles, *Let It Be*
14. "My Girl," The Temptations, *The Temptations Sing Smokey*

15. "Oh! Suzanna," Eight Hand String Band, *Listen to the Mockingbird*
16. "Puff the Magic Dragon," Peter Paul & Mary, *The Very Best of Peter, Paul & Mary*
17. "Silver Bells," Johnny Mathis, *Merry Christmas*
18. "Stand by Me," Ben E. King, *The Very Best of Ben E. King*
19. "Sunrise, Sunset," Fiddler on the Roof, *Original Motion Picture Soundtrack*
20. "Wrapped Around Your Finger," The Police, *Syncronicity*

Check the Answer Key (pp.189–190) to see how you did.

Going the Extra Mile

Activity Three is an excellent chance to work with a partner. After deciding on the song form, discuss with your partner the musical features of each song. Some things to consider:

- What is the time signature of the song?
- Is the song in a major or minor key?
- Do you recognize the chord progressions in the verse (A) or chorus (B) sections?
- How does the musical content of the verse (A) and chorus (B) relate? Are they similar or different?
- If there is an introduction, interlude or ending, how does the musical content of these supporting sections relate to the verse (A) or chorus (B) sections?
- Anything else you might notice as interesting?

Remember, two heads are better than one—imagine what four ears can do!

Collecting Souvenirs

Review your band's song list with an eye and ear out for song form. What songs follow a verse and chorus format? Taking the time now to analyze the forms of songs in your band's repertoire will make it easier to memorize these song arrangements for the gig.

We'll continue our work with song form in the next chapter, examining the standard 32-bar song form. Let's turn our "rhythmetic" attention to quarter note triplets.

INTRODUCING QUARTER NOTE TRIPLETS

In Chapter 6, we studied eighth note triplets, and experienced the "three against two" feel on an eighth note level. We can double up on that concept, and experience the same "three against two" feel, but this time on a quarter note level with quarter note triplets. The time of three quarter note triplets is equal to the time of two normal quarter notes.

If you felt the tug of war of "three against two" was challenging on an eighth note level, don't be surprised if the tension feels even greater with quarter note triplets against straight quarter notes. The slower the tug, the greater is the challenge of keeping the 3:2 ratio steady.

Let's begin our practice with a rhythm grid activity that links eighth note triplets to quarter note triplets.

10 Mapping the Song Form

ACTIVITY FOUR: *Linking Eighth Note Triplets to Quarter Note Triplets*

We can apply the feel of eighth note triplets to help get us in the groove of quarter note triplets. Consider that the time of one quarter note triplet is equal to two tied eighth note triplets.

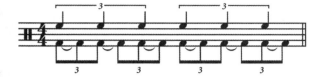

With the following 20-bar rhythm grid, you will be performing each new rhythmic attack with "tah," and performing the sustained tied values with "tah-ah" in order to express a tight connection with the underlying eighth note triplet subdivision. Let me demonstrate the first four bars on Audio track 60. Are you ready?

1. Read through the 20-bar rhythm grid above, applying the singing method of "tah's" and "tah-ah's" for an accurate performance.
2. Notice that the new quarter note triplet figure presented in the even numbered bars will be introduced via tied eighth note triplets in the previous measures.
3. Choose a comfortable, moderate tempo (not too slow!) for your performance.
4. Don't forget to conduct as you perform. Conducting in 4 will emphasize the "three against two" feel in your performance.
5. If you're feeling confident, do away with the "tah-ah" approach when performing the quarter note triplet figures, blending "tah-ah" into one seamless "tahah."

ACTIVITY FIVE: *Combining Duple and Triplet Feel*

Now that you're warmed up from the last rhythm grid activity, read through the following 16-bar example that combines duple and triplet feel rhythmic figures.

1. Perform the example at a variety of tempos. Slower tempos can often be the most demanding.
2. Try performing the rhythms with both a straight and swing eighth note feel. Notice when swinging the eighth notes, they take on almost a triplet feel themselves.
3. Experiment performing the example with, and then without conducting. Did it make a difference in the accuracy of your performance?

Two for the Road

Create your own 12-bar blues rhythm example, following either the A A A or A A B format. Make sure to incorporate some quarter note triplet figures for practice. Perform your rhythm blues for your partner, and have them transcribe it. Remember, a clean performance on your part will give your partner a good shot at success. Then, switch seats.

ACTIVITY SIX: *Sight-Reading from Sher's "New Real Book" Fake Book*

I'm sure you have many wonderful fake books (collection of lead sheets) in your music library. Take one off the shelf and do some rhythmic sight-reading. I'd like to recommend Sher's *New Real Book* fake book as one to add to your collection. Included in this particular fake book are several songs which involve quarter note triplets. A few of my favorites are: "All of Me," "Ana Maria," "Dindi," "I Should Care," "Lady Bird," "Once I Loved," "Out of This World," "Velas," and "Watch What Happens."

Tip: If you listen to "Ana Maria" from Wayne Shorter's *Native Dancer* recording, you'll hear many instances of quarter note triplets in his performance.

We will learn how to create a lead sheet in the next chapter. Reading through them now will give us a good example of what goes into (and what's left out of) a typical lead sheet.

10 Mapping the Song Form

ACTIVITY SEVEN: *Takin' Quarter Note Triplets to the Streets*

Listen to the swingin' arrangement of "Come Rain or Come Shine" from Art Blakey and the Jazz Messenger's recording *Moanin'* on the web. I guarantee that once you hear it, you'll want to add it to your own record collection!

Transcribe just the rhythm of the melody performed by the horns. Hint: there are definitely some quarter note triplets being played! The template provided below will also include the rhythm section kicks, so you can hear/see how the melody converses with the rest of the band.

This song is an excellent example of the A B A C song form, which we'll cover in the next chapter…stay tuned!

Now check the Answer Key (p.191) to see how you did with transcribing the horn melody.

Reading, Writing and Rhythmetic

Two for the Road
Let's play the arrangement of "Come Rain or Come Shine" from the previous activity. With your partner, perform the duet of the horn melody against the rhythm section kicks. Make sure to play all the parts!

Activity Eight: *Round Trip*
Back in Chapter 6 when we discussed 12/8 feel, McCoy Tyner's "Blues on the Corner" was mentioned as an example. Let's revisit this song for notation purposes.

1. Below is a rhythmic transcription of the head (the melody) written out in 12/8 time. Try reading through it before listening to the actual recording. Then, listen to this swingin' blues from the recording *The Real McCoy*. How'd you do?

2. Convert this 12/8 meter notation to 12/8 feel in 4/4 by using swing eighth notes and quarter note triplets where appropriate. A template is provided below for your version. Check the Answer Key (p.191) when you're finished.

3. Listen again to the recording as you read through both notated versions. Which notation do you feel is most appropriate for this particular performance? Why?
   Tip: A lead sheet of "Blues on the Corner" appears in Sher's *New Real Book*—what a bonus!

10 Mapping the Song Form

Approaching the Fork in the Road

In the last two chapters' "Approaching the Fork in the Road" discussions, we focused on the value of the transcription process as a whole, noting the importance of taking all the required steps for a successful transcription journey. We strategized and engaged in a variety of activities in order to internalize music, (careful listening, singing, playing, employing different ways to visualize the musical idea) prior to the final step of writing it down. We also talked about the importance of relying on our musical memory, when we've left the "road map" at home. If we've internalized the music, then our internal GPS will safely and confidently get us where we need to go. Is there really a need to bring the journey to its final destination of notation? Absolutely!

Today, I asked my students this very question, "What are the benefits of notating music?" They unanimously applauded the many rewards that result from notating music. Here's what they had to say...

- Notating the music allows for clear communication between musicians.
- Writing out music helps us to organize the musical concepts, and engages both a tactile and visual dimension to processing the music.
- Seeing the music written down facilitates analyzing the music more easily.
- Writing down the music "frees" memory from the responsibility of having to remember it, and provides a safety zone if we forget.
- "Don't leave home without it." It is practical to have the "road map" available when traveling away from home.
- Notated music can stand the test of time. As composers, it allows our music to be passed down through generations, ensuring it will be performed and interpreted exactly as we intended.
- Writing music is a proactive way of understanding the rules of notation. Reading and writing is a two-way street. Notating music makes us better music readers.
- Notating music requires the 50% "brain-training" part of the transcription process. It demonstrates an educated, disciplined and professional level of musicianship.
- "Eat your vegetables!" Transcribing is hard, but good for you, as we look to be the best and most complete musicians we can be.
- What a sense of accomplishment...need I say more?

11 CREATING A LEAD SHEET

INTRODUCTION

In this chapter we continue exploring song form as we shine our headlights on the 32-bar song form. Making its debut in the early part of the 20th century, this form has become one of the most standard song forms in today's music. We will take a look and give a listen as we examine the three most common combinations—A A B A, A B A B, and A B A C. This will be the first time we encounter a third theme, "C," in the mix.

The lead sheet has been a passenger in our musical journey: now it's time to take the wheel and learn how to create one. The goal is to keep the notation simple and easy to read, and this isn't always so easy to do! What to leave in and what to leave out (when listening to an artist's individual performance) are the decisions we have to make.

We started our "rhythmetic" journey by feeling the beat and learning about familiar time signatures such as $\frac{4}{4}$, or common time. We'll take the road less traveled in this chapter and explore some odd time signatures such as $\frac{5}{4}$ and $\frac{7}{4}$. Fasten your seat belts!

Back on the road again, but this time with a new road map to follow.

32-BAR SONG FORM

Let's continue our discussion of how songs are organized, focusing on the 32-bar song form. This 32-bar form was popular during the 1920's through the 1950's, the era often referred to as the "Great American Songbook." This era featured such important and influential composers as: Harold Arlen, Irving Berlin, Ira and George Gershwin, Jerome Kern, Johnny Mercer, Cole Porter and Richard Rodgers, to mention a few. Their music was often featured on the Broadway stage or in Hollywood films. To this day, the 32-bar song form continues to be a common road map for many of today's contemporary popular songs.

Similar to our work in the last chapter with the binary song form (songs organized with alternating verses and choruses), most 32-bar songs feature only two main ideas, the A and the B themes. There are only so many ways to shuffle these 8-bar A and B themes within the limit of 32 measures. The two most common arrangements are A A B A and A B A B. On occasion, a third theme, "C," might be introduced as the final 8-bar section. Though "C" can sometimes be its own independent theme, it is more often a variation of the B theme.

Listening to songs which demonstrate the 32-bar A A B A, A B A B, or A B A C form will be music to our ears.

A A B A

To begin, let's listen to three songs which demonstrate the most popular of the three forms—the A A B A song form. Letter A continues to mark the first idea presented in a song. However, rather than function as the supportive role of the verse (as in last chapter's verse, chorus setup), here, the A section is the *featured* part of the song. The A theme is stated three times, and in most cases,

READING, WRITING AND RHYTHMETIC

quotes the title of the song. In this setting the B section might be referred to as the "bridge," linking the A sections together. In the A A B A form, the B section plays a supportive role (unlike it's earlier leading role as the chorus in the binary song form).

Do you sometimes forget the bridge, the B section, in an A A B A tune? I'm not surprised! Listen to the following three songs that feature the A A B A form. Notice that the song title appears in each A section.

1. "Every Breath You Take," The Police, *Syncronicity*
2. "Over the Rainbow," Judy Garland, *Over the Rainbow*
3. "Satin Doll," Ella Fitzgerald, *Ella Fitzgerald with the Duke Ellington Orchestra*

A B A B

Next, listen to the following three songs which feature the A B A B song form. This form might look familiar, resembling the verse/chorus organization we saw in Chapter 10, but don't be fooled! This time the leading role can be played by either the A or the B section. In "Gravity" and "Isn't She Lovely," the title is quoted in the A section. But in "In My Life," the leading role is played by the B section.

1. "Gravity," John Mayer, *Continuum*
2. "In My Life," The Beatles, *Rubber Soul*
3. "Isn't She Lovely," Stevie Wonder, *Songs in the Key of Life*

Note: I know, the terms "verse, chorus" can be confusing at times! Their musical definition in a song depends on their context. In the last chapter we learned to associate A with the verse, and B with the chorus. Now we see that the lead role of the chorus might live within either the A or B sections, depending on the context. To make matters even more confusing, the term "chorus" will sometimes mean "once through the song." So for example, completing one A A B A is considered one chorus. We'll discuss this usage of the term "chorus" in Chapter 12 when we discuss the chart, or arrangement of a song. Ugh! Hang in there.

A B A C

Finally, let's listen to three songs which feature the A B A C outline. As you listen, consider whether the C section presents its own theme or is a variation of the B theme.

1. "But Not for Me," Chet Baker, *Chet Baker Sings*
2. "Love Letters," Patti Austin, *The Real Me*
3. "Moon River," Andy Williams, *The Very Best of Andy Williams*

It's time to read the "road map" on your own with the next activity.

ACTIVITY ONE: *Is the Song Form A A B A, A B A B, or A B A C?*
Listen to the following 21 song selections and determine if the 32-bar song form is A A B A, A B A B, or A B A C. Remember to listen for repetition of an idea (or lack of a repetition) when making your decisions. If you're on the fence between A B A B and A B A C, both answers could be right: it's not always a clear-cut decision.

1. "All I Have to Do Is Dream," The Everly Brothers, *The Very Best of the Everly Brothers*
2. "All of Me," Billie Holiday, *The Essential Billie Holiday*
3. "Bad Moon Rising," Creedence Clearwater Revival, *Green River*

4. "Be Good," Gregory Porter, *Be Good*

5. "Beautiful Day," U2, *U218 Singles*

6. "Blue Skies," Willie Nelson, *Stardust*

7. "Come Rain or Come Shine," Art Blakey and the Jazz Messengers, *Moanin'*

8. "Don't Know Why," Norah Jones, *Come Away with Me*

9. "Fly Me to the Moon," Frank Sinatra, *It Might as Well Be Spring*

10. "I Got Rhythm," The Sisters of Swing, *Mood Indigo*

11. "My Romance," Ella Fitzgerald, *Ella Fitzgerald Sings the Rodgers & Hart Book*

12. "Norwegian Wood," The Beatles, *Rubber Soul*

13. "On Green Dolphin Street," Miles Davis, *Kind of Blue*

14. "Proud Mary," Tina Turner, *All the Best: The Hits*

15. "Rudolph the Red-Nosed Reindeer," Roberta Radley, *Swing-a-Jing-a-Lingin'*

16. "Shoot the Moon," Norah Jones, *Come Away with Me*

17. "Surfer Girl," The Beach Boys, *Surfer Girl*

18. "Tango Till They're Sore," Tom Waits, *Rain Dogs*

19. "This Boy," The Beatles, *Meet the Beatles!*

20. "When Lights Are Low," Miles Davis, *Blue Haze*

21. "We Can Work It Out," The Beatles, *Rubber Soul*

Check the Answer Key (p.192) to see how you did. Better yet, have a conversation with a classmate or two about these songs. Identifying the song form is just the tip of the iceberg. Talking about the musical content of the song is where the fun begins!

Going the Extra Mile

If composing is your thing, write a song that follows one of the 32-bar song forms. Remember, most songs incorporate only two different ideas (A and B themes). A good thing is worth repeating!

I've used the term "lead sheet" frequently throughout the book, and I'm sure you've all read one. Now, let's get in the driver's seat and learn more about how to create one. What exactly goes into, or is left out of a typical lead sheet? We'll find out in the next section.

CREATING A LEAD SHEET FROM A TRANSCRIPTION

What's a lead sheet? Typically, it's a simple sketch of a song, capturing the two basic ingredients—notation of the melody and the accompanying chord symbols. If you have fake books in your music library, then you have read through a collection of lead sheets. Fake books are wonderful role model collections: let's pay closer attention to what we see when reading through the lead sheet.

Note: Have you wondered where "fake" book got its name? The simple lead sheet version of a song allows the reader to fake it, to make it up in his/her own personal way when interpreting the song.

It's one thing to be in the passenger seat, reading through a lead sheet. It's another thing to be in the driver's seat, facing the challenges of creating one. What are some of the challenges?

READING, WRITING AND RHYTHMETIC

- The biggest challenge in making a lead sheet is deciding what to leave in and what to leave out when notating a particular artist's performance of a song. When possible, listen to a few different artists' renditions to avoid being overly influenced by any particular performance. Arrive at a composite rendition of the song that you hold in your memory. Sing back this composite melody from memory: that might be exactly what you want to notate.

- This is especially true if you're listening to a jazz artist's rendition of a song. Given the improvisational spirit of jazz, the musician's interpretation of the melody might intentionally vary greatly from the original. This often occurs with an instrumental delivery of the melody. If the original song has lyrics, research them. They can help frame the melody in a simpler way.

- Keep the notation simple — reader-friendly is the rule. Keeping the notation "easy on the eye" allows the reader to interpret the music in his/her own way, not being boxed in by overly intricate detail in the notation.

- Try to be consistent with your notation; don't have some measures appear simple while others appear overly complex. Inconsistency in notation will only confuse the reader. That having been said, no two lead sheets are likely to look exactly the same.

- When notating the melody, keep the rhythms simple, using on-the-beat notation where possible, and avoid unnecessary syncopation, which might just be a particular artist's rendition of the melody. Regarding the pitches, avoid notating what appears to be ornamentation or fillers. Referencing the lyrics of a song can be helpful in determining what's essential to the melody. When in doubt, follow the "less is more" rule.

- And how about the chords? As with the melody, keep things simple. Listen for the chords that fall on the strong beats of the measure (the downbeat in particular). Avoid notating specific chord voicings or tensions, etc., as those might be the artist's interpretation rather than part of the original song.

Why go to the trouble of creating the lead sheet yourself when there are so many excellent fake books out on the market to reference? Here is my anecdotal answer.

When I was gigging full time as a bandleader, I wanted to perform a fresh repertoire of songs and not simply perform the same "standards" that everyone else was using. Often, there wasn't a published lead sheet available, so I had to do the job myself. And I'm so glad I did! Making the effort to listen, transcribe and then make a lead sheet of the song meant that I owned the song in the end. I had created a lead sheet for my bandmates to read, and I had already internalized the music in the process, and, ironically, no longer needed to reference the lead sheet I produced.

Let's get some two-hands-on-the-wheel practice using the tips outlined above, and create some lead sheets in the following activities.

ACTIVITY TWO: *Creating a Rhythm Lead Sheet for "Softly as in a Morning Sunrise"*

In Chapter 8, we transcribed the melody of "Softly as in a Morning Sunrise" from five different artists. Our job then was to capture each artist's exact rhythmic interpretation of the melody. Refer to the Answer Key for Chapter 8, Activity Nine (pp.178–180) to refresh your memory of these five different performances.

Now, let's attempt to create a simplified composite version. Again, we'll only address the rhythmic notation of the melody. In reviewing all five versions, Bobby Darin's vocal delivery is probably the simplest of them all. Remember, using the lyric is a great resource for capturing the basics. If

124

we strip away the syncopation, and bring things closer to the beat, we might end up with something like the following example.

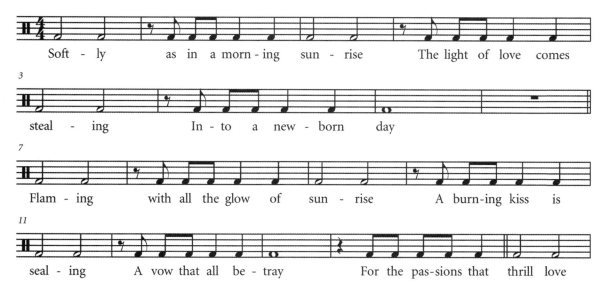

It's unlikely (hopefully!) that anyone will play it this straight. But the benefit of "seeing it straight" allows you the freedom to interpret the music in your own way. Give it a try in the next activity!

ACTIVITY THREE: *Interpreting the Lead Sheet*

Read through the rhythmic lead sheet of "Softly as in a Morning Sunrise" shown above, but *interpret* what you see, speaking the lyric as you would in a natural way. We don't speak like robots—natural speech is actually quite syncopated. Experiment with a few different ways of saying the lyric…it's fun! Record your performances and transcribe your takes. It's interesting to see the natural results on paper!

Here's one of my takes. Read and perform it with a swing eighth note feel in mind.

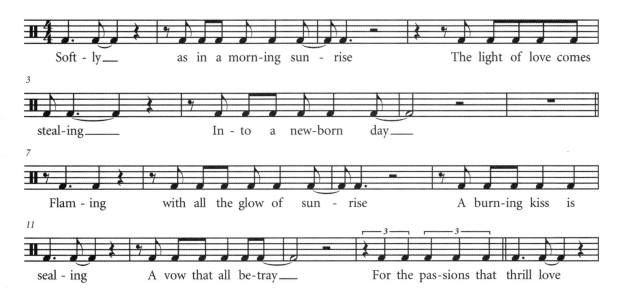

In the next activity, we'll create a complete lead sheet for "Jingle Bells." I've chosen this public domain song so we don't violate any copyright laws.

ACTIVITY FOUR: *Creating a Lead Sheet for "Jingle Bells"*

This time we'll notate both the pitches and rhythm of the melody. I've chosen the well-known song "Jingle Bells." If you're already familiar with this song, you can jump ahead in the process and transcribe the melody from your memory. But if not, take the following steps.

First, look up the lyrics to "Jingle Bells" as a helpful guideline. Then listen to several renditions of the song, until you're able to sing back the melody from memory. Finally, transcribe your memory's recall of the melody, rather than from any one particular artist's version. Your memory will filter through all the wonderful details and produce a simplified version, a version ready-made for the lead sheet.

I've included six versions of "Jingle Bells" for you to listen to. None of these recordings play it straight, so the challenge is on to create a simplified version!

1. Bing Crosby & the Andrew Sisters, *White Christmas*
2. Ella Fitzgerald, *Ella Wishes You a Swinging Christmas*
3. Frank Sinatra, *A Jolly Christmas from Frank Sinatra*
4. Harry Connick Jr., *What a Night!– A Christmas Album*
5. Johnny Mathis, *Christmas Eve with Johnny Mathis*
6. Roberta Radley, *Swing-a-Jing-a-Lingin'*

Each arrangement of "Jingle Bells" listed above is unique. The song is performed in a variety of keys, and the ordering of the verse and chorus differ from one version to the next. What to do? It could be a personal choice to decide on the key. Regarding the ordering of the verse and chorus, typically, the verse precedes the chorus. I've made these two decisions for you in the template provided below.

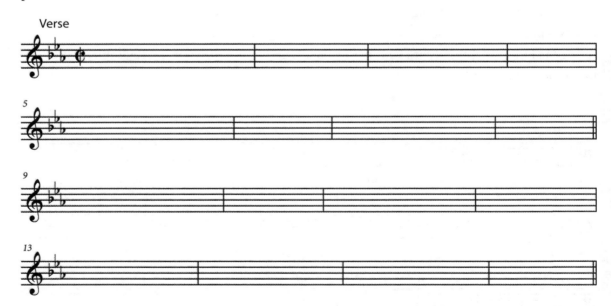

11 CREATING A LEAD SHEET

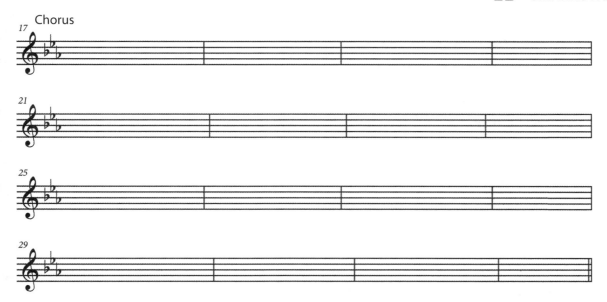

Check the Answer Key (pp.192–193) to compare your lead sheet with mine. There is no one absolute right answer, but "simple" should be the adjective that best describes the results.

ACTIVITY FIVE: *Studying the Arrangements of "Jingle Bells"*

I'm not a composer, but I *love* to create arrangements of other peoples' songs! Many of my ideas have been influenced and inspired by the in-depth study of others' arrangements. Choose one or two of the "Jingle Bells" performances you just listened to and analyze the arrangement in detail. As you lay out the road map (how the sections are organized), also pay attention to how the arranger has orchestrated the music. "Smelling the musical roses" along the way makes this analysis trip quite an enjoyable and enlightening venture!

Here's my analysis of Frank Sinatra's version…my favorite!

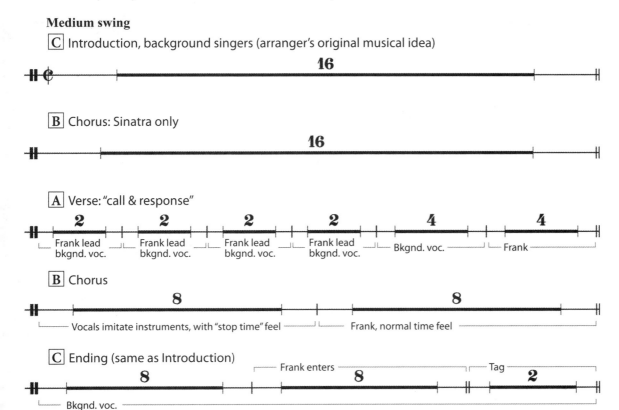

Reading, Writing and Rhythmetic

Two for the Road
You and your partner will create a lead sheet for the same song, but work independently for starters. Each of you is free to do the homework in your own way. When you're finished, compare your two lead sheets. How are they similar and how are they different from each other? Remember, there is no one perfect answer, but it might be interesting to share your thought process with your partner, and vice versa.

Let's steer our "rhythmetic" wheel towards the study of odd time signatures in the next section. We've traveled a long way from our common time home of 4/4!

Odd Time Signatures

We've covered quite a bit of rhythmic territory over the past ten chapters, from feeling the beat to working with quarter note triplets, and lots more in between! Let's take a detour for a moment and explore the road less traveled: odd time signatures. We'll focus on two of the most popular: 5/4 and 7/4. Both time signatures are compound meters, and can be broken down into different combinations of grouping of 2's and 3's.

For example, 5/4 can be felt as 2+3 or 3+2.

2+3   3+2

7/4 can be organized with a few different combinations of 2's and 3's. What would they be? That's right: 2+2+3, 3+2+2, or 2+3+2.

2+2+3   3+2+2

2+3+2

When listening to the following songs that are either in 5/4 or 7/4, identify the sub-divisions as well, the groupings of 2's and 3's. How? Listen for the accented beats.

Activity Six: *Identifying the Odd Time Signatures*
Listen to the following 13 song selections and determine if they're in 5/4 or 7/4 time. In addition, identify the subdivisions within the measures (groupings of 2's and 3's). Are some sub-division groupings more common than others? Which ones?

There's one "ringer" in the group of examples: one of the songs is in 9/8 time. Can you find it?
1. "Blue Rondo à la Turk," Dave Brubeck, *Time Out*
2. "Countdown," Dave Brubeck, *Time in Outer Space*
3. "Do What You Like," Blind Faith, *Blind Faith*
4. "In What Direction Are You Headed?" Lee Morgan, *Lee Morgan*

5. "Living in the Past," Jethro Tull, *Stand Up*
6. "Mission Impossible theme," Lalo Schifrin & John E. Davis, *The Best of Mission Impossible– Then and Now*
7. "Money," Pink Floyd, *The Dark Side of the Moon*
8. "Prints Tie," Bobby Hutcherson, *San Francisco*
9. "River Man," Nick Drake, *Five Leaves Left*, or Brad Mehldau, *Songs: the Art of the Trio, Vol. 3*
10. "Seven Days," Sting, *Ten Summoner's Tales*
11. "Solsbury Hill," Peter Gabriel, *The Round Ones*
12. "Take Five," Dave Brubeck, *Time Out*
13. "Unsquare Dance," Dave Brubeck, *Time Further Out*

Check the Answer Key (p.193) to see the results. Did you find the "ringer?"

Tip: There are several musical artists and bands that are noted for featuring odd metered and mixed time signatures throughout their music. These include: Dream Theater, Frank Zappa, Genesis, King Crimson, Radiohead, Rush and Tool, just to mention a few.

Collecting Souvenirs

Can you find some of your own examples of songs written in $\frac{5}{4}$ or $\frac{7}{4}$? There aren't many songs written in odd time signatures, so these souvenirs will be "collector's items" for sure!

ACTIVITY SEVEN: *Round Trip*

In the last chapter we worked with quarter note triplets, and certainly felt the "tug of war" pull between the triplets and straight quarter notes. But there will be times when the triplet feel will actually sound like you're establishing a new three meter, without the tug.

Listen to the Beatles' "We Can Work It Out," from *Rubber Soul* for an example. In the B section, when the lyrics are "fighting my friends," and "ask you once again," there is the impression of four quick measures of $\frac{3}{4}$ created by the quarter note triplet phrasing. Rather than modulate to a new time signature, it is more practical to stay in the original $\frac{4}{4}$ time and notate the feel as triplets.

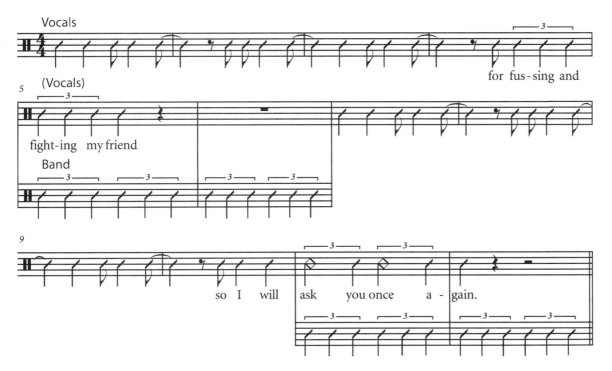

READING, WRITING AND RHYTHMETIC

This occurs in another tune that many of you might be unfamiliar with: Bobby Hutcherson's "Jazz" from his *San Francisco* album. Check out measures 23–26 in particular for this impression of a fast three meter within the overall scope of $\frac{4}{4}$. Bobby Hutcherson was one of jazz's greatest vibraphonist ambassadors: you won't be disappointed!

In the next chapter we will explore songs that involve "metric modulations," where the time signature changes from one section of the piece to another. This is often at the hands of the arranger rather than the original composer.

Approaching the Fork in the Road

From understanding the minute details of a two-beat rhythm word to analyzing song form, and everything else in between, we've spent a tremendous amount of time and effort examining and dissecting the music we listen to. So now, let's talk—have a conversation about music with your musical colleagues and friends; the knowledge you've gained will be a great contribution to that conversation.

The reason every chapter has a "Two for the Road" activity is to offer an opportunity to explore ideas "live," with a musical companion, and to engage in open conversation, perhaps learning something about your partner which is not directly related to music. One thing can lead to another, but the road can always lead back to the music.

Though music can often speak for itself, it's also important to talk about music with others. When all is said and done, note values and pitches can describe much, but not *everything*, about music: only words can complete the description. Have that conversation.

During my early days of development, I confess to being too obsessed at times with studying and transcribing music—alone, with not enough time devoted to making music—with others. There is nothing better than making music with other musicians! It takes the music to the next level, and it's fun! Make sure you have this experience; bandmates can be your friends for life. They might be the only friends you have that can truly engage in deep, meaningful, priceless conversations about music!

12 Transcribing Jazz Solos

Introduction

Our study of song form in the last two chapters focused our attention on the composition itself. Now, in this final chapter, we'll shine the headlights beyond song form and examine the song's overall arrangement. Developing song arrangements is right down my creative alley—how about you?

Continuing our work with song form, we will focus on the "C" section in today's contemporary pop and rock genres. These songs extend far beyond the 32 bar limit, often featuring instrumental solos which give each performance its unique signature.

Our transcription journey has now lead us to the final frontier—transcribing jazz solos. Solo transcription is probably the ultimate ear training challenge, and in fact was my inspiration for writing this book.

The last "rhythmetic" installment is working with songs which incorporate metric modulations—not exactly "danceable" songs, but finding the beat remains the first step to understanding these mixed meters.

This is the final leg of our transcription journey—I hope you continue to enjoy the ride!

Charting the Arrangement

We've spent time over the last two chapters analyzing song form, focusing our attention *within* the composition. In Chapter 11 we learned how to create a lead sheet, capturing only the essentials of the song's melody and chords. The intention then was to strip away the details of an artist's performance, thus producing a generic, easy-to-read notation of the song. Our attention was drawn inward to the essentials of the composition, rather than outward to the unique features of the individual performance.

In this final chapter, let's shine the headlights outward and add back in the details of the artist's performance. How is the performance a unique presentation of the song? To answer that question, we'll examine a song's arrangement and complete our road map with a chart.

An arrangement will often incorporate sections beyond the song form, such as introductions, interludes and endings. These additional sections help expand the song form and provide the performer with additional creative opportunities. Let's take a moment to define and describe these three additional sections.

Most arrangements start with an *introduction*, the main purpose of which is to prepare the listener for the groove and tonality of the song. In most cases, the content of the introduction borrows from the tune itself. It could be the musical content of the A section, minus the melody. Or, it could quote the last part of the song, circling the listener back towards the beginning. Most introductions are short, but there's exceptions. For example, The Eagles' arrangement of "Hotel California" opens with an extensive instrumental feature before getting into the heart of the song. On occasion, the forgotten verse of a song might be re-discovered in the introduction. You can

131

hear this in Chet Baker's version of "But Not for Me" and in my arrangement of "Rudolph the Red-Nosed Reindeer."

Tip: Songs that feature vocals will usually have an introduction for the practical purpose of preparing the singer to come in on the right opening note of the melody.

Interludes are short musical passages inserted into an arrangement. They are often brief instrumental statements that provide breathing room between verses, as in both Dylan's and Hendrix's performances of "All Along the Watchtower." Don't be surprised if the content of the interlude is the same as the introduction, as demonstrated in Sinatra's version of "It Was a Very Good Year."

Endings do just what their name implies: bring arrangements to a close. Endings sometimes will repeat and fade, or add a final section (sometimes referred to as the "tag") to the song. The Everly Brother's "All I Have to Do Is Dream" and the Beach Boys' "Surfer Girl" have these tags. Another popular use of an ending is what I call the "bookends effect." This is where the song's ending is identical to the introduction. This is featured in Etta James' performance of "At Last," Sinatra's "It Was a Very Good Year," and Sarah Vaughan's swingin' delivery of "Lullaby of Birdland."

Some song arrangements are simply a good excuse to feature the artist's improvisation, particularly in the jazz genre. You might not remember the melody as much as recalling the great solos over the changes. You're going to hear some great improvisations as you listen to "But Not for Me" and "Lullaby of Birdland" in Activity One.

Note: Remember that the term "chorus" can have two meanings: it can be the featured section within the song, or it can mean "once through the song form." In the jazz selections that follow, the term "chorus" means the latter.

Let's revisit 15 songs we've listened to earlier, this time listening closely to the arrangements.

ACTIVITY ONE: *Takin' the Arrangements to the Streets*

As we revisit the following songs, create an arrangement chart for each one. To get you started, I've set up the chart for the first selection, "At Last." I've also provided the song form and length of the arrangement for all selections. Include as much detail in your chart as you feel is necessary. Including a narrative description of the orchestration is probably the most vital information of all, along with defining the road map (are there introductions, interludes, or endings involved?) and indicating the number of measures per section. Enjoy the music from the very first hit to the last note played!

1. "At Last," Etta James, *At Last!* Song form is A A B A; once through the song.

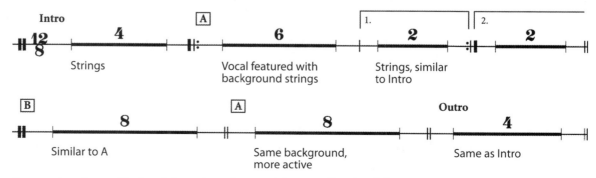

Comments: solo vocal featured throughout; Intro and Outro are "bookends."

2. "It Was a Very Good Year," Frank Sinatra, *Nothing But the Best*. Song form is Verse (A) only; once through the song.

3. "Surfer Girl," The Beach Boys, *Surfer Girl*. Song form is A A B A; once through the song.

4. "We Can Work It Out," The Beatles, *Rubber Soul*. Song form is A A B A; one and one-half times through the song.

5. "All I Have to Do Is Dream," The Everly Brothers, *The Very Best of the Everly Brothers*. Song form is A A B A; one and one-half times through the song.

6. "You Send Me," Sam Cooke, *The Best of Sam Cooke*. Song form is A A B A; twice through the song.

7. "Rudolph the Red-Nosed Reindeer," Roberta Radley, *Swing-a-Jing-a-Lingin'*. Song form is A A B A; twice through the song.

8. "I Just Called to Say I Love You," Stevie Wonder, *The Woman in Red*. Song form is Verse (A)/Chorus (B); twice through the song.

9. "Shoot the Moon," Norah Jones, *Come Away with Me*. Song form is A B A B; twice through the song.

10. "Hotel California," The Eagles, *Hotel California*. Song form is Verse (A)/Chorus (B); features solos.

11. "All Along the Watchtower," Bob Dylan, *John Wesley Harding*. Song form is Verse (A) only; compare with Jimi Hendrix's version.

12. "All Along the Watchtower," Jimi Hendrix, *Electric Ladyland*. Song form is Verse (A) only; compare with Bob Dylan's version.

13. "But Not for Me," Miles Davis, *Bag's Groove (Take Two)*. Song form is A B A C; arrangement features solos. Use of the term "chorus" means once through the song form. Compare with Chet Baker's version.

14. "But Not for Me," Chet Baker, *Chet Baker Sings*. Song form is A B A C; arrangement features solos. Compare with Miles Davis' version.

15. "Lullaby of Birdland," Sarah Vaughan & Clifford Brown, *The Definitive Sarah Vaughan*. Song form is A A B A; arrangement features solos.

Check the Answer Key (pp.194–197) to compare your arrangement charts with mine. Did we both capture the same essentials?

Going the Extra Mile

Select one of the arrangements you charted from the previous activity, and use it as a road map to arrange any song you choose. While attending Berklee, I had the incredible opportunity to study with Herb Pomeroy. As part of his "The Music of Duke Ellington" course, we analyzed some of Duke's arrangements in minute detail, and then composed an original piece of our own which incorporated our analysis of his arrangement. This modeling one of jazz's greatest composer/arrangers was an invaluable learning experience!

Before we conclude our work with song form and charting arrangements, let's take one more look at and listen to the "third wheel," the C section.

READING, WRITING AND RHYTHMETIC

FEATURING THE C SECTION

When we discussed the 32-bar song form in Chapter 11, one of the options was A B A C. In that case, the C section was often a variation of the B theme. Now, we'll highlight the C section as being its own independent theme within the song form.

A popular song form found in today's contemporary rock and pop music stretches beyond 32-bars, incorporating three distinct sections: A (verse), B (pre-chorus), and C (chorus). The new element here is the "pre-chorus" section, which serves as a link between the verse and the chorus, acting to setup the upcoming chorus. There is no absolutely predictable length or ordering of these three sections, so when you're listening you will need to pay close attention to the function of each section. One relatively predictable clue is that the chorus section may likely include the title of the song as the lyrics repeat. It is also common for featured instrumental solos to occur within these lengthy arrangements.

In other songs, the C section might play a supporting role serving as a variation for one of the verses (A). It can also be a third musical theme presented for the sake of breaking away from the predictable A (verse) and B (chorus) themes. In these situations, the C section is often referred to as a bridge. From my ear's perspective, this is often the most interesting part of a song.

ACTIVITY TWO: *Identifying the Role of the C Section*

As you listen to the following 12 song selections, determine the location of the C section and the role it plays within the song form. For example, in Michael Jackson's "Billie Jean," I hear the lyrics, "Billie Jean is not my lover…" as the C section, playing the role of the chorus. In the Beatles' "Ob-La-Di, Ob-La-Da," the lyric, "In a couple of years they have built a home-sweet home…" announces the C section, functioning as a bridge. For the sake of simplicity, label the role of the C section as either "chorus" or "bridge."

1. "Afro Blue," Abbey Lincoln, *Abbey Is Blue*
2. "Another Day in Paradise," Phil Collins, *…But Seriously*
3. "Billie Jean," Michael Jackson, *Thriller*
4. "Don't Stop Believin'," Journey, *Escape*
5. "Don't Take Away My Heaven," Aaron Neville, *The Grand Tour*
6. "Fix You," Coldplay, *X&Y*
7. "Hold My Hand," Hootie and the Blowfish, *Cracked Rear View*
8. "Just My Imagination," The Temptations, *Sky's the Limit*
9. "Livin on a Prayer," Bon Jovi, *Cross Road*
10. "Ob-La-Di, Ob-La-Da, The Beatles, *White Album*
11. "Piano Man," Billy Joel, *Piano Man*
12. "Rolling in the Deep," Adele, *21*

Check the Answer Key (p.197) to see how you did.

TRANSCRIBING THE JAZZ SOLO: DO AS I SAY, NOT WHAT I DID

I am undoubtedly showing my age when I tell you that my early days of transcribing jazz solos involved playing LP's (records) at half speed while I checked the notes on an electric toy organ.

The process required an incredible amount of patience, as I repeatedly dropped the needle at the approximate groove on the record. After grabbing a few notes, I would play them back on the organ to hear if they were correct (or not), then proceed to the next few notes, and so on. Why the toy organ? Because unlike my acoustic piano, it was relatively in tune. My poor record collection got butchered along the way, with multiple scratches showing the wounds from my labored transcription technique—but it was worth it!

I did the best I could with the equipment and tools which were available at the time. Technological innovations have since provided much more efficient and user-friendly tools for today's transcriber. Programs which allow looping and controlling the speed of the music are incredibly helpful. The playback feature of notation software is another asset. Truly amazing stuff!

I was incredibly motivated to learn about jazz improvisation and was wisely advised by my teachers that transcribing solos was the best way to proceed. Your collection of recordings, LP's, CD's, mp3's, etc., is an excellent resource for transcribing the solos of the great jazz artists. Transcribing a solo yourself is the best effort you'll ever make for truly digesting and owning the ideas you transcribe. Though there are published books that have done the transcriptions for you, the benefits do not match the effect of what happens when you take down the solo yourself.

I can still sing back the very first solo I transcribed—Miles Davis on "When Lights Are Low." (You'll be hearing me do just that later in the chapter!)

As a beginner, I relied heavily on that electric toy organ; it was like an appendix to my writing hand. My fingers, not my ears, were searching for the notes. Writing the notes as quickly as possible was my goal, but after a few notes I quickly forgot them as I continued writing more and more notes. Though I had captured the notes on paper, I had not taken the time to internalize their sound. This was not the best approach, but it got me started.

If I could go back in time, I would have done things differently. I would have taken the time to first listen carefully to the musical phrase. I would then have sung back the phrase first before attempting to write it down. They say you can learn from your mistakes…I did! And now I'm passing along my hindsight's advice to you.

MY 12-STEP PROGRAM

1. Love the music you choose to transcribe. Motivation is the fuel needed to keep you going on this challenging, tough journey.

2. Pick a solo that is manageable. If you choose one that is too complicated and lengthy, you might never finish it. As a test, can you sing along with it? I found that starting with Miles Davis' "When Lights Are Low" was a great first choice for me, for this very reason that I could sing it.

3. Live with the music for a while before attempting the detailed, analytical listening required to transcribe it. Remember, listening is the first key step.

4. As you begin to listen for the details, again determine if you can sing back the phrase. If so, you've probably internalized the music.

5. Reference a lead sheet for basic information about the song. Knowing the melody and chord changes will give you an excellent jump-start to frame the notes ahead. Most solos will reference both the melody and changes. Have you heard the phrase, "playing over the changes?"

6. Take advantage of technological tools. Don't hesitate to loop or slow down the music in order to internalize it in a comprehensible way. If the music is flying by way too fast, you may become frustrated.

7. If you're using music notation software, use the playback feature to check what you've just written.

Reading, Writing and Rhythmetic

8. It is *not* cheating to check your work on your instrument as you go along (the old fashioned approach). But don't make the instrument the driver, put it in the passenger's seat.
9. Do *not* attempt to transcribe the entire solo at once. Transcribing requires intense listening and a fresh mind…avoid burning out. Allowing things to sit on the back burner can produce amazing results! I refer to this as the "24-hour" rule. It works every time!
10. For your initial transcriptions, try to stay with the same artist or style of music so you can become familiar with the vocabulary of that artist or style. Having transcribed several Miles' solos, I could almost predict what he was likely to play.
11. When you've completed the transcription, take a moment to enjoy the accomplishment—you've earned it! Now that the solo is notated, take the time to analyze it and reflect on it intellectually. What can you learn from the notes and rhythms written on the page?
12. If you have truly internalized the music, the value of transcribing goes far beyond what's written down (the notes and rhythms). This is the best step of all. You've listened to the artist's voice on a deeper level and you've experienced the artistry of his/her delivery—the musical magic! Whenever I've completed a transcription, I have a greater appreciation of the music; it always enhances the magic.

Tip: It is inevitable when transcribing jazz solos that you will encounter some non-diatonic pitches. Let's pull off the road to study the chromatic scale and its associated solfege syllables.

61 Listen to Audio track 61 as you view the chromatic solfege syllables below. Notice that the syllables change according to their direction. Sharp notes end in an "i" sound, flat notes (except *re*) end in an "e" sound. If a chromatic note is a chord tone, use the syllable that best describes its harmonic function. (*Note:* "i" is pronounced "ee," "e" is pronounced "ay," and "ra" is pronounced "rah.")

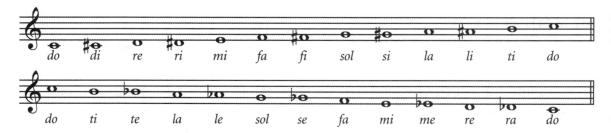

It's time to take the 12-step program out for a test drive with the next series of activities.

Activity Three: *Transcribing the Jazz Solo*

62 Come join me as I re-live Miles Davis' solo on "When Lights Are Low." Due to copyright laws, Miles was unable to make the recording gig, so I'll be singing solo on the CD audio tracks that follow. But you *must* listen to the original Miles' version on *Blue Haze*—his solo was the inspiration for this book!

On Audio track 62, listen to me singing, "la, la, la" on the first 16 bars of Miles' solo. Join me when you're ready and sing along. Listening is the most important step in the transcription process, so take all the time you need with this first step. You can slow down the track if necessary, breaking the solo down into short 2-bar or 4-bar phrases, building the solo as you go.

Activity Four: *Solfegging the Jazz Solo*

On Audio track 63, listen to me translate the "la, la, la's" into meaningful solfege syllables. Before singing along with me, it might be helpful to first write in the solfege syllables on the rhythmic template provided below. (This template was originally used as a reading activity in Chapter 7.) I've also included chord symbols to the template so you can associate the melodic notes with the harmony. Remember, Miles is often "playing over the changes," so knowing the chords up front gives you a head start. Ready, read, sing!

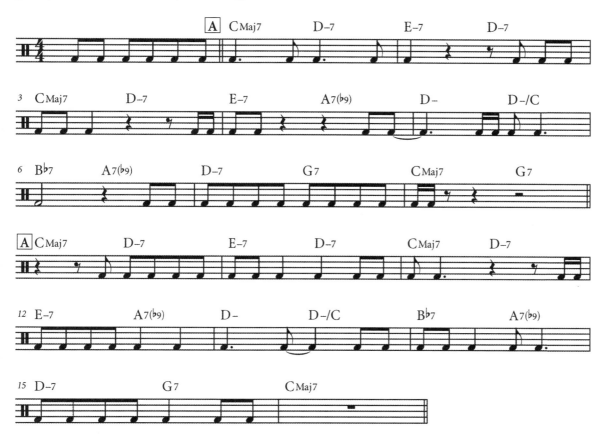

Tip: I'm singing in the key of C, though Miles' original solo was played in the key of F major. I had to transpose the key in order to sing the solo in my comfortable vocal range. We'll talk more about transposition in Activity Six.

Activity Five: *Analyzing the Solo*

Now, write the 16-bar solo in the key of C; it's your job to translate the solfege syllables into the actual key of C because copyright laws forbid me to do it (can't publish this book from the jailhouse!). Take the time to analyze Miles' solo (exercising the 50% "brain-training" of ear training). Consider—at times his solo might relate to the melody, to the sound of the overall key, or to the individual chord changes. Also pay attention to how he develops his ideas, using repetition along the way. A good thing is worth repeating…

Reading, Writing and Rhythmetic

Activity Six: *Memorizing, Transposing and Playing the Solo*

If you've taken the time to thoroughly participate in the previous three activities, then it's likely you've already memorized most, if not all, of these 16 bars. Put that knowledge to work by playing the solo on your instrument in a variety of keys. Transposing will reinforce the usefulness of having analyzed the solo with solfege and/or numbers. Playing the solo is getting the extra mileage out of the transcribing process. Why did I transcribe Miles' solo in the first place— because I wanted to become a better jazz pianist!

Going the Extra Mile

Following the same guidelines used in the previous activities, complete the second half of the solo on "When Lights Are Low."

Collecting Souvenirs

Transcribe solos of your own choosing. Set a weekly goal of transcribing at least 8 bars of improvisation and watch the collection grow and your playing develop! I have some recommendations for choosing the solos to transcribe:

- Choose a particular artist to focus on. As a beginner, I chose several of Miles Davis' solos to get my motor going. I recommend "But Not for Me," "It Could Happen to You," "So What," "Someday My Prince Will Come," "Summertime," and "Walkin'," to get your engine warmed up.
- Choose a particular "set of changes," such as blues, or "rhythm changes" (songs that have the same chord progression as Gershwin's original "I Got Rhythm."). I found this particularly helpful as a beginning improviser.
- Choose artists who play your instrument for that hands-on familiarity.
- Choose artists who play an instrument other than your own in order to give yourself a fresh perspective.

Note: True confession—I might have spent too much time transcribing and not enough time practicing and playing my instrument. If I could go back in time, I would have spent more time nurturing my own musical voice, and less time transcribing. I think I would have benefited from a more balanced approach.

Mixed Meters

Our final rhythmetic equation will involve mixed time signatures within a piece of music. Let's explore the two most common ways this can happen.

Beat Is Constant

With the first situation, the beat remains constant throughout ($\quarternote = \quarternote$), but the number of beats within the measures varies. These variations are most often motivated by the lyrics. It's the words that drive the odd-numbered phrases which end up sounding completely natural. Listen to Paul McCartney's performance of "Blackbird" from the Beatles' *White Album* as you read the charted measures below. We'll focus on just the verse for now.

ACTIVITY SEVEN: *Charting the Mixed Meters, Beat is Constant*

Listen to the following seven song selections which use mixed meters and chart the measures. This can be quite challenging, so I've provided some clues to prime your engine. As you listen to the lyrics, pay attention to where you feel the accents—these are most likely the downbeats of the bars.

1. "All You Need Is Love," The Beatles, *Magical Mystery Tour:* Listen to the 8-bar Verse (A) that combines $\frac{4}{4}$ and $\frac{3}{4}$.

2. "Hiding My Heart," Adele, *21:* Listen to the 8-bar Chorus (B) that inserts one bar of $\frac{2}{4}$ within the overall $\frac{4}{4}$ section.

3. "I Say a Little Prayer," Dionne Warwick, *Dionne Warwick: Her All-Time Greatest Hits:* Listen to the 8-bar Verse (A) that inserts one bar of $\frac{2}{4}$ within the overall $\frac{4}{4}$ section. Listen to the 12-bar Chorus (B) that combines measures of $\frac{4}{4}$ and $\frac{3}{4}$.

4. "Love Letters," Patti Austin, *The Real Me:* Listen to the C section of the first chorus—what happens at the end? Listen to the B section of the second chorus—what happens at the end?

5. "Ponta de Areia," Wayne Shorter, *Native Dancer.* Listen to the Verse that combines measures of $\frac{4}{4}$ and $\frac{5}{4}$.

6. "She's Always a Woman," Billy Joel, *The Stranger:* Listen to the Verse (A) and determine where the $\frac{6}{8}$, $\frac{9}{8}$ and $\frac{12}{8}$ measures occur within this 7-bar section.

7. "Shoot the Moon," Norah Jones, *Come Away with Me:* Listen to the B section that adds one bar of $\frac{2}{4}$ to this overall $\frac{4}{4}$ section. Where does the $\frac{2}{4}$ bar occur?

Check the Answer Key (p.198) to compare your charts with mine.

METRIC MODULATION

The second mixed meter situation is called "metric modulation." In addition to using mixed time signatures, the tempo relationships between the two meters may also be different. Here, the beat may *not* be constant. This usually occurs *between* sections of a song rather than *within* the same section.

The Beatles' "I Me Mine" from the *Let It Be* album is an excellent example of metric modulation. We can consider the Verse (A) to be in $\frac{6}{8}$ and the Chorus (B) to be in $\frac{4}{4}$. The relationship of the two time signatures is: ♩. = ♩ . Another way of saying this is that half a measure of $\frac{6}{8}$ equals half a measure of $\frac{4}{4}$. Have the metronome click this value so you can better grasp how the two time signatures relate to each other.

Note: If you consider the Verse (A) to be in $\frac{3}{4}$ rather than $\frac{6}{8}$, then you will have twice as many measures, and the relationship will now be: ♩. in $\frac{3}{4}$ = ♩ in $\frac{4}{4}$.

ACTIVITY EIGHT: *Identifying the Metric Modulation*

Identify the metric modulations in the following seven song selections. Determining the two time signatures is relatively easy, determining the metric relationship is the challenge. Good luck!

1. "Cherokee," Ahmad Jamal, *The Best of Ahmad Jamal*

2. "Four by Five," McCoy Tyner, *The Real McCoy*

3. "How My Heart Sings," Bill Evans Trio, *Riverside Profiles Bill Evans*

4. "In What Direction Are You Headed?" Lee Morgan, *Lee Morgan*

5. "Love Is Stronger than Justice," Sting, *Ten Summoner's Tales*

READING, WRITING AND RHYTHMETIC

6. "Lucy in the Sky with Diamonds," The Beatles, *Sargent Pepper's Lonely Hearts Club Band*

7. "Whipping Post," The Allman Brothers, *Legendary Hits*

Check the Answer Key (p.199) to see how you did.

ACTIVITY NINE: *Round Trip*

Let's spend a few moments visiting the 16-bar form. It follows many of the same organizational principles as its big sister, the 32-bar form, but it's simply half the length.

When listening to the selections below, consider how the 16 measures are organized into smaller 4- or 8-bar sections. How do these sections relate or contrast? Let's make this a "Two for the Road" activity. You and your partner are now experienced to have this conversation in a meaningful and informed way. Enjoy!

1. "Amazing Grace," Leann Rimes, *You Light Up My Life*
2. "Blue Bossa," Joe Henderson, *Back Road*
3. "Doxy," Dexter Gordon, *Both Sides of Midnight*
4. "Fever," Peggy Lee, *The Best of Peggy Lee*
5. "Fishin' Blues," Taj Mahal, (18-bars)
6. "Mack the Knife," Bobby Darin, *The Ultimate Bobby Darin*
7. "Mockingbird," Carly Simon & James Taylor, *The Best of Carly Simon*
8. "Old MacDonald," traditional children's song
9. "Que Pasa," Horace Silver, *Song for My Father*
10. "She Caught the Katy," Taj Mahal, The Best of Taj Mahal
11. "Summertime," Miles Davis, *Porgy and Bess*
12. "When the Saints Go Marching In," Mel McDaniel, *30 Country Gospel Greats*
13. "Women Be Wise," Bonnie Raitt, *Bonnie Raitt*
14. "Work Song," Nat Adderley, *Work Song*
15. "You Are My Sunshine," Norman Blake, *O Brother, Where Art Thou?*

Approaching the Fork in the Road

As we wrap things up in this final chapter, it's important to reflect on the reasons for transcribing in the first place. I'm certain everyone has his/her own personal answers to this question. Mine is that it changed my musical life substantially in innumerable ways! I don't think I've experienced any ear training practice as demanding as transcribing and as a result, my aural skills have grown tremendously over the years. My trust in making decisions "by ear" has been increased, providing me with greater confidence in my music making. The task of transcribing has been to translate the music we hear into notation on the page; but the rewards are so much greater! What I have learned *about* the music is beyond measure.

I have enjoyed sharing my experiences with you, and wish you the same rewards that transcribing has provided me. You've done an incredible amount of work as you traveled from chapter to chapter, activity to activity. I applaud you for your diligence, work ethic and commitment. Transcribing is hard! Time to take the winner's lap around the racetrack.

And it's time to let the music take a bow. For after all the dissection, analysis and painstaking effort you've made, the music continues to lift the spirit beyond the notes and rhythms. The musical magic is truly bigger than the sum of all the transcribed parts. What could be better than that?

Answer Key

Chapter 1

Activity Five
1. $\frac{3}{4}$ 2. $\frac{3}{4}$ 3. $\frac{2}{4}$ 4. $\frac{3}{4}$ 5. $\frac{2}{4}$

6. $\frac{2}{4}$ 7. $\frac{2}{4}$ 8. $\frac{2}{4}$ 9. $\frac{2}{4}$ 10. $\frac{2}{4}$

11. $\frac{3}{4}$ 12. $\frac{3}{4}$ 13. $\frac{3}{4}$ 14. $\frac{3}{4}$ 15. $\frac{2}{4}$

Activity Six
1. $\frac{2}{4}$ 2. $\frac{3}{4}$ 3. $\frac{2}{4}$ 4. $\frac{2}{4}$

5. $\frac{3}{4}$ 6. $\frac{3}{4}$ 7. $\frac{3}{4}$ 8. $\frac{2}{4}$

9. $\frac{3}{4}$ 10. $\frac{3}{4}$ 11. $\frac{2}{4}$ 12. $\frac{2}{4}$

13. $\frac{3}{4}$ 14. $\frac{2}{4}$ 15. $\frac{3}{4}$ 16. $\frac{3}{4}$

Activity Seven
1. foot stomps and body movement
2. drums and bass
3. vocal chorus
4. guitar strum
5. string section
6. guitar melody
7. left hand chords
8. guitar comping
9. bass drum and bass
10. drums
11. piano
12. opening guitar riff and drums
13. bass drum
14. piano
15. bass
16. bass drum
17. "walking" bass line
18. cowbell
19. opening vocal chorus
20. hand claps and piano

Chapter 2

Activity One

Activity Three

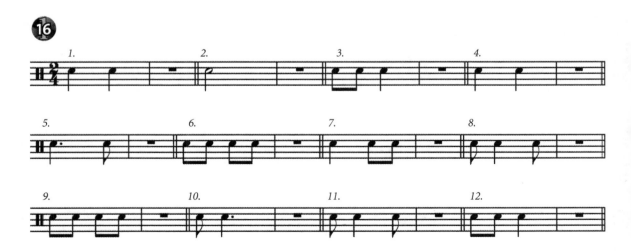

Answer Key

Activity Eight

Activity Nine

1. "All I Have to Do Is Dream" vocal melody, 1st verse

2. "Beat It" vocal melody, 1st verse

3. "Birthday" bass and guitar riff

Reading, Writing and Rhythmetic

4. "Burning Down the House" vocal melody, 1st verse

Ah! Watch out

burn - in' down the house

5. "C Jam Blues" full band melody, 2nd chorus

play 3 times

6. "Fire" guitar introduction

7. "Jeepers Creepers" trumpet melody, 1st verse

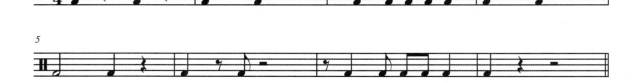

8. "A Little Night Music" 1st movement, 1st four bars

ANSWER KEY

9. "My Girl" guitar riff

10. "River" piano introduction

11. "Uptown Girl" vocal melody, 1st verse

Up-town girl

12. "Walkin'" introduction

Chapter 3

Activity One

1. E	2. D	3. E♭	4. A	5. F
6. B♭	7. C	8. F	9. G	10. D
11. E	12. C	13. D	14. A	15. E♭

Activity Three

1. major	2. major	3. minor	4. major
5. minor	6. major	7. minor	8. minor
9. major	10. minor	11. major	12. minor

Activity Four

1. E minor	2. D minor	3. E♭ major	4. A major	5. F minor
6. B♭ major	7. C major	8. F major	9. G major	10. D major
11. E minor	12. C minor	13. D minor	14. A minor	15. E♭ major

Activity Five

1. C major	2. C♯ or C minor	3. F♯ minor	4. E♭ minor	5. D♭ major
6. C minor	7. E minor	8. A♭ major	9. F major	10. A major
11. D major	12. E major	13. G major	14. F minor	15. C major
16. B♭ major	17. C♯ minor	18. C minor	19. C minor	20. E minor

Activity Eight

Answer Key

ACTIVITY NINE

39 "Happy Birthday"

40 "Minuet in G" 1st 8 bars

41 "When Irish Eyes Are Smiling" 1st 8 bars

42 "U.S. National Anthem" 1st 8 bars

43 "Greensleeves" 1st 8 bars

Reading, Writing and Rhythmetic

Going the Extra Mile

1. "Scarborough Fair" vocals, 1st 24 bars

2. "Moon River" vocal, 1st 16 bars

3. "Sunrise, Sunset" vocals, chorus (B section), 16 bars

ANSWER KEY

4. "Lucy in the Sky with Diamonds" vocal, 1st 19 bars

5. "Chim Chim Cher-ee" vocals, 1st 25 bars

6. "Piano Man" harmonica introduction, 16 bars

149

READING, WRITING AND RHYTHMETIC

7. "Open Arms" vocal, 1st 16 bars

8. "Alice in Wonderland" piano melody, B section, band entrance, 16 bars

9. "Some Day My Prince Will Come" piano chord introduction, 16 bars

ANSWER KEY

CHAPTER 4

ACTIVITY FOUR

1. "Angels We Have Heard on High," *sol, la sol fa mi fa, sol fa mi re mi, fa mi re do re sol sol, do re mi fa mi re do*

2. "Blue Moon," s*ol sol, fa sol la sol sol fa sol, re mi fa mi mi re mi, do re mi do do do do*

3. "Bye Bye Blackbird," *mi mi mi fa mi mi, mi re re, re do do, do, re, do ti, fa fa fa sol fa fa, fa mi mi, mi re re, re mi, re do*

4. "Can't Help Falling in Love," *sol la ti do, re mi fa mi re do*

5. "Fix You," *fa mi re do ti la sol la do, fa mi re do ti la sol la do, fa mi re do mi do*

6. "Fly Me to the Moon," *do ti la sol fa, sol la do ti la sol fa mi, la sol fa mi re, mi fa la si, fa mi re do*

7. "Human Nature," *mi re do ti do ti la sol, la, ti, do do do re do la*

8. "I Want to Hold Your Hand," *do ti la sol fa sol fa mi re mi re do, do ti la sol re do*

9. "Joy to the World," *do ti la sol fa mi re do, sol la, la ti, ti do, do do ti la sol sol fa mi, do do ti la sol sol fa mi, mi mi mi mi mi fa sol, fa mi re re re re mi fa, mi re do do la sol fa mi, fa mi re do*

10. "Lean on Me," *do, do re mi fa, fa mi re do, do re mi mi re, do, do re mi fa, fa mi re do, do re mi ti do*

11. "Minuet in G," *sol do re mi fa sol do do, la fa sol la ti do do do, fa sol fa mi re mi, fa mi re do re, mi re do ti do*

12. "My Romance," *mi fa sol, mi fa sol la ti do do ti la sol, do re mi, do re mi fa sol la la sol fa mi*

13. "Never on Sunday," *sol do ti do re mi fa sol, sol fa sol, sol fa sol, sol fa sol la fa sol mi, sol do ti do re mi fa sol, sol fa sol, sol fa sol, sol fa mi fa re mi do*

14. "Ode to Joy," *mi mi fa sol sol fa mi re do do re mi mi re re, mi mi fa sol sol fa mi re do do re mi re do do*

15. "One Note Samba," *la ti do re do ti la sol fa mi re do ti do re mi ti la, ti do mi ti la*

16. "Overkill," *sol do re mi fa sol, do fa mi re do re mi re do* (repeat)

17. "Pachelbel's Canon in D," *mi re do ti la sol la ti*

18. "Silver Bells," *mi fa sol, la ti do, ti ti do re do ti do sol, mi fa sol, la ti do, ti ti do re do ti do*

19. "Smile," *do, re mi re do ti la, ti, do re do ti la sol, la ti do, la ti do, re mi fa di re mi*

20. "St. Thomas," *mi fa sol, fa mi re, mi re do la, sol do ti do*

21. "There Will Never Be Another You," *sol la ti do re mi sol re do re, mi do re mi sol la do la sol la*

22. "Twinkle, Twinkle Little Star," *do do sol sol la la sol, fa fa mi mi re re do, sol sol fa fa mi mi re, sol sol fa fa mi mi re, do do sol sol la la sol, fa fa mi mi re re do*

23. "The Way You Look Tonight," *sol do, re mi fa mi re, mi fa sol fa mi, fa sol la sol fa sol la ti do do, re mi sol fa mi re do*

24. "Will You Be There," *do do, do re do re mi mi, mi fa mi fa sol sol, sol la sol fa mi re*

25. "With a Little Help from My Friends," *mi fa sol sol, fa mi re mi fa fa, fa fa mi re re re, do re mi*

151

Activity Six

Activity Seven

1. "Don't Worry, Be Happy," Bobby McFerrin, *Simple Pleasures:* whistle introduction

2. "Esconjuros," Serge Mendes, *Brasilerio:* female vocals, 1st 8 bars (excluding pickup)

ANSWER KEY

3. "Fix You," Coldplay, *X & Y:* vocal, B section (chorus)

4. "Humoresque No. 7 in G♭ Major, Opus 101," Dvořák, *Classic Perlman: Rhapsody:* 1st 16 bars

5. "I Want You Back," Jackson 5, *The Essential Michael Jackson:* bass line introduction

6. "Let's Dance," David Bowie, *Let's Dance:* bass line

7. "Livin' in America," James Brown, *Gravity:* background horns at chorus

153

Answer Key

12. "We Will Rock You," Queen, *News of the World:* vocal, first 8 bars

Going the Extra Mile

50 "Joy to the World"

Activity Eight

Chapter 5

ACTIVITY TWO

1. "All of Me," *do sol mi*
2. "Bicycle Built for Two," *sol mi do sol*
3. "Black or White," *sol do mi fa mi do sol fa mi fa sol*
4. "First Suite in D," *mi re do sol do re mi fa mi re do*
5. "Jingle Bells," *mi mi mi, mi mi mi, mi sol do re mi*
6. "Just My Imagination," *sol mi do sol mi do, sol fa mi do do do do la sol*
7. "NBC," *sol mi do*
8. "Oh My Darling, Clementine," *do do do sol, mi mi mi do, do mi sol sol*
9. "On Top of Old Smokey," *do do mi sol do (la)*
10. "Please Don't Talk About Me When I'm Gone," *do mi sol do*
11. "Row, Row, Row Your Boat," *do do do, sol sol sol, mi mi mi, do do do*
12. "Someone Like You," *sol mi re do, sol sol mi re do*
13. "Taps," *sol sol do, sol do mi, sol do mi, sol do mi, sol do mi, do mi sol mi do sol, sol sol do*
14. "U.S. National Anthem," *sol mi do mi sol do, mi re do mi fi sol*
15. "When the Saints Go Marching In," *do mi fa sol, do mi fa sol, do mi fa sol mi do mi (re)*

ACTIVITY FOUR

1. "Twinkle, Twinkle Little Star"
2. "Happy Birthday"
3. "My Country 'Tis of Thee"

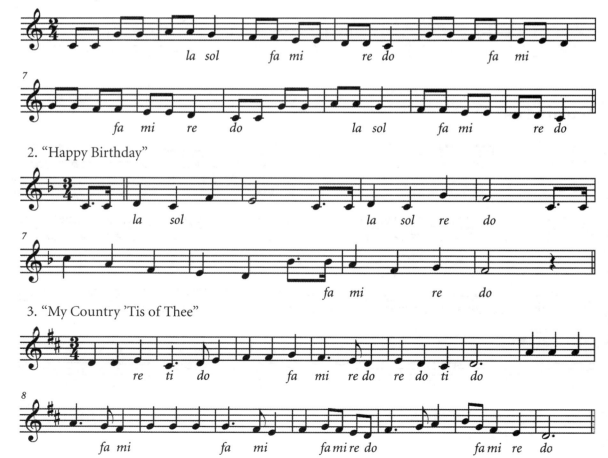

Answer Key

4. "Here Comes the Bride"

Activity Five

1. "C Jam Blues," *sol sol, sol sol, sol sol, sol do*
2. "Dancing Queen," *ti do do, ti do do, re do do ti do do*
3. "Freddie Freeloader," *la sol, la sol, re do, la sol*
4. "I Just Called to Say I Love You," *do do la, do ti, sol ti do do*
5. "Just My Imagination," *sol mi do sol mi do, sol fa mi do do do do la sol*
6. "Moonlight in Vermont," *la sol mi re mi, la sol mi do re mi le*
7. "One Note Samba," *sol's, do's, sol's and do's*
8. "She," *do ti do ti re do ti la do…fa mi fa mi sol fa mi re mi*
9. "Star Eyes," *mi sol re do, sol do re mi sol mi sol re do*
10. "Theme Song from TV Show Jeopardy," *sol do sol do sol do sol, sol do sol do mi…*
11. "Time After Time," *re do do do, re do do do, re do do re mi mi*
12. "Walkin'," *la sol mi do fa mi do, sol do fa mi do te*
13. "We Can Work It Out," *do do do do re do, mi mi sol do re re re re re do do do do*

Activity Six

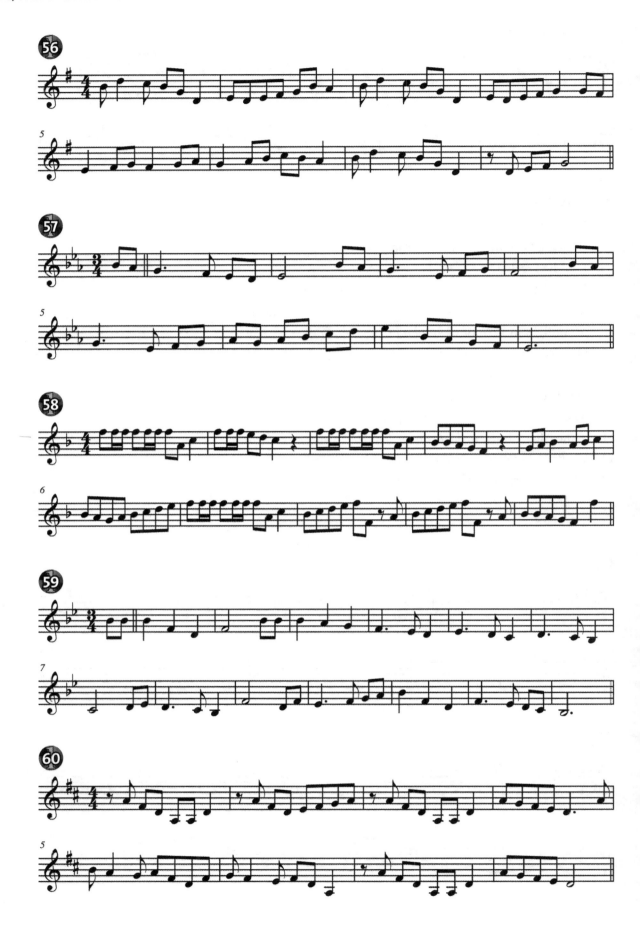

Chapter 6

Activity One

1. "Frère Jacques"
2. "London Bridge Is Falling Down"
3. "Oh My Darling, Clementine"
4. "Old MacDonald"
5. "On Top of Old Smokey"

Reading, Writing and Rhythmetic

6. "Row, Row, Row Your Boat"

7. "Three Blind Mice"

8. "Twinkle, Twinkle Little Star"

Activity Two

1. "Blowin' in the Wind," Bob Dylan, *The Freewheelin' Bob Dylan*

ANSWER KEY

2. "I Still Haven't Found What I'm Looking For," U2, *The Joshua Tree*

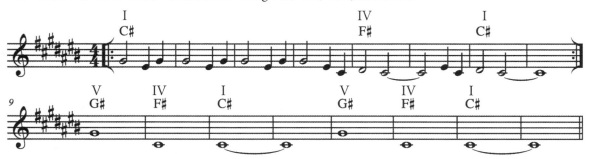

3. "Lean on Me," Bill Withers, *The Best of Bill Withers*

4. "Matilda," Harry Belafonte, *The Essential Harry Belafonte*

5. "Ob-La-Di, Ob-La-Da" (A section only), The Beatles, *White Album*

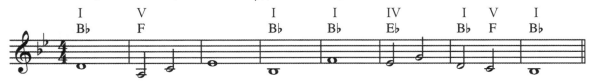

6. "When the Saints Go Marching In," Mel McDaniel, *30 Country Gospel Greats*

7. "You Are My Sunshine," Norman Blake, *O Brother Where Art Thou?*

Reading, Writing and Rhythmetic

ACTIVITY THREE

72 "Frère Jacques"

73 "Old MacDonald"

ANSWER KEY

74 "Three Blind Mice"

75 "Twinkle, Twinkle Little Star"

Reading, Writing and Rhythmetic

Activity Four

1. "Ain't Too Proud to Beg," A section, The Temptations, *Motown's 1's*

2. "All I Have to Do Is Dream," A and B sections, The Everly Brothers: *The Very Best of the Everly Brothers*

3. "Birdland," A section, Weather Report, *Heavy Weather*

4. "Carolina in My Mind," 1st A section, James Taylor, *James Taylor Greatest Hits, Vol. 1*

5. "Don't Stop Believin'," A section, Journey, *Escape*

ANSWER KEY

6. "Every Breath You Take," 2 A sections, The Police, *Synchronicity*

7. "In the Midnight Hour," 1st A section, Wilson Pickett, *The Very Best of Wilson Pickett*

8. "Let It Be," A and B sections, The Beatles, *Let It Be*

9. "Ob-La-Di, Ob-La-Da," A section, The Beatles, *White Album*

10. "Piano Man," A section, Billy Joel, *Piano Man*

11. "Shoot the Moon," A and B sections, Norah Jones, *Come Away with Me*

12. "When Lights Are Low," 1st A section, Miles Davis: *Blue Haze*

Activity Six

Going the Extra Mile

"Summertime," Janis Joplin, *Pearl*

ANSWER KEY

Chapter 7

Activity One

1. major   2. major   3. minor   4. major   5. minor   6. minor
7. major   8. minor   9. major   10. minor   11. minor   12. major

Activity Two

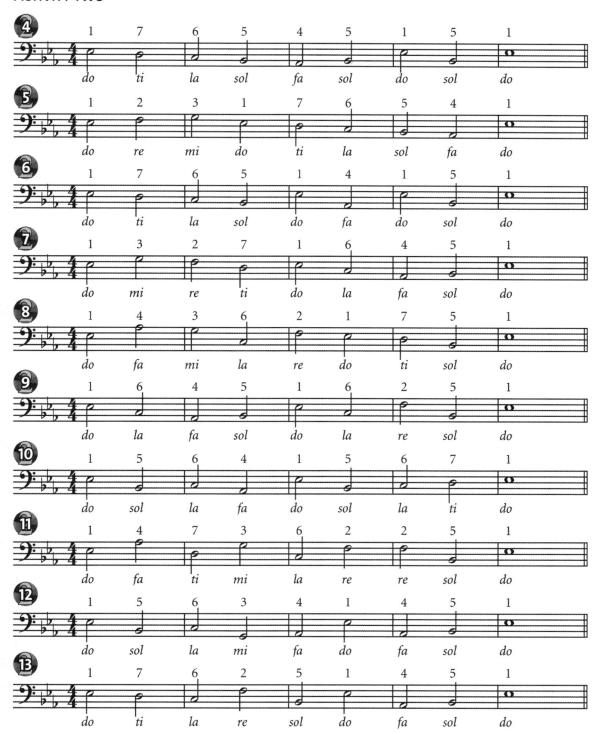

Reading, Writing and Rhythmetic

Activity Five

1. "All I Have to Do Is Dream," The Everly Brothers, *The Very Best of the Everly Brothers* (key of E, first A section)

2. "Always with You, Always with Me," Joe Satriani, *Surfing with the Alien* (key of B, A section)

3. "At Last," Etta James, *At Last!* (key of F, A section)

4. "Blowin' in the Wind," Stevie Wonder, *Up-Tight* (key of B♭, entire song)

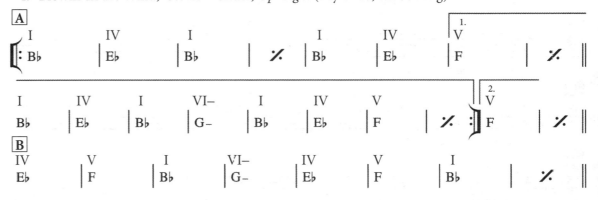

5. "Blue Eyes Cryin' in the Rain," Willie Nelson, *Red Headed Stranger* (key of E, A and B sections)

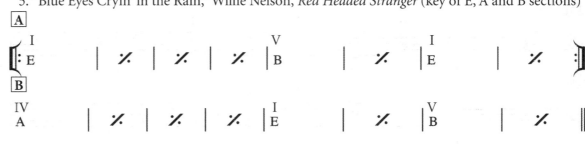

Answer Key

6. "Come Away with Me," Norah Jones, *Come Away with Me* (key of C, B section)

7. "Don't Stop Believin'," Journey, *Escape* (key of E, A section)

8. "Every Breath You Take," The Police, *Synchronicity* (key of A, two A sections)

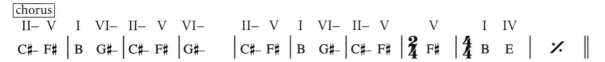

9. "Hey, Soul Sister," Train, *Save Me, San Francisco* (key of E, A section)

10. "Hiding My Heart Away," Adele, *21* (key of B, chorus)

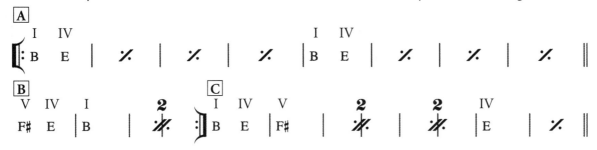

11. "Hold My Hand," Hootie and the Blowfish, *Cracked Rear View* (key of B, entire song)

12. "I Still Haven't Found What I'm Looking For," U2, *The Joshua Tree* (key of C♯, A and B sections)

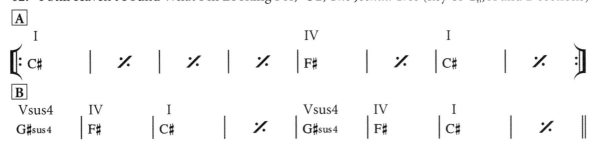

READING, WRITING AND RHYTHMETIC

13. "Lean on Me," Bill Withers, *The Best of Bill Withers* (key of C, entire song)

A

I	IV	I	V	I	IV	I	V	I
C	F	C	G	C	F	C	G	C

14. "Let It Be," The Beatles, *Let It Be* (key of C, A section)

A

I	V	VI–	IV	I	V	IV	I	I	V	VI–	IV	I	V	IV	I
C	G	A–	F	C	G	F	C	C	G	A–	F	C	G	F	C

15. "Love Letters," Patti Austin, *The Real Me* (key of B♭, A section)

A

I		VI–		IV	Vsus4	I	
B♭	✗	G–	✗	E♭	F sus4	B♭	✗

16. "Love Is a Verb," John Mayer, *Born and Raised* (key of E, A section)

A

I	IV	Vsus4	I	**2**	I	IV	Vsus4	VI–	I	IV	Vsus4	I	**2**
E	A	B sus4	E	✗.	E	A	B sus4	C♯–	E	A	B sus4	E	✗.

17. "Mandeville," Bill Frisell, *Rarum V* (key of E, entire song)

A

I	IV	V	I	I	IV	V	I
E	A	B	E	E	A	B	E

B

IV	I	Vsus4	I	IV	I	Vsus4	I
A	E	B sus4	E	A	E	B sus4	E

18. "Ob-La-Di, Ob-La-Da," The Beatles, *White Album* (key of B♭, A section)

A

I	V	V	I	I	IV	I	V	I
B♭	F	F	B♭	B♭	E♭	B♭	F	B♭

19. "So Lonely," The Police, *Message in a Box* (key of C, entire song)

A

I	V	VI–	IV	**2**	**2**	**2**
C	G	A–	F	✗.	✗.	✗.

Answer Key

20. "Someone Like You," Adele, *21* (key of A, chorus)

| chorus |
| I   V   VI–   IV   2   2   2   I   V/3   VI–   IV   IV |
| A   E |F#–   D | %. | %. | %. | A   E/G# |F#–   D |2/4 D || |

21. "Stand by Me," Ben E. King, *Be My Valentine: From Him to Her* (key of A, entire song)

| A |
| I   VI–   IV   V   I |
| A | %. |F#– | %. | D | E | A | %. || |

22. "This Boy," The Beatles, *Meet the Beatles!* (key of D, A section)

| A |
| I   VI–   II–   V   2   2   2 |
| D   B– |E–   A | %. | %. | %. || |

23. "Viva La Vida," Coldplay, *Viva La Vida or Death and All His Friends* (key of Ab, A section)

| A |
| IV   Vsus4   I   VI–   IV   Vsus4   I   VI– |
| Db |Ebsus4 |Ab |F– |Db |Ebsus4 |Ab |F– || |

24. "You Are My Sunshine," Norman Blake, *Oh Brother, Where Art Thou?* (key of F#, entire song)

| A |
| I   IV   I   IV   I   I   V   I |
| F# | %. |B |F# |B |F# |F#   C# |F# || |

25. "You Send Me," Sam Cooke, *The Best of Sam Cooke* (key of G, A section)

| A |
| I   VI–   II–   V   2   2   2 |
| G   E– |A–   D | %. | %. | %. || |

Reading, Writing and Rhythmetic

Activity Seven

Chapter 8

Activity Five

1. "Afro Blue," Abbey Lincoln, *Abbey Is Blue*

2. "Ain't No Sunshine When She's Gone," Bill Withers, *The Best of Bill Withers*

3. "Another Day in Paradise," Phil Collins, *…But Seriously*

4. "Billie Jean," Michael Jackson, *Thriller*

5. "Blue Bossa," Joe Henderson, *Back Road*

6. "Evil Ways," Santana, *Santana*

7. "Equinox," John Coltrane, *Coltrane's Sound*

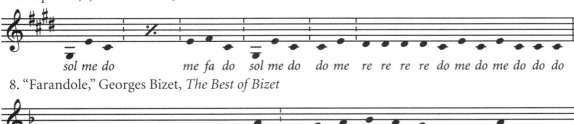

8. "Farandole," Georges Bizet, *The Best of Bizet*

Reading, Writing and Rhythmetic

9. "Fever," Peggy Lee, *The Best of Peggy Lee*

10. "Kiss from a Rose," Seal, *Seal: Hits*

11. "Mas Que Nada," Sergio Mendez and Brasil '66, *Greatest Hits*

12. "Mr. P.C.," John Coltrane, *Giant Steps*

13. "New World Symphony, 4th Movement," Dvořák, *Bernstein: The 1953 American Decca Recordings*

14. "Rolling in the Deep," Adele, *21*

15. "Russians," Sting, *The Dream of the Blue Turtles*

24. "While My Guitar Gently Weeps," The Beatles, *White Album*

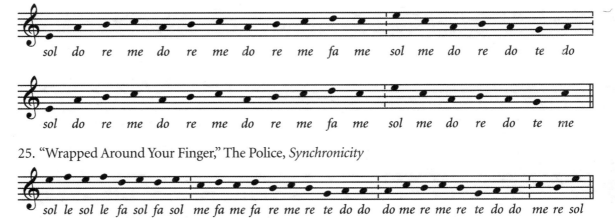

25. "Wrapped Around Your Finger," The Police, *Synchronicity*

ACTIVITY SEVEN

1. B   2. A   3. A   4. B
5. A   6. A   7. B   8. B
9. A   10. B   11. A   12. B

ACTIVITY NINE

1. Chet Baker

Answer Key

2. Michael Brecker

3. Paul Chambers

179

Reading, Writing and Rhythmetic

4. Bobby Darin

5. McCoy Tyner

Chapter 9

Activity Two

㊴ *do me | sol fa | me re | do*

㊵ *do te | le te | do sol | do*

㊶ *do te | le sol | do te | do*

㊷ *do me | re do | te sol | do*

㊸ *do re | me do | re sol | do*

㊹ *do me | re sol | sol te | do*

㊺ *do fa | do sol | le te | do*

㊻ *do me | re sol | do fa | do*

㊼ *do me | le sol | fa te | do*

㊽ *do fa | te me | le te | do*

Activity Three

(pick up measure)*do re me, sol do re, me fa sol, le ti re |*
do ti do, sol, do ti do, le | do ti do, sol le sol fa me re, me re do ti do re, me fa le |
sol, sol fa me, fa, fa me re | me sol, fa, me, re do ti | do, re, me, fa |
sol, le sol fa me, re me re, do ti | do…re…| me, fa, sol, le sol | do…

Activity Six

1. "Afro Blue," Abbey Lincoln, *Abbey Is Blue* (key of C–, 16-bar A section)

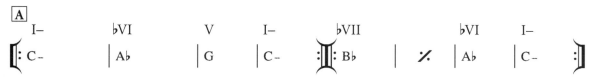

2. "Ain't No Sunshine When She's Gone," Bill Withers, *The Best of Bill Withers* (key of A–, 8-bar A section)

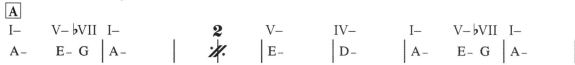

3. "All Along the Watchtower," Jimi Hendrix, *Electric Ladyland* (key of C–, 2-bar repeated phrase, entire song)

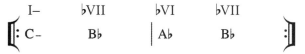

4. "The Animal," Steve Vai, *Passion and Warfare* (key of D–, 14-bar minor blues)

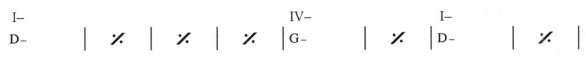

5. "Another Day in Paradise," Phil Collins, *…But Seriously* (key of F♯–, 2-bar repeated phrase, A section)

6. "Beat It," Michael Jackson, *Thriller* (key of E♭–, 8-bar A section)

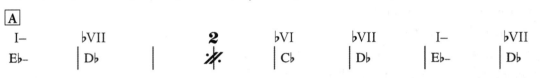

7. "Black Orpheus," Paul Desmond, *Take Ten* (key of G–, first 5 bars)

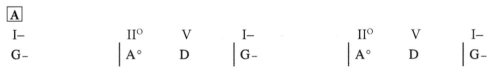

8. "Blue Bossa," Joe Henderson, *Back Road* (key of C–, 8-bar A section)

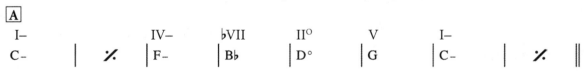

9. "Contemplation," McCoy Tyner, *The Real McCoy* (key of C–, 16-bar phrase, entire song)

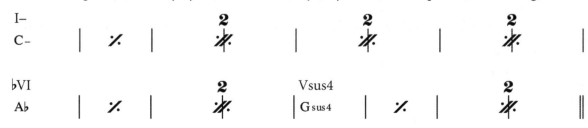

Answer Key

10. "Django," Grant Green, *Idle Moments* (key of F–, 8-bar intro/same as last 8 bars of song)

[Intro]

I–	IV–	V	I–	I–	IV–	V	I–
F–	| B♭–	| C	| F–	| F–	| B♭–	| C	| F– ‖

11. "Equinox," John Coltrane, *Coltrane's Sound* (key of C♯–, 12-bar minor blues)

I–			**2**	IV–	
C♯–	| ✗	|	✗	| F♯–	| ✗ |

I–		♭VI	V	I–	
C♯–	| ✗	| A	| G♯	| C♯–	| ✗ ‖

12. "Fever," Peggy Lee, *The Best of Peggy Lee* (key of A–, 8-bar phrase, entire song)

I–		**2**	**2**	V	I–
A–	| ✗	| ✗	| ✗	| E	| A– ‖

13. "Fragile," Sting, *Nothing Like the Sun* (key of E–, 8-bar A section, 8-bar B section)

[A]   [B]

I–	IV–	V	I–	♭VI	V	I– V	I–
‖: E–	| A–	| B	| E–	:‖: C	| B	| E– B	| E– :‖

14. "House of the Rising Sun," The Animals, *The Animals* (key of A–, 11-bar phrase, entire song)

I–	♭III	IV–	♭VI	I–	♭III	V	I–	♭III	IV–	♭VI
A–	C	| D–	F	| A–	C	| E	| A–	C	| D–	F |

I–	V	I–	♭III	IV–	♭VI	I–	V	I–	V	
A–	E	| A–	C	| D–	F	| A–	E	| A–	E ‖

15. "Livin' on a Prayer," Bon Jovi, *Cross Road* (key of E–, 8-bar A section)

[A]

I–		**2**	♭VI	♭VII	I–	
E–	| ✗	| ✗	| C	| D	| E–	| ✗ ‖

Reading, Writing and Rhythmetic

16. "Mr. P.C.," John Coltrane, *Giant Steps* (key of C–, 12-bar minor blues)

17. "Red Rain," Peter Gabriel, *So* (key of E–, 10-bar B section, chorus, song starts with B section)

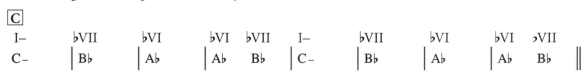

18. "Rolling in the Deep," Adele, *21* (key of C–, 8-bar C section, chorus)

19. "Sixth Sense," Dave Brubeck, *In Their Own Sweet Way* (key of G–, 8-bar A section)

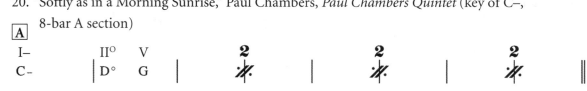

20. "Softly as in a Morning Sunrise," Paul Chambers, *Paul Chambers Quintet* (key of C–, 8-bar A section)

21. "Song for My Father," Horace Silver, *Song for My Father* (key of F–, 8-bar A section)

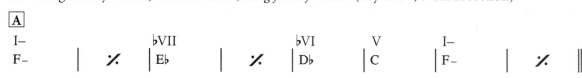

ANSWER KEY

22. "Tango Till They're Sore," Tom Waits, *Rain Dogs* (key of F–, 8-bar A section, 8-bar B section)

A

I–	IV–	V	I–	I–	IV–	V	I–
F–	|Bb–	|C	|F–	|F–	|Bb–	|C	|F– |

B

IV–	V	I–	bVI	V	I–	IV– V	I–
Bb–	|C	|F–	|Db	|C	|F–	|Bb– C	|F– ‖

23. "Three Sheets to the Wind," Joe Satriani, *Unstoppable Momentum* (key of C–, 8-bar A section)

A

I–		bVII		IV–		I–	
C–	| ∕.	|Bb	| ∕.	|F–	| ∕.	|C–	| ∕. ‖

24. "The Thrill Is Gone," B. B. King & Eric Clapton, *80* (key of A–, 12-bar minor blues)

I–		**2**	IV–	I–	bVI	V	I–	
A–	| ∕.	| ∕.	|D–	| ∕. |A–	| ∕. |F	|E	|A–	| ∕. ‖

25. "You Know I'm No Good," Amy Winehouse, *Back to Black* (key of D–, 8-bar A section (verse), 8-bar B section (pre-chorus), 8-bar C section (chorus, modulates to key of A–)

A

I–	IV–	V	I–	I–	IV–	V	I–
D–	|G–	|A	|D–	|D–	|G–	|A	|D– ‖

B

IV–		II		bIII		II	V
G–	| ∕.	|E	| ∕.	|F	| ∕.	|E	|A ‖

C (key change to A minor)

IV–	I–	V	I–	IV–	I–	V	I–
D–	|A–	|E	|A–	|D–	|A–	|E	|A– ‖

Reading, Writing and Rhythmetic

Activity Seven

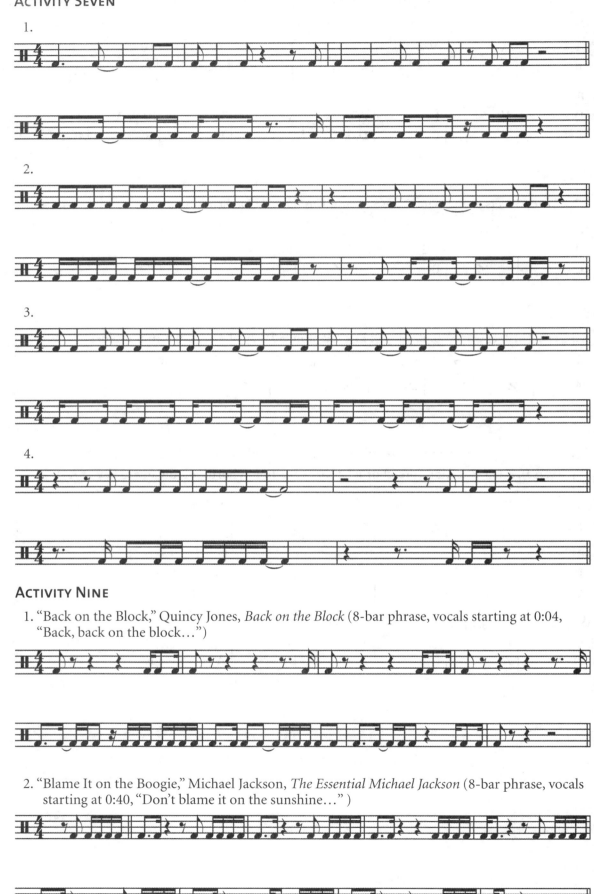

Activity Nine

1. "Back on the Block," Quincy Jones, *Back on the Block* (8-bar phrase, vocals starting at 0:04, "Back, back on the block…")

2. "Blame It on the Boogie," Michael Jackson, *The Essential Michael Jackson* (8-bar phrase, vocals starting at 0:40, "Don't blame it on the sunshine…")

ANSWER KEY

3. "Chameleon," Herbie Hancock, *Head Hunters* (4-bar phrase played 4x, horn melody starting at 1:29)

4. "Get Up, Stand Up," Bob Marley, *Burnin'* (8-bar phrase, vocals starting at 0:08, "Get up, stand up...")

5. "Human Nature," Michael Jackson, *Thriller* (8-bar phrase, vocals starting at 0:50, "If they say why...")

6. "Hylife," Marcus Miller, *Afrodeezia* (8-bar phrase, horn melody starting at 1:12)

7. "Kalimba," Sergio Mendes, *Brasiliero* (14-bar vocal phrase, starting at 0:35)

READING, WRITING AND RHYTHMETIC

8. "Rockit," Herbie Hancock, *Future Shock* (8-bar phrase, synth melody starting at 0:44)

9. "Say It Loud," James Brown, *Say It Loud—I'm Black and I'm Proud* (10-bar phrase, background horns starting at 0:03)

10. "Strasbourg/St. Denis," Roy Hargrove, *Earfood* (8-bar phrase, horn melody starting at 0:19)

ACTIVITY TEN

55

I	V	♭VI	♭VII	I	
C	G	A♭	B♭	C	‖

56

I	VI–	IV	IV–	I	
C	A–	F	F–	C	‖

57

I	♭VII	♭VI	V	I	
C	B♭	A♭	G	C	‖

58

I	IV	♭VII	V	I	
C	F	B♭	G	C	‖

59

I	IV	IV–	♭VII	I	
C	F	F–	B♭	C	‖

CHAPTER 10

ACTIVITY TWO

1. "Bag's Groove," Milt Jackson, *The Birth of the MJQ:* A A A
2. "Bessie's Blues," John Coltrane, *Crescent:* A A B
3. "Born Under a Bad Sign," Albert King, *Born Under a Bad Sign:* A A B
4. "C Jam Blues," Duke Ellington, *Duke Ellington's Greatest Hits:* A A A
5. "Crossroads," Cream, *Wheels of Fire:* A A B
6. "Freddie Freeloader," Miles Davis, *Kind of Blue:* A A B
7. "Gate Walks to Board," Clarence "Gatemouth" Brown, *Texas Swing:* A A A
8. "Going to Chicago Blues," Ernestine Anderson, *When the Sun Goes Down:* A A B
9. "Hound Dog," Elvis Presley, *The Essential Elvis Presley…:* A A B
10. "If You're Goin' to the City," Mose Allison, *The Best of Mose Allison:* A A B
11. "Johnny B. Goode," Chuck Berry, *The Anthology:* A A A
12. "Lateral Climb," Robben Ford, *Truth:* A A B (6 bars)
13. "Love Me Like a Man," Bonnie Raitt, *The Bonnie Raitt Collection:* A A B
14. "Night Train," James Brown, *Gold: James Brown:* A A A
15. "Saturday Afternoon Blues," Ben Webster, *The Soul of Ben Webster:* A A A
16. "Stagger Lee," Taj Mahal, *Giant Step:* A A B (5 bars)
17. "She Walks Right In," Professor Longhair & the Meters, *Best of Professor Longhair:* A A A
18. "Stormy Monday," The Allman Brothers, *The Allman Brothers Band at Fillmore East:* A A B
19. "Sweet Home Chicago," Robert Johnson, *The Complete Recordings:* A A B
20. "The Thrill Is Gone," B. B. King & Eric Clapton, *80:* A A B

ACTIVITY THREE

1. "Blowin' in the Wind," Bob Dylan, *The Freewheelin' Bob Dylan*
   intro │ A A A B │ A A A B │ A A A B │ B
2. "Carey," Joni Mitchell, *Blue*
   intro │ A A B │ A A B │ A A B │ A A B
3. "Compared to What," Less McCann & Eddie Harris, *Swiss Movement*
   long intro │ A B instr │ A B instr │ A B instr │ A B instr │ (long inter, like intro) │
   A B instr │ extended ending
4. "Get Up, Stand Up," Bob Marley, *Legend*
   intro │ B B A A │ B B A A │ B B A A │ B B B (fade)
5. "Give Peace a Chance," John Lennon, *Serve3: Artists Against Hunger & Poverty*
   intro │ A B │ A B │ A B │ A B │ then B is stated six more times
6. "Higher Ground," Stevie Wonder, *Innervisions*
   intro │ A A B │ A A B │ repeat last 4 of B as fade ending

READING, WRITING AND RHYTHMETIC

7. "Hotel California," The Eagles, *Hotel California*
   intro (instr A A) | A A B | A A B | A A | solo on 5 A's (fade out)

8. "Human Nature," Michael Jackson, *Thriller*
   intro | A A B | A B | inter, similar to intro | A B | B B | ending (similar to intro)

9. "I Just Called to Say I Love You," Stevie Wonder, *The Woman in Red*
   intro | A A B | A A B | B (last two B's modulate up ½ step) | ending

10. "I Still Haven't Found What I'm Looking For," U2, *The Joshua Tree*
    intro | A A B | A A B | instr on A | A A B B | ending

11. "Iko Iko," The Dixie Cups, *Chapel of Love*
    intro | A B inter | A B inter | A B inter | A B inter | B | ending

12. "Jingle Bells," Roberta Radley, *Swing-a-Jing-a -Lingin'*
    A A B B | A A B B | B B | ending

13. "Let It Be," The Beatles, *Let It Be*
    intro | A B | A B | (instr inter) | A (solo) B | A B | ending

14. "My Girl," The Temptations, *The Temptations Sing Smokey*
    intro | A B | A B | (8 bar interlude sets up ½ step modulation) | A B | ending

15. "Oh! Suzanna," Eight Hand String Band, *Listen to the Mockingbird*
    (intro: instr A A B) | A A B instr | A A B | (instr A A B) | A A B B | ending

16. "Puff the Magic Dragon," Peter Paul & Mary, *The Very Best of Peter, Paul & Mary*
    intro | A B | A B | A A B

17. "Silver Bells," Johnny Mathis, *Merry Christmas*
    intro | B A B | (original lyric intro) | B | ending

18. "Stand by Me," Ben E. King, *The Very Best of Ben E. King*
    A A B | A A B | (instr on two A's) | B B

19. "Sunrise, Sunset," *Fiddler on the Roof* soundtrack
    intro | A A B B | inter | A A B | ending

20. "Wrapped Around Your Finger," The Police, *Syncronicity*
    intro | A A B | inter (like intro) | A B inter | A B inter | ending (like intro)

Chapter 11

Activity One

1. "All I Have to Do Is Dream," The Everly Brothers, *The Very Best of the Everly Brothers*: A A B A
2. "All of Me," Billie Holiday, *The Essential Billie Holiday*: A B A C
3. "Bad Moon Rising," Creedence Clearwater Revival, *Green River*: A B A B
4. "Be Good," Gregory Porter, *Be Good*: A A B A
5. "Beautiful Day," U2, *U218 Singles*: A B A B
6. "Blue Skies," Willie Nelson, *Stardust*: A A B A
7. "Come Rain or Come Shine," Art Blakey and the Jazz Messengers, *Moanin'*: A B A C
8. "Don't Know Why," Norah Jones, *Come Away with Me*: A A B A
9. "Fly Me to the Moon," Frank Sinatra, *It Might as Well Be Spring*: A B A B
10. "I Got Rhythm," The Sisters of Swing, *Mood Indigo*: A A B A
11. "My Romance," Ella Fitzgerald, *Ella Fitzgerald Sings the Rodgers & Hart Book*: A B A C
12. "Norwegian Wood," The Beatles, *Rubber Soul*: A B A B
13. "On Green Dolphin Street," Miles Davis, *Kind of Blue*: A B A C
14. "Proud Mary," Tina Turner, *All the Best: The Hits*: A B A B
15. "Rudolph the Red-Nosed Reindeer," Roberta Radley, *Swing-a-Jing-a-Lingin'*: A A B A
16. "Shoot the Moon," Norah Jones, *Come Away with Me*: A B A B
17. "Surfer Girl," The Beach Boys, *Surfer Girl*: A A B A
18. "Tango Till They're Sore," Tom Waits, *Rain Dogs*: A B A B
19. "This Boy," The Beatles, *Meet the Beatles!*: A A B A
20. "When Lights Are Low," Miles Davis, *Blue Haze*: A A B A
21. "We Can Work It Out," The Beatles, *Rubber Soul*: A A B A

Activity Four

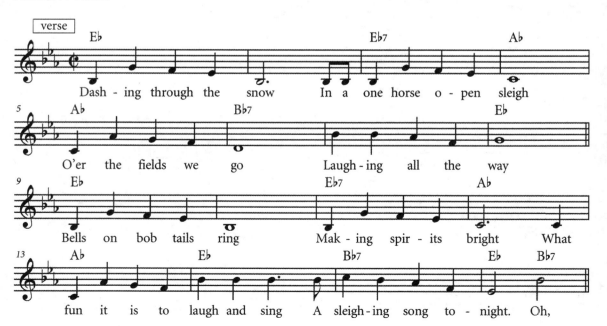

Answer Key

ACTIVITY FOUR (cont'd)

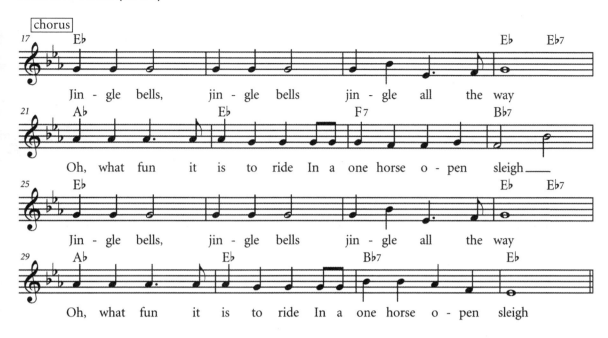

ACTIVITY SIX:

1. "Blue Rondo à la Turk," Dave Brubeck, *Time Out*: 9/8 (2+2+2+3)
2. "Countdown," Dave Brubeck, *Time in Outer Space*: 5/4 (3+2)
3. "Do What You Like," Blind Faith, *Blind Faith*: 5/4 (3+2)
4. "In What Direction Are You Headed?" Lee Morgan, *Lee Morgan*, 7/4 (2+2+3)
5. "Living in the Past," Jethro Tull, *Stand Up*: 5/4 (3+2)
6. "Mission Impossible theme," Lalo Schifrin & John E. Davis, *The Best of Mission Impossible–Then and Now*: 5/4 (3+2)
7. "Money," Pink Floyd, *The Dark Side of the Moon*: 7/4 (3+2+2)
8. "Prints Tie," Bobby Hutcherson, *San Francisco*: 7/4 (2+2+3)
9. "River Man," Nick Drake, *Five Leaves Left*, or Brad Mehldau, *Songs: the Art of the Trio, Vol. 3*: 5/4 (3+2)
10. "Seven Days," Sting, *Ten Summoner's Tales*: 5/4 (3+2)
11. "Solsbury Hill," Peter Gabriel, *The Round Ones*: 7/4 Intro, (3+2+2), then at vocal entrance (2+2+3)
12. "Take Five," Dave Brubeck, *Time Out*: 5/4 (3+2)
13. "Unsquare Dance," Dave Brubeck, *Time Further Out*: 7/4 (2+2+3)

Chapter 12

Activity One

1. "At Last," Etta James, *At Last!*

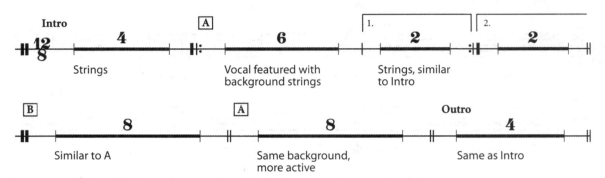

Comments: solo vocal featured throughout; Intro and Outro are "bookends."

2. "It Was a Very Good Year," Frank Sinatra, *Nothing But the Best*

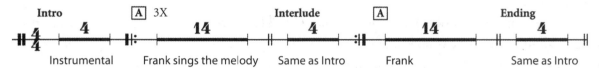

Comments: Intro, Interlude and Ending are the same theme with different orchestration. The orchestration of the arrangement is of equal interest to the melody—as character ages with each verse, the orchestration compliments this "aging."

3. "Surfer Girl," The Beach Boys, *Surfer Girl*

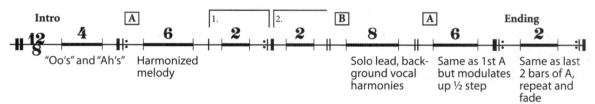

Comments: arrangement features Beach Boys vocal harmonies and uses modulation to develop the arrangement at the very end.

4. "We Can Work It Out," The Beatles, *Rubber Soul*

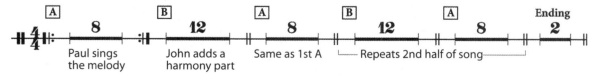

Comments: no Introduction, song sections are unequal length (8 and 12 bars). Repeating only the 2nd half of a song is common, repeating from the Chorus on out.

ANSWER KEY

5. "All I Have to Do Is Dream," The Everly Brothers, *The Very Best of the Everly Brothers*

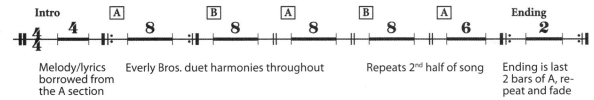

Comments: Intro borrows from A section; Intro and Ending are the same "bookends." Similar to "We Can Work It Out" the song repeats from the 2nd half.

6. "You Send Me," Sam Cooke, *The Best of Sam Cooke*

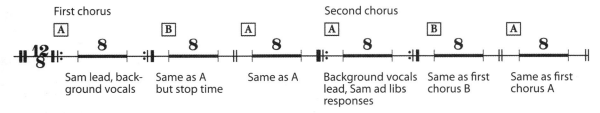

Comments: no Intro, or ending; twice through the song—the only difference in each chorus is the arrangement of first 2 A sections for variety.

7. "Rudolph the Red-Nosed Reindeer," Roberta Radley, *Swing-a-Jing-a-Lingin'*

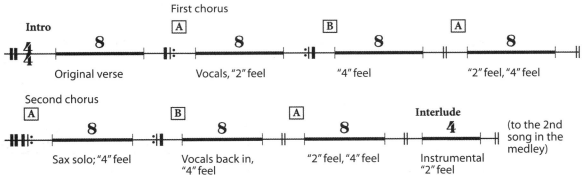

Comments: the Intro uses original song verse; chart features 3-part vocals. It's fairly common to have an instrumental solo for the first half of the second chorus; I've noted the different rhythm section time feels as points of interest; a brief interlude links to the second song, establishing a key change in the medley.

8. "I Just Called to Say I Love You," Stevie Wonder, *The Woman in Red*

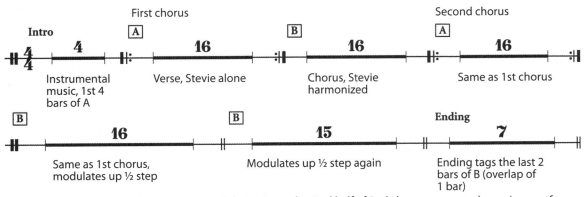

Comments: Intro borrows from A verse; modulation is used in 2nd half of 2nd chorus to create drama (many of Stevie's arrangements use modulation for added interest).

READING, WRITING AND RHYTHMETIC

9. "Shoot the Moon," Norah Jones, *Come Away with Me*

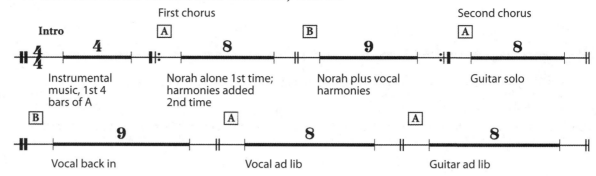

Comments: similar to "I Just Called…" in that the Intro borrows from the A section; this song has a 9-bar B section; the 2nd chorus features improvisation for variety and also changes the form to A B A A.

10. "Hotel California," The Eagles, *Hotel California*

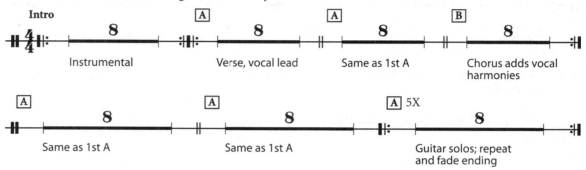

Comments: this arrangement primarily features guitar solos; notice that the chorus is stated only one time, more "verse heavy."

11. "All Along the Watchtower," Bob Dylan, *John Wesley Harding*

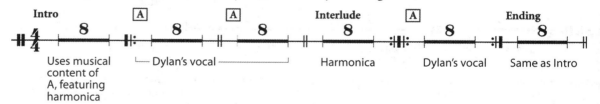

Comments: this arrangement uses a string of verses broken up by occasional instrumental interludes; Intro, Interludes and Ending share the same material.

12. "All Along the Watchtower," Jimi Hendrix, *Electric Ladyland*

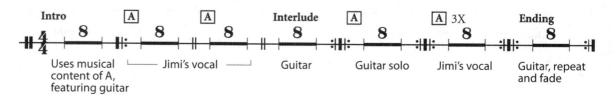

Comments: almost identical to Dylan's arrangement, the only difference being the greater use of guitar solos.

Answer Key

13. "But Not for Me," Miles Davis, *Bag's Groove (Take Two)*

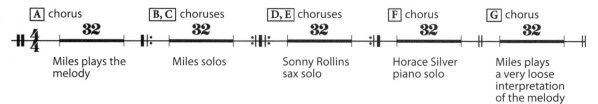

Comments: song form is 32-bar A B A C; the focus of the arrangement is the performers' improvisations.

14. "But Not for Me," Chet Baker, *Chet Baker Sings*

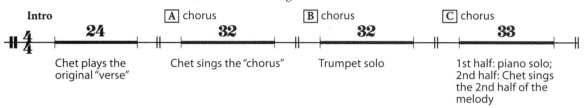

Comments: compared to Miles' version, there is more of a distinct balance between presenting the song's elements and improvisations; the original "verse" is used as the introduction; the term "chorus" in this example means once through the entire song.

15. "Lullaby of Birdland," Sarah Vaughan & Clifford Brown, *The Definitive Sarah Vaughan*

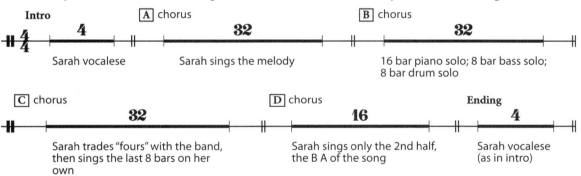

Comments: in this arrangement the Intro and Ending are "bookends"; Sarah is featured as the soloist and singing the melody; for the last chorus (D) she sings only the 2nd half of the song (as in some earlier arrangements we've seen).

Activity Two

1. "Afro Blue," Abbey Lincoln, *Abbey Is Blue:* Bridge
2. "Another Day in Paradise," Phil Collins, *…But Seriously:* Bridge
3. "Billie Jean," Michael Jackson, *Thriller:* Chorus
4. "Don't Stop Believin'," Journey, *Escape:* Chorus
5. "Don't Take Away My Heaven," Aaron Neville, *The Grand Tour:* Bridge
6. "Fix You," Coldplay, *X&Y:* Second Chorus
7. "Hold My Hand," Hootie and the Blowfish, *Cracked Rear View:* Chorus
8. "Just My Imagination," The Temptations, *Sky's the Limit:* Bridge
9. "Livin on a Prayer," Bon Jovi, *Cross Road:* Chorus
10. "Ob-La-Di, Ob-La-Da, The Beatles, *White Album:* Bridge
11. "Piano Man," Billy Joel, *Piano Man:* Chorus
12. "Rolling in the Deep," Adele, *21:* Chorus

Reading, Writing and Rhythmetic

ACTIVITY SEVEN

1. "All You Need Is Love," The Beatles, *Magical Mystery Tour*

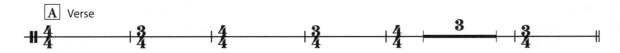

2. "Hiding My Heart," Adele, *21*

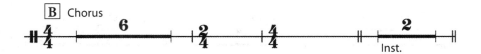

3. "I Say a Little Prayer," Dionne Warwick, *Dionne Warwick: Her All-Time Greatest Hits*

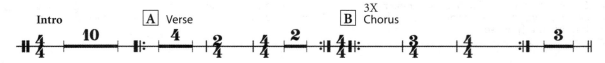

4. "Love Letters," Patti Austin, *The Real Me*

5. "Ponta de Areia," Wayne Shorter, *Native Dancer*

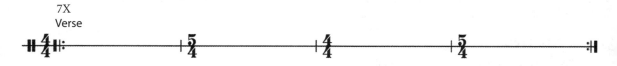

6. "She's Always a Woman," Billy Joel, *The Stranger*

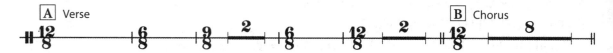

7. "Shoot the Moon," Norah Jones, *Come Away with Me*

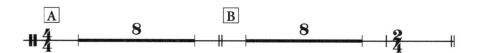

ANSWER KEY

ACTIVITY EIGHT

1. "Cherokee," Ahmad Jamal, *The Best of Ahmad Jamal*
   A section is fast 4/4
   B is slow 3/4 waltz where 4/4 ♩ = 3/4 ♪

2. "Four by Five," McCoy Tyner, *The Real McCoy*
   A section is 4/4
   B section is 5/4, ♩ = ♩

3. "How My Heart Sings," *Riverside Profiles Bill Evans*
   A section is 3/4
   B section is 4/4, ♩ = ♩

4. "In What Direction Are You Headed?" Lee Morgan, *Lee Morgan*
   A 8/4
   interlude 1 7/4
   B 7/4 + one 8/4
   interlude 2 8/4
   solos in 8/4 ♩ = ♩

5. "Love Is Stronger than Justice," Sting, *Ten Summoner's Tales*
   Verse (A) is in 7/8
   Chorus (B) is in 4/4 ♪ = ♪

6. "Lucy in the Sky with Diamonds," The Beatles, *Sargent Pepper's Lonely Hearts Club Band*
   Verse (A) is in 3/4
   B is in 4/4 where 3/4 ♩. = 4/4 ♩

7. "Whipping Post," The Allman Brothers, *Legendary Hits*
   intro is in 11/8
   tune is in 12/8 ♪ = ♪

199

DISCOGRAPHY

Song	Composer	Artist/Album
A Little Night Music	W. A. Mozart	
Afro Blue	Mongo Santamaría	Abbey Lincoln: Abbey Is Blue
Ain't No Sunshine When She's Gone	Bill Withers	Bill Withers: The Best of Bill Withers
Ain't Too Proud to Beg	Norman Whitfield, Edward Holland, Jr.	Temptations: Motown's 1's
Alice in Wonderland	Sammy Fair, Bob Hilliard	Bill Evans: Sunday at the Village Vanguard
All Along the Watchtower	Bob Dylan	Bob Dylan: John Wesley Harding
—	—	Jimi Hendrix: Electric Ladyland
All Blues	Miles Davis	Miles Davis: Kind of Blue
All I Have to Do Is Dream	Felice & Boudleaux Bryant	The Everly Brothers: The Very Best of the Everly Brothers
All of Me	Gerald Marks, Seymour Simons	Billie Holiday: The Essential Billie Holiday
All You Need Is Love	Lennon & McCartney	The Beatles: Magical Mystery Tour
Always with You, Always with Me	Joe Satriani	Joe Satriani: Surfing with the Alien
Amazing Grace	Traditional (words John Newton)	Leann Rimes: You Light Up My Life
Ana Maria	Wayne Shorter	Wayne Shorter: Native Dancer
Angels We Have Heard on High (Gloria)	Traditional	
Another Day in Paradise	Phil Collins	Phil Collins: …But Seriously
Armando's Rhumba	Chick Corea	Chick Corea: My Spanish Heart
At Last	Mack Gordon, Harry Warren	Etta James: At Last!
Au Privave	Charlie Parker	Charlie Parker: The Genius of Charlie Parker
Autumn Leaves	Joseph Kosma	Eva Cassidy: Songbird
Back on the Block	Jones, Rod Temperton, Siedah Garrett, Caiphus Semenya, Ice-T, Melle Mel, Kane, Kool Moe Dee	Quincy Jones: Back on the Block
Bad Moon Rising	John Fogerty	Creedence Clearwater Revival: Green River
Bag's Groove	Milt Jackson	Milt Jackson: The Birth of the MJQ
Beat It	Michael Jackson	Michael Jackson: Thriller
Beautiful Day	U2	U2: U218 Singles
Be Good (Lion's Song)	Gregory Porter	Gregory Porter: Be Good
Be Ever Wonderful	Larry Dunn, Maurice White	Earth, Wind and Fire: The Eternal Dance
Bessie's Blues	John Coltrane	John Coltrane: Crescent

READING, WRITING AND RHYTHMETIC

Song	Composer	Artist/Album
Billie Jean	Michael Jackson	Michael Jackson: Thriller
Birdland	Joe Zawinul	Weather Report: Heavy Weather
Birthday	Lennon & McCartney	The Beatles: White Album
Bits and Pieces	Dave Clark, Mike Smith	Dave Clark Five: Glad All Over
Black or White	Michael Jackson, Bill Bottrell	Michael Jackson: Dangerous
Black Orpheus	Luiz Bonfá, Antônio Maria	Paul Desmond: Take Ten
Blackbird	Lennon & McCartney	The Beatles: White Album
Blame It on the Boogie	Michael George Jackson-Clarke, David Jackson, Elmar Krohn	Michael Jackson: The Essential Michael Jackson
Blowin' in the Wind	Bob Dylan	Bob Dylan: The Freewheelin' Bob Dylan
—	—	Stevie Wonder: Up-Tight
Blue Bossa	Kenny Dorham	Joe Henderson: Back Road
Blue Eyes Cryin' in the Rain	Fred Rose	Willie Nelson: Red Headed Stranger
Blue Moon	Richard Rodgers & Lorenz Hart	Billie Holiday: Solitude
Blue Rondo à la Turk	Dave Brubeck	Dave Brubeck: Time Out
Blue Skies	Irving Berlin	Willie Nelson: Stardust
Blues March	Benny Golson	Art Blakey & The Jazz Messengers: Moanin'
Blues on the Corner	McCoy Tyner	McCoy Tyner: The Real McCoy
Born Under a Bad Sign	Booker T. Jones, William Bell	Albert King: Born Under a Bad Sign
Breaking the Girl	Flea, John Frusciante, Anthony Kiedis, Chad Smith	Red Hot Chili Peppers: Greatest Hits
Burning Down the House	Byrne, Weymouth, Harrison, Frantz	Talking Heads: Speaking in Tongues
But Not for Me	George Gershwin	Chet Baker: Chet Baker Sings
—	—	Miles Davis: Bag's Groove (Take Two)
Bye Bye Blackbird	Ray Henderson, Mort Dixon	Miles Davis: Round About Midnight
Call Me Back Again	Paul McCartney	Wings: Venus and Mars
C Jam Blues	Duke Ellington	Duke Ellington: Duke Ellington's Greatest Hits
Can't Help Falling in Love	Hugo Peretti, Luigi Creatore & George David Weiss	Elvis Presley: Blue Hawaii
Canon in D	Johann Pachelbel	
Carey	Joni Mitchell	Joni Mitchell: Blue
Carmina Burana	Carl Orff	
Carolina in My Mind	James Taylor	James Taylor: Greatest Hits, Vol. 1
Chameleon	Herbie Hancock	Herbie Hancock: Head Hunters
Cherokee	Ray Noble	Ahmad Jamal: The Best of Ahmad Jamal
Chim Chim Cher-ee	Robert B. Sherman, Richard M. Sherman	Mary Poppins soundtrack
Come Away with Me	Norah Jones	Norah Jones: Come Away with Me

DISCOGRAPHY

Song	Composer	Artist/Album
Come Rain or Come Shine	Harold Arlen, Johnny Mercer	Art Blakey and the Jazz Messengers: Moanin'
Compared to What	Gene McDaniels	Less McCann & Eddie Harris: Swiss Movement
Con Alma	Dizzy Gillispie	Stan Getz: The Very Best of Stan Getz
Contemplation	McCoy Tyner	McCoy Tyner: The Real McCoy
Countdown	Dave Brubeck	Dave Brubeck: Time in Outer Space
Crossroads	Robert Johnson	Cream: Wheels of Fire
Daisy Bell (Bicycle Built for Two)	Harry Dacre	Nat King Cole: Those Lazy Hazy Crazy Days of Summer
Dancing Queen	Benny Andersson, Björn Ulvaeus & Stig Anderson	ABBA: Arrival
Dat Dere	Bobby Timmons	Art Blakey and the Jazz Messengers: The Big Beat
Django	John Lewis	Grant Green: Idle Moments
Do What You Like	Ginger Baker	Blind Faith: Blind Faith
Don't Give Up	Peter Gabriel	Peter Gabriel: So
Don't Know Why	Jesse Harris	Norah Jones: Come Away with Me
Don't Stop Believin'	Jonathan Cain, Steve Perry & Neal Schon	Journey: Escape
Don't Take Away My Heaven	Aaron Neville	Aaron Neville: The Grand Tour
Don't Try to Explain	Kevin Moore	Keb' Mo': Keb' Mo'
Don't Worry, Be Happy	Bobby McFerrin	Bobby McFerrin: Simple Pleasures
Doxy	Sonny Rollins	Dexter Gordon: Both Sides of Midnight
Edelweiss	Richard Rodgers	Sound of Music soundtrack
Eleanor Rigby	Lennon & McCartney	The Beatles: Revolver
Equinox	John Coltrane	John Coltrane: Coltrane's Sound
Esconjuros	Aldir Blanc, Carlos "Guinga" Escobar	Serge Mendes: Brasilerio
Europa	Carlos Santana, Tom Coster	Carlos Santana: Precious Lounge Moments
Every Breath You Take	Sting	The Police: Synchronicity
Every Day I Have the Blues	Aaron "Pinetop" and Milton or Marion Sparks	John Mayer: Where the Light Is: John Mayer Live…
Evil Ways	Clarence "Sonny" Henry	Santana: Santana
First Suite in D (Masterpiece Theater theme song)	Jean-Joseph Mouret	New York Trumpet Ensemble: 100 Hits: Greatest Classical Composers
Farandole	Georges Bizet	Georges Bizet: The Best of Bizet
Fever	Eddie Cooley, Otis Blackwell	Peggy Lee: The Best of Peggy Lee
Fire	Jimi Hendrix	Jimi Hendrix: Are You Experienced
Fishin' Blues	Henry Thomas	Taj Mahal: The Best of Taj Mahal
Fix You	Coldplay	Coldplay: X & Y
Fly Me to the Moon	Bart Howard	Frank Sinatra: It Might as Well Be Spring
Four	Eddie "Cleanhead" Vinson	Miles Davis: Workin' with the Miles Davis Quintet
Four by Five	McCoy Tyner	McCoy Tyner: The Real McCoy

READING, WRITING AND RHYTHMETIC

Song	Composer	Artist/Album
Four on Six	Wes Montgomery	Wynton Kelly Trio, Wes Montgomery: Smokin' at the Half Note
Fragile	Sting	Sting: Nothing Like the Sun
Freddie Freeloader	Miles Davis	Miles Davis: Kind of Blue
Funeral March	Frédéric Chopin	
Gate Walks to Board	Clarence "Gatemouth" Brown	Clarence "Gatemouth" Brown: Texas Swing
Get Up, Stand Up	Bob Marley	Bob Marley: Burnin'
Give Peace a Chance	John Lennon	John Lennon: Serve3: Artists Against Hunger & Poverty
Going to Chicago Blues	Wm. James "Count" Basie	Ernestine Anderson: When the Sun Goes Down
Goodbye Yellow Brick Road	Elton John, Bernie Taupin	Elton John: Goodbye Yellow Brick Road
Gravity	John Mayer	John Mayer: Continuum
Happy Xmas (War is Over)	John Lennon, Yoko Ono	John Lennon: Power to the People: The Hits
Have a Heart	Bonnie Hayes	Bonnie Raitt: Nick of Time
Here Comes the Sun	George Harrison	The Beatles: Abbey Road
Hey Joe	Billy Roberts	Jimi Hendrix: Are You Experienced
Hey, Soul Sister	Patrick Monahan, Amund Bjørklund, & Espen Lind	Train: Save Me, San Francisco
Hiding My Heart (Away)	Tim Hanseroth	Adele: 21 (UK Limited Edition)
Higher Ground	Stevie Wonder	Stevie Wonder: Innervisions
Held My Hand	Mark Bryan, Dean Felber, Darius Rucker & Jim Sonefeld	Hootie and the Blowfish: Cracked Rear View
Hotel California	Don Henley, Glen Frey, Don Felder	The Eagles: Hotel California
Hound Dog	Jerry Leiber, Mike Stoller	Elvis Presley: The Essential Elvis Presley…
House of the Rising Sun	Traditional	Animals: The Animals
How My Heart Sings	Earl Zindars	Bill Evans Trio: Riverside Profiles Bill Evans
Human Nature	Steve Porcaro, John Bettis	Michael Jackson: Thriller
Humoresque no. 7 in G-flat Major, Opus 101	Antonín Dvořák	Classic Perlman: Rhapsody
Hylife	Marcus Miller	Marcus Miller: Afrodeezia
I Got It Goin' On	Tone Lōc	Us3: Hand on the Torch
I Got Rhythm	George Gershwin	The Sisters of Swing: Mood Indigo
I Just Called to Say I Love You	Stevie Wonder	Stevie Wonder: The Woman in Red
I Me Mine	George Harrison	The Beatles: Let It Be
I Mean You	Thelonious Monk	Thelonious Monk: Art Blakey's Jazz Messengers with Thelonious Monk
I Only Have Eyes for You	Harry Warren, Al Dubin	The Flamingos: Flamingo Serenade
I Say a Little Prayer	Burt Bacharach, Hal David	Dionne Warwick: Dionne Warwick: Her All-Time Greatest Hits
I Still Haven't Found What I'm Looking For	U2	U2: The Joshua Tree
I Want to Hold Your Hand	Lennon & McCartney	The Beatles: Meet the Beatles!

DISCOGRAPHY

Song	Composer	Artist/Album
I Want You Back	Berry Gordy, Freddie Perren, Alphonzo Mizell, Deke Richards	Jackson 5: The Essential Michael Jackson
I Will Survive	Freddie Perren, Dino Fekaris	Gloria Gaynor: I Will Survive
I'm Walking to New Orleans	Bobby Charles	Fats Domino: Hit's of the 60s
If You're Goin' to the City	Mose Allison	Mose Allison: The Best of Mose Allison
Iko Iko	James "Sugar Boy" Crawford, Barbara Hawkins, Rosa Hawkins	The Dixie Cups: Chapel of Love
In My Life	Lennon & McCartney	The Beatles: Rubber Soul
In the Midnight Hour	Wilson Pickett, Steve Cropper	Wilson Pickett: The Very Best of Wilson Pickett
In What Direction Are You Headed?	Harold Mabern	Lee Morgan: Lee Morgan
In Your Eyes	Peter Gabriel	Peter Gabriel: Secret World Tour, 1993
Isn't She Lovely	Stevie Wonder	Stevie Wonder: Songs in the Key of Life
It Was a Very Good Year	Ervin Drake	Frank Sinatra: Nothing But the Best
Jazz	Bobby Hutcherson	Bobby Hutcherson: San Francisco
Jeepers Creepers	Harry Warren, Johnny Mercer	Louis Armstrong: C'est Si Bon
Jingle Bells	James Lord Pierpont	Harry Connick Jr.: What a Night!– A Christmas Album
—	—	Bing Crosby & the Andrew Sisters: White Christmas
—	—	Ella Fitzgerald: Ella Wishes You a Swinging Christmas
—	—	Johnny Mathis: Christmas Eve with Johnny Mathis
—	—	Roberta Radley: Swing-a-Jing-a-Lingin'
—	—	Frank Sinatra: A Jolly Christmas from Frank Sinatra
Johnny B. Goode	Chuch Berry	Chuck Berry: The Anthology
Joy to the World	Traditional	
Just My Imagination	Norman Whitfield, Barrett Strong	Temptations: Sky's the Limit
Kalimba	Vitor Martins, Ivan Lins	Sergio Mendes: Brasiliero
Kiss from a Rose	Seal	Seal: Seal: Hits
Lateral Climb	Robben Ford	Robben Ford: Truth
Lean on Me	Bill Withers	Bill Withers: The Best of Bill Withers
Let It Be	Lennon & McCartney	The Beatles: Let It Be
Let's Dance	David Bowie	David Bowie: Let's Dance
Like Sonny	John Coltrane	John Coltrane: A Giant Step in Jazz
Lil' Darlin'	Neal Hefti	Count Basie: Count Basie & His Orchestra
Livin' in America	Dan Hartman, Charlie Midnight	James Brown: Gravity
Livin' on a Prayer	Jon Bon Jovi, Richie Sambora, Desmond Child	Bon Jovi: Cross Road
Living for the City	Stevie Wonder	Stevie Wonder: Innervisions

205

READING, WRITING AND RHYTHMETIC

Song	Composer	Artist/Album
Living in the Past	Ian Anderson	Jethro Tull: Stand Up
Love Is a Verb	John Mayer	John Mayer: Born and Raised
Love Is Stronger than Justice	Sting	Sting: Ten Summoner's Tales
Love Letters	Victor Young, Edward Heyman	Patti Austin: The Real Me
Love Me Like a Man	Chris Smither	Bonnie Raitt: The Bonnie Raitt Collection
Lucy in the Sky with Diamonds	Lennon & McCartney	The Beatles: Sgt. Pepper's Lonely Hearts Club Band
Lullaby of Birdland	George Shearing	Sarah Vaughan and Clifford Brown: The Definitive Sarah Vaughan
Mack the Knife	Kurt Weill	Bobby Darin: The Ultimate Bobby Darin
Magalenha	Sergio Mendes	Sergio Mendes: Brasilerio
Man in the Mirror	Glen Ballard, Siedah Garrett	Michael Jackson: The Essential Michael Jackson
Mandeville	Paul Motian	Bill Frisell: Rarum V
Mas Que Nada	Jorge Ben Jor	Sergio Mendez and Brasil '66: Greatest Hits
Matilda	Norman Span	Harry Belafonte: The Essential Harry Belafonte
Memory	Trevor Nunn, Andrew Lloyd Webber	Cats soundtrack
Mexican Hat Dance	Traditional	Macarena Kids Party: Macarena Kids Party
Minuet in G Major (from the Anna Magdalena notebook)	J. S. Bach	
Mission Impossible Theme	Lalo Schifrin	Lalo Schifrin & John E. Davis: The Best of Mission Impossible–Then and Now
Mockingbird	Inex & Charlie Foxx	Carly Simon & James Taylor: The Best of Carly Simon
Money	Roger Waters	Pink Floyd: The Dark Side of the Moon
Moon River	Henry Mancini, Johnny Mercer	Andy Williams: The Very Best of Andy Williams
Moonlight in Vermont	John Blackburn, Karl Suessdorf	Ella Fitzgerald: Ella and Louis
Morning Mood (from Peer Gynt Suite No. 1)	Edvard Grieg	London Philharmonic Orchestra: 50 Greatest Pieces of Classical Music
Most Like Lee	Lee Morgan	Lee Morgan: Cornbread
Mr. P.C.	John Coltrane	John Coltrane: Giant Steps
My Girl	Smokey Robinson, Ronald White	The Temptations: The Temptations Sing Smokey
My Romance	Richard Rodgers, Lorenz Hart	Ella Fitzgerald: Ella Fitzgerald Sings the Rodgers and Hart Songbook
Natural Woman	Carole King, Gerry Goffin, Jerry Wexler	Aretha Franklin: The Best of Aretha Franklin
NBC	TV theme	
Never on Sunday	Manos Hadjidakis	Melina Mercouri: Never on Sunday
New World Symphony, 4th Movement	Antonín Dvořák	Bernstein: The 1953 American Decca Recordings
Night Train	Jimmy Forrest	James Brown: Gold: James Brown
Nobody Knows You When You're Down and Out	Jimmy Cox	Eric Clapton: Unplugged

Song	Composer	Artist/Album
Norwegian Wood	Lennon & McCartney	The Beatles: Rubber Soul
Ob-La-Di, Ob-La-Da	Paul McCartney	The Beatles: White Album
Ode to Joy (from the Ninth Symphony)	Ludwig van Beethoven	(Various orchestras): Ninth Symphony
Off the Wall	Rod Temperton	Michael Jackson: Off the Wall
Oh Darling	Lennon & McCartney	The Beatles: Abbey Road
Oh My Darling, Clementine	Percy Montrose (sometimes credited to Barker Bradford)	Malcolm Forest: Legends
Oh! Suzanna	Stephen Foster	Eight Hand String Band: Listen to the Mockingbird
Old MacDonald	Traditional	
On Green Dolphin Street	Bronisław Kaper	Miles Davis: Kind of Blue
On Top of Old Smokey	Traditional	Gene Autry: The Essential Gene Autry
One Note Samba	Antonio Carlos Jobim, Newton Mendonça	Astrud Gilberto: Getz Au Go Go
Open Arms	Steve Perry, Jonathan Cain	Journey: Escape
Over the Rainbow	Harold Arlen, E.Y. Harburg	Judy Garland: Over the Rainbow
Overkill	Colin Hay	Men at Work: Cargo
Penny Lane	Lennon & McCartney	The Beatles: Magical Mystery Tour
Pent-Up House	Sonny Rollins	Sonny Rollins: Sonny Rollins Plus 4
People Get Ready	Curtis Mayfield	Blind Boys of Alabama: Higher Ground
Piano Man	Billy Joel	Billy Joel: Piano Man
Piano Sonata No.9, Movement 1	Mozart	Academy of St. Martin in the Fields: The Complete Mozart Edition: The Symphonies, Vol. 1
Please Don't Talk About Me When I'm Gone	Sam H. Stept, Sidney Clare	Willie Nelson: Moonlight Becomes You
Pomp and Circumstance, March No.1	Sir Edward Elgar	
Ponta de Areia	Milton Nascimento	Wayne Shorter: Native Dancer
Prints Tie	Bobby Hutcherson	Bobby Hutcherson: San Francisco
Proud Mary	John Fogerty	Tina Turner: All the Best: The Hits
Puff the Magic Dragon	Leonard Lipton, Peter Yarrow	Peter Paul & Mary: The Very Best of Peter, Paul & Mary
Purple Haze	Jimi Hendrix	Jimi Hendrix: Are You Experienced
Que Pasa	Horace Silver	Horace Silver: Song for My Father
Red Rain	Peter Gabriel	Peter Gabriel: So
River	Joni Mitchell	Joni Mitchell: Blue
River Man	Nick Drake	Nick Drake: Five Leaves Left
—	—	Brad Mehldau: Songs: the Art of the Trio, Vol. 3
Rockit	Herbie Hancock, Bill Laswell, Michael Beinhorn	Herbie Hancock: Future Shock
Rocky Raccoon	Lennon & McCartney	The Beatles: White Album
Rolling in the Deep	Adele, Paul Epworth	Adele: 21
Route 66	Bobby Troup	Nat King Cole: The World of Nat King Cole
Row, Row, Row Your Boat	Traditional	Elizabeth Mitchell: Kids' Club-Family Songbook

READING, WRITING AND RHYTHMETIC

Song	Composer	Artist/Album
Run Baby Run	Bill Bottrell, David Baerwald, Sheryl Crow	Sheryl Crow: Tuesday Night Music Club
Rudolph the Red-Nosed Reindeer	Johnny Marks	Roberta Radley: Swing-a-Jing-a-Lingin'
Russians	Sting	Sting: The Dream of the Blue Turtles
Sailor's Hornpipe	Traditional	101 Strings Orchestra: 20 Best of Celtic Moods
Satin Doll	Red Garland, Billy Strayhorn, Johnny Mercer	Ella Fitzgerald: Ella Fitzgerald with the Duke Ellington Orchestra
Saturday Afternoon Blues	Johnny Hodges	Ben Webster: The Soul of Ben Webster
Say It Loud	James Brown	James Brown: Say It Loud—I'm Black and I'm Proud
Scarborough Fair	Traditional	Simon and Garfunkel: Parsley, Sage, Rosemary and Thyme
Serenade to a Cuckoo	Roland Kirk	Roland Kirk: I Talk with the Spirits
Seven Days	Sting	Sting: Ten Summoner's Tales
Sgt. Pepper's Lonely Hearts Club Band	Lennon & McCartney	The Beatles: Sgt. Pepper's Lonely Hearts Club Band
She	Charles Aznavour, Herbert Kretzmer	Elvis Costello: The Very Best of Elvis Costello
She Caught the Katy	Taj Mahal, James Rachell	Taj Mahal: The Best of Taj Mahal
She Walks Right In	Professor Longhair	Professor Longhair & the Meters: Best of Professor Longhair
She's Always a Woman	Billy Joel	Billy Joel: The Stranger
Shoot the Moon	Jesse Harris	Norah Jones: Come Away with Me
Silver Bells	Jay Livingston, Ray Evans	Johnny Mathis: Merry Christmas
Sir Duke	Stevie Wonder	Stevie Wonder: Songs in the Key of Life
Sixth Sense	Dave Brubeck	Dave Brubeck: Impressions of New York
—	—	Dave Brubeck: In Their Own Sweet Way
Smile	Charlie Chaplin, John Turner, Geoffrey Parsons	Nat King Cole: The Nat King Cole Story
Só Danço Samba	Antônio Carlos Jobim	João Gilberto, Stan Getz: Getz/Gilberto
So Lonely	Sting	Police: Message in a Box
Softly as in a Morning Sunrise	Sigmund Romberg, Oscar Hammerstein II	Chet Baker: Chet Baker/Wolfgang Lackerschmid Artists Favor
—	—	Michael Brecker: Live at Jazz Baltica 2003
—	—	Paul Chambers: Paul Chambers Quintet
—	—	Bobby Darin: Bobby Darin: That's All
—	—	McCoy Tyner: Coltrane "Live" at the Village Vanguard
Solsbury Hill	Peter Gabriel	Peter Gabriel: The Round Ones
Someday My Prince Will Come	Larry Morey, Frank Churchill	Miles Davis: Someday My Prince Will Come
Someone Like You	Adele, Dan Wilson	Adele: 21
Song for My Father	Horace Silver	Horace Silver: Song for My Father
Sonnymoon for Two	Sonny Rollins	Sonny Rollins: Jazz 1 – Timeless Legends
Spoonful	Willie Dixon	Howlin' Wolf: The Chess 50th Anniversary…

DISCOGRAPHY

Song	Composer	Artist/Album
St. Thomas	Sonny Rollins	Sonny Rollins: Saxophone Colossus
Stagger Lee	American folk song	Taj Mahal: Giant Step
Stand by Me	Ben E. King, Jerry Leiber, Mike Stoller	Ben E.King: Be My Valentine: From Him to Her
Star Eyes	Gene de Paul, Don Raye	Charlie Parker: Bird at St. Nick's
Stars and Stripes Forever	John Philip Sousa	J. F. Sousa: The US Army Field Band
Stay with Me	Sam Smith	Sam Smith: In the Lonely Hour
Stayin' Alive	Barry, Robin and Maurice Gibb	Bee Gees: Saturday Night Fever soundtrack
Stolen Moments	Oliver Nelson	Oliver Nelson: The Blues and the Abstract Truth
Stormy Monday	T-Bone Walker	The Allman Brothers: The Allman Brothers Band at Fillmore East
Strasbourg/St Denis	Roy Hargrove	Roy Hargrove: Earfood
Summertime	George Gershwin	Janis Joplin: Pearl
—	—	Miles Davis: Porgy and Bess
Sunrise, Sunset	Jerry Bock, Sheldon Harnick	Fiddler on the Roof soundtrack
Superstition	Stevie Wonder	Stevie Wonder: Talking Book
Surfer Girl	Brian Wilson	Beach Boys: Surfer Girl
Sweet Home Chicago	Robert Johnson	Robert Johnson: The Complete Recordings
Symphony No.5 in C Minor, First Movement Theme	Ludwig van Beethoven	
Take Five	Paul Desmond	Dave Brubeck: Time Out
Tango Till They're Sore	Tom Waits	Tom Waits: Rain Dogs
Taps	Traditional	United States Navy Band Music for Honors and Ceremonies
Tell Her About It	Billy Joel	Billy Joel: An Innocent Man
Tenor Madness	Sonny Rollins	Sonny Rollins: Tenor Madness
The Animal	Steve Vai	Steve Vai: Passion and Warfare
The Entertainer	Scott Joplin	Scott Joplin: Ragtime
The Kicker	Joe Henderson	Horace Silver: Song for My Father
The Rose	Amanda McBroom	Bette Midler: The Rose
The Star-Spangled Banner (U.S. National Anthem)	John Stafford Smith, Francis Scott Key	US Army Band: A Patriotic Salute to the Military Family
The Thrill Is Gone	Rick Darnell, Roy Hawkins	B. B. King & Eric Clapton: 80
The Times They Are a Changin'	Bob Dylan	Bob Dylan: Bob Dylan's Greatest Hits
The Way You Look Tonight	Dorothy Fields, Jerome Kern	Frank Sinatra: Nothing but the Best
The Way You Make Me Feel	Michael Jackson	Michael Jackson: Bad
There Will Never Be Another You	Harry Warren, Mack Gordon	Chet Baker: Chet Baker Sings
They Won't Go When I Go	Stevie Wonder, Yvonne Wright	Stevie Wonder: Fulfillingness' First Finale
Thick as a Brick	Ian Anderson	Jethro Tull: The Very Best of Jethro Tull
Think	Merv Griffin	(theme Song from TV Show Jeopardy)

READING, WRITING AND RHYTHMETIC

Song	Composer	Artist/Album
This Boy	Lennon & McCartney	The Beatles: Meet the Beatles!
Three Sheets to the Wind	Joe Satriani	Joe Satriani: Unstoppable Momentum
Time After Time	Cyndi Lauper	Cyndi Lauper: She's So Unusual
Time Has Come Today	Willie & Joseph Chambers	The Chambers Brothers: Time Has Come: The Best of the Chambers Brothers
Twinkle, Twinkle Little Star	Traditional	
Unchained Melody	Alex North, Hy Zaret	Righteous Brothers: Just Once in My Life
Unit 7	Sam Jones	Wes Montgomery: Wes Montgomery and Wynton Kelly Trio: Smokin' at the Half Note
Unsquare Dance	Dave Brubeck	Dave Brubeck: Time Further Out
Uptown Girl	Billy Joel	Billy Joel: An Innocent Man
Viva La Vida	Coldplay	Coldplay: Viva La Vida or Death and All His Friends
Walkin'	Miles Davis (?), Gene Ammons (?)	Miles Davis: Walkin'
Waltz of the Flowers, from the Nutcracker Suite	Pyotr Tchaikovsky	
We Can Work It Out	Lennon & McCartney	The Beatles: Rubber Soul
We Three Kings (of Orient Are)	John Henry Hopkins, Jr.	Dolly Parton: Home for Christmas
We Will Rock You	Brian May	Queen: News of the World
When Johnny Comes Marching Home	Patrick Gilmore, (pseud. Louis Lambert)	Ross Moore: Southern Son
When Lights Are Low	Benny Carter, Spencer Williams	Miles Davis: Blue Haze
When the Saints Go Marching In	Traditional	Mel McDaniel: 30 Country Gospel Greats
Where Did Our Love Go	Brian Holland, Lamont Dozier, Eddie Holland	The Supremes: Anthology
While My Guitar Gently Weeps	George Harrison	The Beatles: White Album
Whipping Post	Gregg Allman	The Allman Brothers: Legendary Hits
Whole Lotta Love	Led Zeppelin (Willie Dixon)	Led Zeppelin: Led Zeppelin II
Will You Be There	Michael Jackson	Michael Jackson: The Essential Michael Jackson
With a Little Help from My Friends	Lennon & McCartley	Joe Cocker: With a Little Help from My Friends
Women Be Wise	Sippie Wallace	Bonnie Raitt: Bonnie Raitt
Work Song	Nat Adderley	Nat Adderley: Work Song
Wrapped Around Your Finger	Sting	Police: Synchronicity
Yardbird Suite	Charlie Parker	Charlie Parker and Miles Davis: Birdsong
You Are My Sunshine	Jimmie Davis, Charles Mitchell	Norman Blake: Oh Brother, Where Art Thou?
You Know I'm No Good	Amy Winehouse	Amy Winehouse: Back to Black
You Really Got a Hold on Me	Smokey Robinson	Smokey Robinson and the Miracles: Ooo Baby Baby: the Anthology
You Send Me	Sam Cooke	Sam Cooke: The Best of Sam Cooke

About the Author

Roberta Radley is the author of her much-celebrated book *The Real Easy Ear Training Book*, published by Sher Music Co.

An accomplished performer and a seasoned educator, she walks the walk, bringing professional experience as a jazz vocalist, pianist and arranger into her classrooms, both "live" and "virtual." It is her strong belief that true learning can only occur when students apply their new knowledge and skills to their own personal music making— there is no substitute for experience.

Ms. Radley is currently the Assistant Chair of the Ear Training department at Berklee College of Music. A Berklee graduate herself, she has been a member of the faculty since 1976. In many ways, the classroom is Roberta's best and most preferred performing stage. Her accomplishments as an educator earned her the "Outstanding Achievement in Music Education" award from the College. She has taught a wide range of ear training classes, using innovative methods to help students hear music more analytically, and to inspire students to develop their own unique musical voice.

As former founding member of the jazz vocal trio The Sisters of Swing, Roberta created many arrangements for the group—giving the jazz standards her own fresh and personal sound. The group released two CD's: "Mood Indigo," and the holiday collection "Swing-a-Jing-a-Lingin'." Several of these recordings are featured in this new book.

She has authored two courses "Basic Ear Training" and "Harmonic Ear Training," through Berklee Online, produced the DVD "Harmonic Ear Training," through Berklee Press, and co-authored the Ear Training department's *Core Ear Training Textbooks, Volumes 1–4*. Roberta has traveled across the U.S. and internationally on behalf of the College, presenting seminars and performances. She has also spoken at various educational venues and conferences, (such as the Jazz Education Network) sharing with colleagues her specialty on harmonic hearing pedagogy.

Roberta is now honored to present her second book *Reading, Writing and Rhythmetic: the ABCs of Music Transcription*, where she shares her insights and strategies on every detail of the transcription process—the ABCs.